COUPS AND COCAINE

Anthony Daniels' journeys are not epics of endurance by canoe or mule, though in his second trek he does achieve his modest aim of crossing South America without recourse to planes or private vehicles. He is not in search of adventure so much as the spirit of people and place. The trail takes him from the smartest hotel in Lima to the freezing doss-houses of the high Andes; a package tour into the Amazon forest reveals one version of the truth, but so
does some Bolivian prison visiting in La Paz.

Anthony Daniels talked to many characters en route from a neo-Facist dispossessed landowner in a Cuzco nightspot to the widow of an ex-president of Ecuador, hoarding her gold figures in a shoebox for safe keeping. His outstanding skills as a writer show both the desperation and the fascination of the Continent. *Coups and Cocaine* is Anthony Daniels' first book, and he is at present working on another work of non-fiction.

'This is a lively traveller's tale' *Times Literary Supplement*

'Full of pleasant surprises' *Standard*

Also published in the Century Classics

The cover shows a view in the Cordilleras

ANTHONY DANIELS

Coups and Cocaine

TWO JOURNEYS IN SOUTH AMERICA

Century
London Melbourne Auckland Johannesburg

First published in 1986 by John Murray (Publishers) Ltd

© Anthony Daniels 1986

This edition first published in 1987 by Century, an imprint of
Century Hutchinson Ltd, Brookmount House, 62–65 Chandos
Place,
London WC2N 4NW

Century Hutchinson Australia Pty Ltd
PO Box 496, 16–22 Church Street, Hawthorn, Victoria 3122,
Australia

Century Hutchinson New Zealand Limited
PO Box 40–086, Glenfield, Auckland 10, New Zealand

Century Hutchinson South Africa (Pty) Ltd
PO Box 337, Berglvei, 2012 South Africa

ISBN 0 7126 1770 1

CONTENTS

Maps will be found on pages x and 148

PREFACE

As a child, South America excited my imagination as no other continent: the Andes, the Amazon, the Atacama Desert, were all names to which I gave a visionary landscape. Then, as my education took another turn, the visions faded.

Having qualified as a doctor, I took a post in the Gilbert Islands in the South Pacific. The remoteness of those coral atolls enabled me – indeed, required me – to travel extensively, and my fascination with South America revived with the opportunity to go there. I travelled twice to the continent and, far from assuaging my interest, my journeys served only to stimulate it further. South America may be the most unstable region of the globe; it is so much in debt that it could ruin us all; violence is never far below the surface; but life there is never dull. It is the perfect antidote to numbing routine.

ACKNOWLEDGEMENTS

The poem by Antonio Machado on p. ix came from *Times Alone: Selected Poems*, ed Robert Bly, Wesleyan University Press, Connecticut, 1983 (my own translation); the extracts on pp. 28 and 29 are from *Paraguay: Power Game*, anon, Latin America Bureau, London, 1980; the three lines on p. 31 are by Wilfrid Owen; the extracts on pp. 44 and 48 are from *Exploration Fawcett*, P.H. Fawcett, Hutchinson, London, 1955; the extracts on pp. 55 and 65 are from *Pueblo Enfermo*, Alcides Argüedas, Ediciones Isla, La Paz, n.d.; the quotations by Nuñez del Prado on p. 57 and by Fernando Belaúnde on p. 115 are from *Power and Society in Contemporary Peru*, François Bourricaud, Faber, London, 1970; the quotation by Manuel Belzu on p. 71 is from *Bolivia, Land Divided*, Harold Osborne, Gordon Press, New York, 1976; the quotation on p. 91 is from *We Eat the Mines and the Mines Eat Us*, June Nash, Columbia University Press, New York, 1979; the quotation by García Meza on p. 92 is from *Coup in Bolivia*, anon, Latin America Bureau, London, 1980; the lines by Nicanor Parra on p. 99 and Julián del Casal on p. 114 are from *Latin American Poetry: Origins and Presence*, Gordon Brotherston, Cambridge University Press, 1975; the lines by Pablo Neruda on p. 115 are from his *Selected Poems*, Penguin, London, 1975 (my own translation); the lines by Pablo Neruda on p. 116 are from *Twenty Poems*, Rapp & Whiting, London, 1967 (my own translation); the quotation by Fray Tomás Ortiz on p. 117 is from *A Cultural History of Latin America*, Germán Arciniegas, Frank Cass, London, 1966; the Ecuadorian bishops' instruction on p. 128 is from *El Poder Político en el Ecuador*, Osvaldo Hurtado, Ariel, Madrid; the quotations on pp. 156 and 174 (bottom) are from *Letters on Paraguay*, J.P. and W.P. Robertson, John Murray, London, 1839; the quotation on p. 162 is from *Madame Lynch and Friend*, Alyn Brodsky, Cassell, London, 1976; the quotations on pp. 182 and 183 are from *Indians, Missionaries and the Promised Land*, Luke Holland, Survival International, London, 1980; the quotations on pp. 184 and 185 are from *Fishers of Men or Founders of Empire?*, David Stott, Zed Press, London, 1982.

He andado muchos caminos,
he abierto muchas veredas,
he navegado en cien mares,
y atracado en cien riberas.

En todas partes he visto
caravanas de tristeza,
soberbios y melancólicos
borrachos de sombra negra . . .

ANTONIO MACHADO

I have walked many roads,
I have opened many paths,
I have sailed a hundred seas,
and landed on a hundred shores.

Everywhere I have seen
excursions of sadness,
angry and melancholy
drunks with black shadows . . .

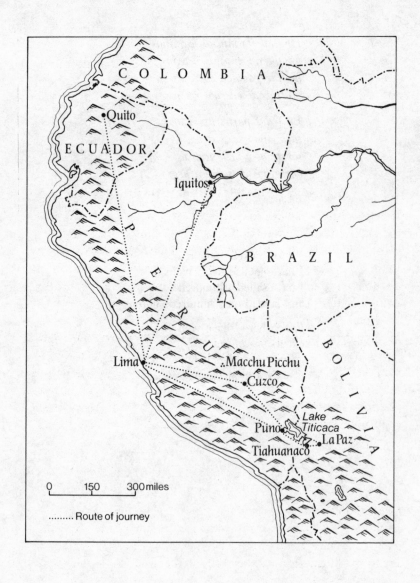

.... Route of journey

ONE

Lima, Peru

M OST JOURNEYS to South America begin in Miami. It is itself a half-Latin city; as much Spanish is spoken on its streets as English. Miami is the city to which the nervous rich of the southern continent remit their money against a rainy – or more likely, a bloody – day. It is the city in which the exiles of twenty Latin republics plot their triumphant returns to their *patria*. It is the dream capital of Latin America. It is the murder capital of the United States.

Miami sprawls. There is the famous beach, swept clean every morning before the sunbathers arrive, fringed with an endless arc of towering motels and condominiums with names like 'Casablanca', 'Marrakesh' and 'Jade Garden'. One of the motels, a Hollywood-Aztec palace, has an illuminated hurricane-proof plastic palm tree outside, advertising the happy hour. Above these exotically furnished but carefully standardised motels flies a monoplane trailing an advertisement:

KELLY'S SEAFOOD HOUSE. ALASKA CRAB LEGS
AND SALAD BAR $8.95

I waited for the bus to take me downtown. There was an old lady at the bus-stop who eyed me nervously, as though she expected me to mug her. When the attack failed to materialise she said, in apparent contradiction to her present situation:

'I never go downtown.'

'In that case,' I asked, 'why are you waiting for a bus?'

'Today is different. But I'm coming straight back, as soon as I can.'

'Why?'

'Hispanics. They mug you in the street.'

'Even in the daytime?'

'Even in the daytime.'

Violence seems part of everyday life in Miami. A lady I met in a bar, the widow of an air force general, told me she had recently been in a restaurant with a colleague of her husband's when three armed men stormed in, took seventy dollars from the till and shot a waitress dead.

'Niggers!' she exclaimed, her voice quivering with two centuries of Southern emotion.

The old lady at the bus-stop dabbed her forehead with a lace-frilled handkerchief.

'I can't take the heat,' she said. 'I been living in Miami for eighteen years and I still can't take the heat.'

'Why don't you move?'

She looked at me ruefully for a few moments.

'I can't take the cold,' she said.

The bus came. Its interior was covered with indelible graffiti. Above the driver's seat, in thick black lettering, was:

SEX HAS NO CALORIES

'I don't care no more about calories,' said one of the old ladies behind me.

'You mean you still care about sex?' asked her companion.

No-one on the bus was less than twice my age. Not surprisingly, perhaps, the main topic of conversation was health and how to achieve it.

'I wouldn't go there even if I was dead,' said the lady behind me, pointing to the hospital outside which we had stopped.

'My husband died in that hospital,' said her companion.

'I'm not surprised.'

Two younger people who had just attended the hospital got on the bus. They both carried X-rays. One of them, a young lady of intimidatingly immaculate appearance, was very angry.

'They said my X-ray was O.K. They said there was nothing wrong with me. But it's *my* body. *I* know how I feel.'

She had hoped for a serious, but completely curable, disease.

The ladies behind me discussed their latest encounters with the medical profession.

'I said to this doctor, you're the first man in thirty years to ask me to take off my clothes.'

'My doctor gave me kwy-nine for my cramps.'

In downtown Miami, the Anglos – as Americans of Polish, Yugoslav or Italian origin are known there – were distinguishable from the Latins by their dress and the speed at which they walked. The Cubans and other Latin Americans had taken over the small shops, and stood outside them, chatting and trying to re-create the atmosphere of the countries from which they were exiled. But the looming glass and steel office blocks served to remind them of their exile, and of the repulsive-attractive power of *gringo* civilisation.

To wait in dreary places for flights or ships or trains is the price travellers pay for their restlessness. It is their form of purgatory. I spent a day or two by the pool of my hotel, among tropical pot plants and fountains. Meandering and tuneless music without percussion permeated the air, from a source impossible to locate. Men with lobster-pink bellies over tight trunks refreshed themselves every ten minutes or so with long drinks taken from a glass with a hibiscus flower and a piece of pineapple attached to the rim, served by waitresses with a flower above their right ear. It was paradise, Dakron, Ohio.

Sometimes two streams of music emanated from different sources at the same time, creating discord. I pointed this out to a waiter.

'We're used to it,' he said. 'We don't even notice it.'

'But *I* notice it.'

'Some people like it,' he said and left me to take an order for a cocktail.

Messages interrupted the music. 'Will Jim Dragelski please

contact reception. Will Jim Dragelski please contact reception. Thank you and have a nice day.'

I flew to Lima aboard Aero Peru, or Aero Peor – Air Worst – as it is familiarly known in Peru. Until the military coup of 1968 it had been the air transport wing of the Peruvian air force. Peru possessed another airline which flew once a week from Miami to Manaus and on to the jungle city of Iquitos. It was called Faucett, a somewhat unfortunate name, one might have thought, for an airline overflying the Amazon jungle.

We landed at dawn. The *garúa*, a thick grey mist that some-times lasts for months, obscured completely from the air the arid coastal plain on which the Spanish elected to build their City of Kings, as Lima was first called. Fifty miles to the east, majestic and imperious, rose the Andes.

Bored but edgy *mestizo* soldiers, their hands resting on auto-matic weapons slung round their necks, waited for the passengers inside the terminal. The flight from Moscow and Havana had also just arrived, and there had been a recent revival of revolutionary guerrilla activity in Peru. The garúa turned everything grey, a phenomenon instantly familiar to anyone who has ever lived in England. It was something of a disappointment, for my arrival in a new continent, though hardly in the mould of a Cortés or Pizarro, had raised hopes that here everything, including the spectrum, would be different.

The customs officials worked slowly – so slowly, in fact, that the line seemed scarcely to move, and one disgruntled American passenger said he already regretted leaving the States, and if this was what abroad was like he would never leave again. A Peruvian behind me told me that the men worked this slowly in the hope that frustrated passengers would offer them bribes. If so, their strategy failed; it takes time to accustom oneself to a climate of petty corruption.

Looking into my case, the customs official found mainly books. 'You are starting a library, señor?'

'Just preparing for customs,' I replied.

The car that took me from the airport was a battered silver monster, reprieved from a North Amercan scrap heap. It made more noise than a goods train in the night.

The outlying industrial districts of the city were squat and ugly. The factory walls were covered with political slogans: No to Hunger, Down With Fascism, The Strike Is Our Only Weapon. Workers were gathering by the gates which were not yet open, and they bought their breakfast of roasted maize cobs from Indian women vendors.

Peru had recently returned to democracy, or at least to an elected presidency, after twelve years of military rule. Señor Fernando Belaúnde Terry, who was overthrown by the army in 1968, had been re-elected in 1980. The political situation was, as ever, fragile, and the President's relations with the army, always the predominant force in Peruvian politics, were of a Byzantine complexity. Sr Belaúnde spoke eloquently of the return to democracy after military dictatorship, but his own commitment to the electoral process was less than rock-solid, and he had once used the army to further his own ambitions. The guerrillas' activities started during his first term of office, when they had been led by unlikely scions of the privileged classes: Javier Heraud, a spoilt young poet, Luis de la Puente, a lawyer, and Hugo Blanco, an agronomist. They were defeated with ease, but the recrudescence looked like being more serious.

Suddenly we were in the centre of Lima. The abrupt transition from periphery to hub reflected Lima's phenomenal growth, or hypertrophy. Sixty years ago it had been a city of less than a quarter million; now it was a city of more than six million. The centre had not been able to keep pace with this expansion of population.

We entered a hexagonal plaza in the grandiose style of Baron Haussmann. In the middle, atop a column, a winged lady dressed in Greek robes tripped lightly forward, one leg extended grace-fully behind her, holding aloft laurels or olive branches. She represented Victory or Peace, or both, though neither has hitherto been a prominent feature of Peruvian history.

The plan of the plaza envisaged six grand boulevards radiating from it. However, the money must have run out before the completion of the project, which was started during one of Peru's periodic commodity booms, when its international credit stood high. Several times in its history a single commodity – silver, guano, rubber, fishmeal, oil – has been expected to relieve Peru from its desperate poverty for ever. Unfortunately, booms are always followed by crashes, leaving grand hexagonal plazas radiating six ugly streets of no particular distinction.

My hotel, the Gran Hotel Bolívar, was in the Plaza San Martín. Opposite the entrance stood an equestrian statue of San Martín, a gift to Peru from the Argentine Republic on the centenary of Peru's independence. It was an equivocal gift at best: a permanent reminder to Peruvians that their independence came not as a result of their own struggle – they remained, on the whole, steadfastly loyal to the Spanish Empire – but as a gift of others, among whom was the Argentinian, San Martín. His summary of his life's work does not appear on the plinth of the statue: 'The attempts of twenty-four years to promote liberty have resulted in nothing more than calamities . . . Liberty? Give a child of two a box of razors to play with and see what happens!'

The Gran Hotel Bolívar was Lima's grandest. Standing to attention by corinthian columns were a host of blue and gold liveried flunkys with Indian faces, whose sole function appeared to be to bow to guests as they passed. Three of them helped me into the elaborately mirrored lift; one bowed, one opened the gate, and one pressed the button for my floor. Over this little scene presided the portrait of Simón Bolívar, el Libertador, the Liberator.

How much the Byronic hero he looked! 'War is my element,' said Bolívar, 'danger my glory.' His dark saturnine features seemed to disapprove sourly of all that passed before them; one would never have guessed from his portrait that he was excessively fond of dancing. Exiled from the lands he supposedly liberated, he wrote: 'There is no good faith in America, neither between men nor between nations. Treaties are pieces of paper, constitutions books; elections, battles; liberty, anarchy; and life, a torment.' When he died, however, his words were soon forgotten, and he underwent secular canonisation, since when he has become an all-purpose icon, brought out and displayed on every national occasion like a miracle-working virgin.

I took breakfast amongst gilt and plush. The waiter, an elderly mestizo, wore a dazzlingly starched white jacket and a satin bow tie. The worn soles of his shoes, however, were separating from their scuffed uppers, and I felt ashamed to look him in the face.

I went out into the Plaza San Martín, which was just coming alive for the day. The exclusive clubs modelled on English institutions – the Círculo Militar, the Club Nacional, where more of the nation's business is conducted than in the National Congress – remained closed, but the bootblacks had already set up their stalls under the colonnades. The magazine stalls were opening too. Censorship having recently been abolished, they sold everything from dry Marxist theoretical journals with obligatory quotations from the *Obras Completas* of Lenin, to lurid crime magazines with cover pictures of murder victims lying on cold mortuary slabs, their split chests sewn up with thick post-mortem sutures.

On every corner stood soldierly policemen in steel helmets and battle dress. They were accompanied by policewomen in smart bottle-green suits with incongruous slits up the skirts. They wore long black boots, were heavily made up, and carried revolvers. They looked as though they were cast for a sado-masochist adventure film, in which the violence is done to men by women.

One side of the square was a hive of lawyers' chambers, their brass plates rendering the wall almost entirely metallic.

SCHMIDT ALEXANDER
ABOGADO
ENGLISH SPOCKEN

I went down the Jirón de la Unión, Lima's principal shopping street. Most of the faces in the crowd were mestizo; those with more European features looked more prosperous, though the relation between social position and racial origin is one which many South Americans prefer to ignore.

In its few hundred yards, the Jirón de la Unión recapitulates the history of architecture from Spanish baroque to ultramodern which, in its Latin American incarnation, makes use of huge, brutal, angular concrete blocks that stain easily in Lima's polluted atmosphere. These barbarous *edificios* – mostly banks, offering sixty-five per cent annual interest on deposits – display a regard for size as a value in itself. In a frantic effort after North American modernity, the architects have resorted to the aesthetics of the torture chamber.

Every inch of wall within reach was hung with political posters from last year's election. Shreds of the faces of defeated candidates flapped disconsolately above shop windows.

ARMANDO TIENE FUERZA PARA SALVAR AL PERU
(Armando has the strength to save Peru)

The Plaza de Armas, at the far end of the Jirón de la Unión, is the inner sanctum of Peruvian life. The Presidential Palace, the Cathedral, the City Hall, and the Archbishop's Palace are all there, conforming to the ancient Spanish plan, though only the Cathedral has any claim to antiquity, and even that has been rebuilt several times. Everything else, though colonial in style, is comparatively recent. The City Hall was built in 1945; the Presidential Palace in 1938, in partial replication of Pizarro's original, which was demolished shortly before; and the Archbishop's Palace, with its magnificent wooden balcony, in 1924, when it was presented to the Archbishop of Lima by President Agusto Leguía, as a token of 'the harmony existing between Church and State'. When that Peruvian dictator was removed from office in 1930 he had amassed one of the largest fortunes in the world.

I entered the gloomy cathedral. A long line of tiny Indian children entered with me, led by their teacher. They marched up to the altar rail with military precision and, on the orders of their teacher, deposited their identical aluminium luncheon boxes on the stone floor, making a clatter that would have woken the dead of a millennium ago. They crossed themselves and said a prayer. When it was done, they picked up their luncheon boxes and marched out, leaving the Cathedral to a pious old lady, and me.

She was kneeling at the first chapel. Her religious reflections were inspired by the shrivelled remains of a man in a glass sarcophagus on the right. She touched the railings with her shawl, asking for his intercession in heavenly quarters. The man in the sarcophagus, however, was no saint; far from it, though he died (murdered) with the name of Jesus on his lips. He was Francisco Pizarro, killed in an internecine dispute with Pedro de Alvarado over the spoils of the Inca Empire they had conquered together.

The memory of Pizarro has fared better in Peru than that of Cortés in Mexico, where tributes to the greatest of the *conquistadores* are as common as statues of Trotsky in Moscow. Outside Lima Cathedral, however, in the far corner of the Plaza de Armas, stands an equestrian statue of Pizarro, an exact copy of the one that stands in the main square of his birthplace, Trujillo in Estremadura. With his plume flying stiffly erect behind his helmet, he is the very embodiment of Spanish *hidalguía*: noble, cruel, brave, proud, rapacious, treacherous, passionate, implacable.

Nevertheless, a first step in Pizarro's demotion has been taken. General Velasco, the head of the military junta of 1968 who was fond of radical gestures, renamed the Sala Pizarro in the Presidential Palace the Sala Tupuc Amaru, after the leader of the famous Indian rebellion against the Spanish and *criollos* of 1781. The uprising was put down with the maximum of ferocity, and Tupuc Amaru, who was descended from the Inca Emperors, was publicly hanged, drawn and quartered. Velasco was currying favour with the masses but, as he later found out, playing with symbols of revolt is a dangerous business.

At the rear of the Presidential Palace, my next diversion, ran the Río Rimac. It was reduced to a trickle when I saw it, but the smell was overpowering: urine. From the balcony of the palace, the President would have had a view of the low brown hills in whose valleys run the *pueblos jóvenes* (or *barriadas* as they used to be known before another fiat of General Velasco's changed their name, but not their condition, to the more euphemistic and hopeful 'young towns'). They are the mile on mile of slums where immigrants to the city build their homes of cardboard boxes, tin and polythene. High above one of the buildings, the President would have seen a giant neon exhortation, supported by metal scaffolding, to drink Inka Cola, 'Peru's National Flavour'.

Across the Puente de Piedra, the famous bridge built in 1610 with mortar containing the whites of hundreds of thousands of eggs, is the oldest quarter of Lima. The buildings there are one storey, painted pastel shades. One storey buildings survived best in Lima because of the numerous earthquakes that punctuated the city's history. Every earthquake was taken as a sign of God's wrath with a wicked and luxurious city, but the warnings were clearly insufficient because it was found necessary to repeat them, on average, once every seven years throughout the two hundred and eighty years of colonial rule. The earthquake of 1746 left only twenty houses standing and killed four thousand out of fifty thousand inhabitants. In 1981 the Peruvian tourist industry was almost ruined by an American scientist who predicted (erroneously) that there would be a severe earthquake that year, with Lima at its centre.

I stood on the bridge, gagging at the smell. An old man in astonishingly tattered rags, his bronze face canyoned by time and troubles, his back bent nearly double by the weight of the sack he was carrying, shuffled towards me. Before he reached me he took his sack, which contained rubbish, and emptied it over the side of the bridge. As scraps of paper still fluttered downwards, he shuffled on.

There was a small open air market on the palatial bank of the river. The stalls sold mainly cheap clothing, but there were also individual vendors with trays hanging from their necks, selling envelopes or cigarettes one by one. How many would they have to sell, I wondered, to make enough profit for one meal? Two nurses in white uniforms stood behind a table set up in a doorway. They were offering to measure for nothing the blood pressures of passers-by. A notice on the table said: Peruvian League for the Fight Against Hypertension. Several young men – mestizos – lined up to have their blood pressures taken. They found the fight against hypertension highly amusing, and a macho competition developed among them to discover who had the highest blood pressure. They clenched their fists and flexed their muscles to make their blood pressures go higher. Though a doctor, I too found the fight against hypertension slightly absurd. It reminded me of the Rumanian proverb; the whole village is on fire, but grandma wants to finish combing her hair.

A young woman with strangely protuberant eyes, who was dressed as though Lima's cold were intense, approached me and asked me whether she could practise her English on me. I must have been very conspicuous as a *gringo*. She was a law student, she said, and as proof she flashed an ordinary exercise book in front of my face.

It transpired that Spanish was a more practical means of communication between us, since her English was almost non-existent. She asked me whether I had yet been to the church of San Francisco, to which I replied that I had been in Lima only two hours. I must go, she said, and putting her arm in mine, led me off.

We walked the short distance to the church. Completed in 1674, it is famous for having survived many earthquakes, for its paintings by Zurbarán, its catacombs (beware of the scorpions, says the *South American Handbook*), and its monastery library containing twenty thousand volumes of theology.

My companion crossed herself as we entered, and every time we passed one of the numerous chapels. Each chapel contained religious statuary of the most extravagant Spanish variety. Blood and baroque agony were everywhere; Christ crowned with thorns, the sacred blood dripping down His face; Christ crucified; the deposition from the cross. No detail was too gory to be lingeringly portrayed. The Virgin Mary seemed to have reached a kind of ecstasy through suffering. Sceptical myself, I found it all slightly ridiculous, like a chamber of horrors in a travelling waxwork museum. But as Paul Theroux once pointed out to a disapproving American protestant, Christ's suffering must be depicted graphically indeed if it is to appear greater in kind than the ordinary experience of Latin Americans.

She took me to her favourite corner of the church where, set on a table, was a glass box that contained a small doll of the Infant Jesus, cherubic and rosy-cheeked, dressed in cloth of silver and gold, a star-studded halo suspended above His head by a wire. At His feet were crumpled banknotes, stuffed into the box through a slit thoughtfully provided in the top. Pinned to the box was a prayer on a card:

> Small child of my heart, I come before you full of trust, to ask for yet more favours. Pour your grace on me, give me health of body and soul. Oh my sweet child! Send down on me a rain of flowers, flowers of your grace, enraptured in their own perfumes. Give me the smile of your lips and the sky of your eyes. Your caresses are worth more to me than all the joys of the world. With your little hands extended, press me tight in your arms. Take me along the way, and never depart from me, I beg you. Amen.

Tears welled up in her eyes as she read the prayer. What was her motive in bringing me here? Accustomed to thinking the worst, I admitted in the end that this rather unattractive girl was simply deeply religious, and subject to emotions I could neither share nor understand. She took a small note from her thin purse and pushed it into the box. She asked me whether I wanted to buy a candle and I said yes, to prevent her from using more of her pitiful supply of money.

We went to the tomb and reliquary of San Martín de Porres, passing over an iron grille in the floor which covered the stairs down to the catacombs. On the steps were skulls and femurs lying across one another; money had been flung down to them.

St Martín of Porres died in 1639, and since then has been the object of a cult among the poor and downtrodden of Lima. He was a lay brother who tended the poor of the city with great devotion; such was his prestige and reputation that he was able to intercede on their behalf with the Viceroy himself. In 1962 he was canonised by Pope John XXIII, to demonstrate to the poor the new alignment of the Church, thus justifying *post facto* the three hundred years of devotion his remains had received.

My companion touched the reliquary and her body relaxed, like a man in severe pain receiving a shot of morphine. Marx's famous dictum suddenly seemed no more than the literal truth.

We left the church and, although it was only eleven o'clock, she said it was time for lunch. We went to the café used by working men where we bought some bullet-like dry rolls, and some sour and salty goatsmilk cheese. In payment I offered a thousand *soles*. The owner of the café exclaimed immediately that it was a sum completely impossible to change, though it was scarely more than two dollars. He went off grumbling that he would have to scour the whole street for my change.

My companion asked me what I wished to do next. I was by now anxious to detach myself from her, but could not steel myself to say so.

'I'm a doctor,' I said. 'I'd like to see a hospital.'

It was an odd request, as her face plainly showed. But she agreed to take me, and she thought for a moment about where to go. She said we should visit a hospital in the north of the city, reached by bus.

At the front of the bus was a religious shrine. In India it would have been dedicated to Ganesh or Krishna, with garlands and incense. In Lima it was dedicated to the Virgin Mary, a plastic statuette of whom was hung with rosary beads, under whose protection the driver was absolved from all responsibility to drive carefully.

The bus was full – more than full. The people were mestizo or Indian, obviously poor. But when a woman climbed on with her shopping a man immediately offered his seat and bowed courteously. A kind of solidarity seemed to subsist between them; when my companion offered one of the half-eaten bread rolls and cheese which she had brought from the café to a perfect stranger on the bus, he took it and ate it at once. It was as though in hard times, and all times were hard, people automatically shared the little they had.

We reached the northern edge of the city, where the hospital was the last of the permanent structures, before the shacks and huts began. My companion stopped a young man with a bushy black beard, owlish round glasses, and a corduroy jacket, at the hospital gate. He was carrying a large volume on the inequities of the world economic system under his arm – in English. She told him I was an important visitor from Europe and the director of the hospital must show me around at once. This was not a claim I made for myself, and in her wild protuberant eyes I suddenly recognised the source of her oddness; she was mad. The man with the beard tried patiently to explain to her that as the director was presently giving a lecture, he could not show me round. My companion said the lecture must be interrupted, postponed, cancelled, and stamped her feet. The man turned to me and spoke in English.

He was a Catholic lay brother from the United States called Paul who had come to Peru straight after graduating seven years ago. He was now training at the hospital to become a medical assistant (or barefoot doctor), and was also taking a course in philosophy and science at an independent Catholic university.

My companion grew impatient and jealous of the instant intimacy which fluency in a foreign language conferred on us. For Paul it was a pleasure to speak English again after seven years, but when he offered to show me round the hospital himself, my companion stamped her foot again and said I must choose between Paul and her. I chose Paul, and she flung off down the street, leaving me feeling like the personification of Perfidious Albion.

We walked round the hospital together. The corridors were full of pregnant women, or women with several small children clutching their skirts, waiting to be seen at a clinic. We did not enter the wards as Paul felt this would be a gratuitous exhibition of the patients' suffering. In any case, I was interested in what he was telling me. He wanted to be a medical assistant, he said, because he felt the Catholic Church must involve itself in the everyday problems of the people, rather than offer them perfect solace in the indefinite future. He had a high regard for the hospital and the doctors who worked there, who were almost the only ones in Lima with a concern for the poor and sick rather than an urge to accumulate money quickly by treating the rich. The hospital served the poor, but not the poorest of the poor, *los olvidados*, the forgotten ones, who could not even afford to transport their sick to the hospital for its free treatment. Besides, los olvidados were the superstitious ones, who brought their sick only in extremis, whereupon they usually died, thus reinforcing their idea that hospital was only a place in which to die. I said I was familiar with this vicious cycle from the Pacific islands where I worked.

But Paul had come to doubt in any case the value of the therapeutic measures he was being taught to apply. What was the point of curing a child in hospital of a disease, when he would be discharged into the environment which caused the disease in the first place? The more Paul studied medicine, the more he was convinced that it was the environment which needed transformation. And to transform the environment, in Peru at least, required a revolution. Only a Marxist revolution would answer the need.

But how, I asked, did he reconcile his Marxism with his Catholicism?

Before he could answer, we met Rosa, his wife. She was a mestiza who worked as a technician in the laboratory. She greeted me with an open smile – two of her teeth were rimmed in gold – and she kissed me. Any friend of her husband's must be her friend too. She pulled his beard and called him 'my gringo'. Their love for one another was evident.

Farther down the corridor we met Rosa's mother, a fat, comfortable woman waiting to attend a diabetic clinic.

Paul, Rosa and I agreed to meet at my hotel for a drink before dinner. Paul told me 'the Movement' was holding a demonstration against hunger that evening in the Plaza San Martín; perhaps

I should like to join it after dinner? I said I could think of no better way to spend my first night in South America.

Now, however, I had to go to the British Embassy, where I had arranged to meet two friends, Richard and Frances, who had come out to Peru a week before me. We had arranged to go to the British Embassy every afternoon at four o'clock until we met. The Embassy, in accordance with Britain's greatly reduced place in the world, was on an upper floor in the Edificio Washington, on the corner of the Avenida Arequipa. The building also housed a travel agency and the embassy of South Africa. Four o'clock was clearly well past the hour at which our diplomats did any work; the Embassy was so firmly closed that it looked as though it had never been, and never would be, open.

Richard and Frances did not arrive. Feeling suddenly alone in an alien world, I left a message with the Edificio doorman and walked back to my hotel.

I passed the American Embassy, known to Limeños as *la casa del virrey* – the house of the viceroy – and entered the Plaza Grau, named after the Peruvian naval hero, Admiral Miguel Grau. His grim, mutton-chopped visage appears on the thousand soles note which had given me trouble earlier in the day. Admiral Grau led the Peruvian naval forces in the War of the Pacific against Chile in 1879, his heroic command of the ironclad *Huáscar* delaying Chile's eventual victory.

Grau, it so happens, had a brief and abortive connection with the remote Pacific atolls where I worked. In the early 1860s Peruvian vessels visited the islands to recruit, often forcibly, labour for the coastal plantations of Peru. Some of the islands were depopulated as a result. Grau, then a captain, set out in the schooner *Margarita*, but unfortunately for him, and fortunately for the islands, it sank before leaving Callao harbour.

In the Plaza San Martín a crowd was gathering. It was as yet small and passive: there were as many people queuing for admission to two cinemas, one showing *Grease Brillantina* with John Travolta, the other *Prostitución Clandestina*, whose stars preferred to remain anonymous.

From the balcony of one of the exclusive clubs hung a huge red banner: 'No to Civilian Dictatorship. Instead of Hunger – no more price rises! Instead of Torture – Freedom! Instead of foreign exploitation – national ownership! The United Left repudiates the 'Antiterrorist' Law!'

The Communist Party of Peru was going through one of its Popular Front phases. Sr Belaúnde was called a dictator by the Party, which lost no opportunity of reminding the crowd of his social origins from among the old Peruvian gentry. The Party's objections to torture were, on the other hand, tactical rather than categorical. To be categorical is, in their parlance, to be undialectical. In the words of one Peronist asked for his attitude towards torture: it depends on who is tortured and who is doing the torturing. As for the 'antiterrorist' law, the Party seemed incensed that the Government should actually take seriously the threats of what the Party called 'left-wing adventurists'.

The speeches had begun from a covered platform set high above the ground near the entrance to the Gran Hotel Bolívar. It was impossible to see the speakers, whose voices came from behind an impenetrable red screen. It was as though the cult of personality, as the Stalin years are quaintly known, had been replaced by the cult of impersonality, which was just as sinister in its own way. The speakers quickly reached a crescendo of indignation, which they maintained heroically for minutes on end. The mestizo crowd, still thin, remained impassive; all the indignation on their behalf called forth no echoes in their immobile faces.

Occasionally, but not often, a speech came to an end, and a snatch of music from the *sierra* was played before the next speech began. The emotions vibrated immediately to the haunting pipes and flute, the *quena*, which seemed to sob with grief. It was music of a melancholy landscape, a melancholy past, and a melancholy future. It was music deeply subversive of the communist message of hope; by its very beauty, it almost reconciled a man to his suffering.

I slipped into the Gran Hotel Bolívar. It was the tea-time of the bourgeoisie. Music tinkled as waiters pushed around little carts of cakes between the coffee tables, while ladies with ringed fingers pointed to a tart or an eclair, which the waiters then lifted carefully with silver tongs on to a porcelain plate. The waiters hovered as the first bite was taken, anxious that the ladies had made the right choice. This was *té inglés* – English tea. It was different, though, from the ceremony as it is known in Tunbridge Wells or Harrogate. In the first place, slogans wafted in on the air through the revolving doors from the Plaza San Martín. 'Down with hunger! Down with unemployment! Death to the bourgeoisie!' In the second place, the tea was overseen by police-men with machine-guns at the ready to repel any over-zealous demonstrators. The waiter adjusted the little woollen muff on the handle of my silver teapot so I should not burn my fingers. 'Long live the proletariat!'

After tea, I rejoined the demonstration. The square had filled up, but still the crowd was listless. The vendors of state lottery tickets, however, were doing a brisk trade.

I met Paul and Rosa outside the hotel. By this time large Mercedes water cannon and long green articulated trucks had drawn up to the kerb next to the hotel. There were no windows in the trailers of the green trucks. Paul said they were called *gusanos* (worms) or *caimanes* (alligators) by the Limeños. They were used by the police for removing anyone inconvenient.

'But still,' I said, 'it *is* something that the government allows demonstrations like this.'

Paul disagreed. He said that, if anything, the new freedom of expression was a retrograde step. It would delude the Peruvian working class into thinking it was free, and sidetrack it into watching trash like *Prostitución Clandestina*. I said I doubted whether the people watching *Prostitución Clandestina* would otherwise be plotting the Revolution.

We went into the hotel's Bar Colonial for a drink, I first having ascertained that they had no ideological objections to doing so. The bar was a wood-panelled room with ceiling-high windows and crystal chandeliers, a superlative target for radical missiles.

The windows overlooked the Avenida Nicholás de Piérola (after the populist dictator of that name) down which students, linking arms *à la rive gauche*, now came trotting, shouting slogans.

A young American lady, dressed expensively in *crêpe de chine*, looked out of the windows.

'It's real creepy,' she said.

'That's democracy for you,' I replied.

'But they're *communists.*'

She returned to her table and took a gulp of her drink.

We drank pisco sours, a cocktail made from Peruvian *aguardiente*, beaten egg white and lemon juice. Soon we were tipsy, and Rosa said this was the grandest building she had ever been in. She went to the toilet and returned with travellers' tales of its marmoreal splendour. The doors were polished brass, the basins marble, the air and soap scented. Above all, a servant came forward to turn on the tap for you and hand you your perfumed towel. We laughed at the pretentiousness of it all.

We left the hotel and sought a small restaurant Paul knew, threading our way through the demonstrators who were growing more excited: riot police had arrived. In the restaurant Paul ordered a bottle of Chilean white wine, and I chaffed him about its political impurity. It was better wine than Peruvian, he said, and if he refused to buy it only the Chilean peasants would suffer.

'That's precisely why we buy South African fruit in England,' I said.

He grew expansive under the influence of the wine, and talked only of large subjects. Paul launched into a description of the future he envisaged, when Man will be truly Man (as compared with what he is now). He will no longer want to watch John Travolta; he will prefer Shakespeare and Goethe. Moreover, his creative energies will be so liberated that he will himself create works of equal stature.

I said I found this vision of the future somewhat intimidating.

Paul warmed to the subject of Man in general. Reactionaries, he said, believed that society would be good only when men were good. Scientific progressives, on the other hand, knew that men would be good only when society was good.

I turned to Rosa. I asked her whether either of them, Man or Society, would ever be any good. She pulled Paul's beard.

'Only my gringo,' she said, 'only my gringo is good.'

With that, we left the restaurant. Returning to the hotel I found I was not yet ready for bed, and I walked down the Avenida Nicholás de Piérola, through the crowds listening to the twentieth speech, past an arcade in which less seriously inclined Limeños played electronic games, down as far as the Hotel Crillon, Lima's second most famous luxury establishment. The windows at the front glittered; people in evening dress were arriving and departing. I walked round the back of the hotel, down a dark narrow street. There, the first three storeys of the hotel consisted only of a blank concrete wall without windows. Against the wall, smelling of urine, a line of young couples were making love. It was more private there than in their shacks in the pueblos jóvenes.

Paul, Rosa and I met again early next morning. The worms and alligators were still parked by the kerb, but no-one had been arrested in the night. Paul said this was just another example of the cunning of the bourgeoisie, led by Sr Belaúnde, to deceive the Peruvian working class that it now had a government that respected its own laws. But in reality it was just as lawless as the rest.

We went to the main food market of Lima to buy lunch. Paul warned me to keep my money close about me, and to try to look poor, for the pickpockets were numerous and skilful. Crowds of ordinary Limeños were shopping with the fine discrimination that a devotion to good food but a small budget dictates. The choice of produce was vast. I had never seen many of the fruits and herbs before. When the Spaniards conquered the Inca Empire, the Incas knew a greater variety by far of food crops than were known to the whole of Europe. Indian women in bowler hats, with babies strapped to their backs by beautiful multicoloured blankets, sat on the ground with their produce spread out before them. There were exotic fruits, and bouquets of peppers of all colours: yellow, orange, red, green, mauve and even blue. My fascination with these humble things amused Rosa; I, whom she thought dwelt in a world of marble latrines.

We walked between the butchers' stalls. Mock-angry butchers berated housewives for being foolish, for ignoring such bargains as were not to be had in the rest of the market, if not the world. No portion of a carcass was too despised to be on sale. Even the trachea found favour. One stall sold only heads, another only lungs.

Rosa bought garlic (it was sold by the kilo) and some maize that was jet black. I thought it had been burnt to charcoal, but she assured me that black was its natural colour. When immersed in water it produced a purple drink, the colour of potassium permanganate. Paul bought some giant seed pods, eighteen inches long and an inch and a half wide. Inside the pods large green beans nestled on a white velvety lining. It was the lining we ate, sweet and succulent. Rosa laughed at my surprise.

We took a taxi to their flat – a great luxury for them. They said they could afford a taxi only once a month.

Their flat was in an area inhabited by what Paul called 'the established working class,' by which he meant those in regular employment. A few years ago it had been one of the pueblos jóvenes, the jerrybuilt and illegal squatter settlements that migrants to the city erect on the fringe of what is already built. If the settlement survives attempts to destroy it, eventually the authorities, with the same pragmatism that allowed the Catholic church to incorporate Indian festivals into the Christian calendar, recognise the settlements as permanent, and provide them with power lines and water, in return for the right to levy certain local taxes.

The flat was on the second floor of the building that looked as though it would dissolve into mud if it rained. We approached it through a maze of washing lines, from which their next door neighbour was plucking garments like fruit. It was small but not uncomfortable and I have seen much worse in England. There was a bedroom, a study, and a kitchen with a dining area. There was electric light, cold running water, and a one-ring gas stove working off a cylinder. It was simple but not spartan. The rent for two months was less than my hotel bill for one night.

While Rosa prepared lunch, Paul showed me the study. Above the bookcase was a crucifix modelled in clay in the rough but expressive indigenist style of contemporary Peruvian sculpture. The books in the bookcase were, with the exception of the Bible, all of the Marxist bent (and even the Bible, I learnt from Paul, was Marxist in tendency). Lenin was there, in fifty-four volumes, and Stalin in thirteen. There were selected works of Mao Tse-Tung in four; and the speeches of Enver Hoxha, Great Leader, Philosopher, Helmsman, Literary Critic, etc., of the Albanian people, also in four volumes, published by the Foreign Languages Publishing House in Tirana. There was a Short History of the Albanian Workers' Party. I said I thought it was an odd selection for a devout Catholic. Paul handed me a book which would explain everything to me, he said. It was *Teología de la liberación, Perspectivas* by a man called Gustavo Gutiérrez.

Gutiérrez started out to train as a doctor, but was deflected from this course by his observation of the mass misery of Peru, which medicine alone could never hope to dent. He turned to the study of politics, philosophy and theology instead; he is now a famous professor of theology in the Catholic University of Lima. Gutiérrez is not a clear writer; his style is heavy and academic, and would hardly be understood by the subjects of his forth-coming liberation, the Indians and mestizos. This is odd, because his basic ideas are not difficult. The Church in South America, he says, has traditionally been the handmaiden of the oligarchy. It has done the oligarchy's ideological work for it. By stressing the life to come; by persuading the poor and oppressed that present social arrangements were ordained by God rather than man; by emphasising that life on earth was but a prelude to the life eternal elsewhere; and by absorbing the Indian's attention in a ceaseless round of religious fiestas; the Church implicitly and explicitly supported some of the vilest exploitation of Man by men in the history of the world. But in the gospels Christ enjoins Man to love his neighbour as himself. In Peru, his neighbour is overwhelmingly likely to be poor, oppressed and miserable. To love one's neighbour as oneself in such a situation can only mean to relieve his poverty, oppression and misery. And this is where Marxism comes in. It is the only system of thought that can uncover the causes of all these phenomena, and therefore Catholics must also be Marxists. A Marxist analysis soon shows that Peru's problems all stem from its dependent role in the world capitalist system. Therefore, it is the first duty of Peruvian Catholics to work for the withdrawal of Peru from that system, and towards a socialist Peru. Gutiérrez says they must develop a 'revolutionary praxis'. He does not say what this actually entails, but others have drawn the conclusion that it means violent revolution, in the traditional Marxist sense. The Gospels not merely permit revolutionary violence: they require it.

Paul was a follower of Gutiérrez. Taking his line of thought to its ultimate conclusion, he considered Stalin, Enver Hoxha and the rest better Catholics and more orthodox than St Thomas Aquinas. This rather odd conclusion, which a man with less integrity than Paul might consider a *reductio ad absurdum*, reminded me of a friend who, after listening to a sermon during which the congregation was castigated by the preacher for not acting on its professed religious beliefs, exclaimed, 'My husband's an atheist, but he's a better Christian than any of you.'

We had quite a heated discussion about Marxism and Christianity. I said that at the most the Sermon on the Mount was compatible with some form of Utopian Socialism, of the kind for which Marx himself had nothing but contempt, to say nothing of his militant atheism. Paul said I had absorbed a distorted view of Marxism from anti-Soviet propaganda. In any case, from the Peruvian standpoint nothing in the Soviet Union looked too bad. I said the history of the Soviet Union was not without blemishes. Paul replied quoting Lenin: You can't make an omelette without breaking eggs.

'Yes,' I retorted, 'but you can break eggs without making an omelette.'

At this point our voices were raised, and Emilia announced that lunch was ready.

We sat down to *cebiche*, a dish of marinaded octopus, fish and prawns, which was so delicious that it soothed our differences away. Over the meal Paul and Rosa described their future as they saw it. It held no terrors for them, for they had abandoned ambition of the usual sort. Paul did not wish ever to return to the comfort of the United States. Rosa did not want to go either, unusually in a Peruvian girl marrying a *norteamericano*. Indeed, for a girl to marry thus was known locally as *comprar un boleto de Braniff* – to buy a Braniff ticket.

No; when Paul was qualified as a medical assistant, they would both go out to a village in the Sierra and work to improve the health of the people. They wanted nothing more.

I left them after lunch and never saw them again. They were deeply in love; they had a cause in which they believed whole-heartedly. I envied them.

Once again Richard and Frances were not at the Embassy at four o'clock. Disconsolately, I entered the National Museum of Art on my way back to the hotel. It was housed in the Palacio de la Exposición, built for an international exhibition which, in the heady days of the guano boom, was intended to demonstrate Peru's arrival as a nation.

A vast tapestry of Simón Bolívar hung in the entrance hall. Once again he looked unhappy: perhaps he had just heard of a recent survey carried out in Ecuador, a country which he liberated a century and a half ago, which revealed that seven out of ten rural Ecuadorian Indians were unable to name the country in which they were living.

The first thing that strikes the casual observer about South American art of the two great colonial schools, those of Cuzco and Quito, is the almost total lack of local reference. To the untutored eye, the two and a half centuries of Virgins, Depositions, Cruci-fixions and Viceroys might just as well have been painted in the workshops of Spain. The sober portraits of nineteenth-century

Republican worthies would not be out of place in a London club. Only in the twentieth century did Peruvian artists make the momentous discovery that Peru has a landscape of its own. They made a further discovery: the Indian. To make up for past neglect, and with the zeal of converts, they proceeded to paint nothing else. There was something forced, theoretical and even insincere about this *indigenismo*. The admiration and sympathy for the Indian was from afar; it was the exorcism of four hundred years of bad conscience. The artists rarely succeeded in portraying Indian life from the inside. The gulf between the cultures of the European and the Indian remained as wide as ever.

Richard and Frances had traced me to my hotel. Our reunion among the tea cups, cakes and machine guns was exuberant and most un-British.

Their week in Peru before my arrival had not been entirely trouble-free. They were glad to see me, not only for the sake of my company, but because they had lost all their money, their credit cards, their clothes, passport and camera. They were sitting in Huancayo station, waiting for a train. Their valuables were in a bag between Richard's feet. Suddenly, pandemonium broke out behind them. A peasant woman had dropped her eggs on the platform, and was screaming as though she had lost her children: ¡Oh, mis huevos, mis huevos! It was impossible not to look round, of course, but in that moment their bag was snatched. The thieves made off so quickly there was no hope of catching them. As for the decoy, she quickly forgot her eggs – her working capital, as it were – and scuttled away. Even at the moment of their loss, Richard and Frances were able to admire the skill with which it had been effected.

Their experience was not unusual. But the thieves of Peru are pacific on the whole. They rob you, but they do not kill you. I met a man who was robbed in an ingenious way: he was sitting at a station with two pieces of luggage, one large and one small. Two men approached him; one of them grabbed the small piece and ran away. The man's accomplice merely smiled at the victim. If he were to give chase carrying his large piece he would have no chance of catching the first thief; if he were to give chase without it, the second thief would merely walk away with it. He had no alternative but to accept his misfortune.

The worst part of Richard and Frances' experience was yet to come. This was dealing with the British Embassy to obtain new passports. They were treated with the superciliousness of official-dom once it has the upper hand. The woman in the Embassy, whose job it was to deal with precisely such cases, had formed the impression that she had been sent out to Lima exclusively to finish her knitting, into which any work was therefore an unwarrantable intrusion. Having been told by this Madame Defarge of the Foreign Office that it was impossible to issue new passports in under a month, Frances began to cry and Richard to shout. To avoid any repetition of such scenes, passports were issued next day.

The following day, Sunday, was the day of the National Census. No-one was allowed out of the building in which he spent the night until he had been enumerated. We sat on the verandah of the hotel overlooking the utterly deserted Avenida Nicholás de Piérola. As we stared at the buildings opposite, we noted their walls were pockmarked with bullet holes from the great anti-government riots of 1977. Suddenly the thickness of the plate glass separating us from the street became explicable: it was bullet-proof. An amenity of the Gran Hotel Bolívar is that its guests may sit and watch coups, riots and other civil disorders while eating good food, in perfect comfort and safety.

We went to be enumerated in the census. A lady in a silk dress sat in the hotel lobby at an escritoire with spindly golden legs. Behind and to the right of her was a flunkey in blue and gold livery. I sat in a blue plush chair.

I gave my name, age and nationality. The lady asked me what was my level.

'Level of what?' I asked.

'Education, señor.'

'I am a doctor.'

'Then I don't have to ask you whether you can read.'

'No,' I replied. 'The great majority of doctors can read.'

Her questions answered, the lady signalled to the flunkey, who stepped forward, picked a little paper sticker in the colours of the Peruvian flag from a board, and pressed it to my chest as though he were decorating me for bravery.

'You may now leave the hotel, señor,' she said.

The streets were eerily deserted, apart from the water cannon, worms and knots of soldiers on the street corners. Their task, apart from arresting pedestrians not bearing the census sticker, was to preserve public order. Census day evidently provided an opportunity for a public demonstration of discontent, though in the event occurred. The inhabitants of the pueblos jóvenes were afraid the information gathered in the census might be used by the authorities against their interests; amongst other ways, by removing them to their home provinces. Mistrust of authority runs deep in Peru, as well it might. In the eighteenth century censuses were undertaken to provide mine and textile factory owners with forced labour. The dreaded *mita de minas* and *mita de obrajes* levied on vast areas of Peru and Alto Peru (now Bolivia) brought millions of Indians to work in scarcely describable conditions. To be enumerated in a census was to be recruited for the mita; to be recruited for the mita meant death in all probability. Every year for two hundred years fifteen thousand Indians were sent to the mercury mines of Huancavelica or the silver mines of Potosí of whom two thirds died within a year. Some never even reached the mines: fettered together on the way from their villages by a long halter around their necks, if one of them stumbled through weakness or illness his head was severed from his body by the sword of a guard, so that he should not slow the others on their way to the mine. The Peruvian author González Prada wrote: 'Peru is a mountain crowned with a cemetery.' It was hardly a figure of speech, and the soldiers on National Census day looked nervous.

Gradually Lima thawed as people were counted in their houses. Old men ambled out on to the streets and sat on benches, reading the newspapers. Boys played football rowdily in the road,

while slightly older males discussed things knowingly in doorways. Being Sunday, it was a day of rest, essentially not different
from such days anywhere in the world. Work is oppressive and
dull, but Sundays are boring and futile.

The worms and water cannon remained outside the hotel, whose
inside was still patrolled by police with guns they looked all too
ready to use. The reason was now clear: a conference of all the
Latin American ministers of justice was convened in the hotel.
Men in immaculately tailored suits, with clumps of aides behind
them, sat round a highly polished wooden table set up on a dais,
with little flags of their various countries at their places. Discussion was earnest but *sotto voce*.

Among these well turned-out gentleman (and a few ladies in
silk dresses), perhaps the most distinguished for his services to
the cause of justice was Señor Sabino Agusto Montanaro, the
representative of Paraguay. Here is how justice was done to
Miguel Soler, leader of the Paraguayan Communist Party, by the
ministry of which Señor Montanaro was the highest official:

[He] was arrested in the house in which he had been secretly
living . . . Miguel Soler was tied by the feet and hands with rope
and gagged to prevent him from screaming. To disguise the
noises, the torturers played guaraní records of José Asunción
Flores, at full volume. Soler was beaten with truncheons, whips
and with iron bars for approximately four hours. Afterwards they
began to amputate his hands and arms. While dying, Soler
shouted to Pastor Coronel [his torturer] 'criminal, murderer,
dealer in white women, drug-traffficker' and spat in his face.
Pastor Coronel responded by kicking him in the chest which
caused heart failure. Soler had died . . . From that moment deep
silence fell over the Department of Investigations. After a while
some policemen came out of a room and began to shout in alarm,
'he's committed suicide! he's committed suicide!' The following
day a sheet appeared in the toilets completely saturated in blood
and the floor was covered in coagulated blood . . .

This was no mere aberration or oversight, however. This is what happened to his colleague in the Communist Party, Rubén Gonzalez:

[He] was beaten with truncheons over his whole body until there was not a square centimetre of his skin which was not bruised, and put into the bath full of water and excrement, with hands and feet tied. After several hours of torment during which Rubén did not once open his mouth except to swallow the excrement or insult his torturers, he was hung upside down, by the feet, from a beam in the ceiling, while being beaten with iron bars until he was dead.

His body was later found, along with two others, floating down the river. The river police and local magistrate ordered some local dockers to bury the bodies in shallow graves. The dockers were offered a similar fate if they ever spoke of what they had done.

There was an old joke in Nazi Germany: a Nazi official visits Luxembourg, and is shown the Luxembourg Ministry of the Navy. 'But you have no navy,' says the Nazi. 'So what?' says his Luxembourg guide. 'There is a Ministry of Justice in Berlin.'

We went out into the city. In the Plaza de Armas the Guatemalan minister of justice was being received with some pomp at the City Hall. A crowd had gathered to watch the guards presenting arms and marching up and down. 'A ceremony a day keeps revolution away,' said Richard.

We made our way to the Museum of the Inquisition. It was in the building where the Holy Office held its deliberations from 1570 until 1820, when it was formally abolished. Lima was one of the two principal seats of the Inquisition in the Indies (the other was Mexico). For all their formidable reputation, the two branches managed only a very low rate of productivity by the exalted standards of our day; in their quarter millennium of existence they executed – 'relaxed' is the technical term – less than a hundred unrepentant heretics. They functioned more as a political police than as guarantors of religious orthodoxy.

Another reason for the comparative unproductiveness of the

Inquisition in the Americas was that the Indians were excluded from its purview, which extended only to fully rational beings. In 1550 a public debate had been held in Valladolid between Fray Bartolomé de Las Casas and Juan Ginés de Sepúlveda as to whether the Indian was or was not truly human. The former answered in the affirmative, the latter in the negative. De Las Casas is generally agreed to have won the debate, but it was nevertheless considered that, legally speaking, the Indian was only a minor. Thus the scope of the Inquisition was restricted, though it managed to exert a dampening effect on the intellectual life of the colonies up to the very end of Spanish rule. As late as 1774 the doctor and mathematician José Celestino Mutis was denounced in Bogotá to the Inquisition for saying the earth revolved around the sun, while Baltasar de los Reyes Morrero was removed from his chair in Mexico in 1788 merely for *mentioning* Descartes.

Around the walls of the vaults were hung wooden plaques, like those in schools listing the names of distinguished old boys, giving the names in gold lettering of those investigated by the Inquisition. The commonest crimes alleged were crypto-Judaism and following the rites of Moses, of which nearly all those charged were found guilty, though a few were found innocent after having been tortured to death. In the vaults were tableaux of the tortures. One exhibit was called 'Los dos métodos de desarticulación' – the two methods of disarticulation – as though it were knowledge usefully to be imparted, like two methods of solving quadratic equations. The isolation cells, where heretics were kept sometimes for decades, were scarcely more than holes the size of a coffin: there was not room even to sit. Small coins had been thrown down to the dummies that suffered imprisonment in this way.

We had lunch in a restaurant called '*Tea Roon*'. The waiter looked as though he used the lapel of his once-white jacket to strain soup. He met our disconcerted glance with a defiant glare: if you can't stand the dirt, get out of the restaurant.

The Historical Museum, to which we went in the afternoon,

was in the old colonial house in which Simón Bolívar had stayed while he was in Lima. His bedroom was arranged as he left it. Portraits of him, and of his contemporary Antonio José Sucre, hung on the walls. Sucre, the third of the great foreign liberators of Peru, was a Venezuelan of Flemish descent. He was a man of stunning looks and one, moreover, of almost saintly character, which his enemies interpreted as weakness. Without personal ambition or avarice, Sucre was later assassinated by men who in turn met violent deaths. No doubt the thread of blood could be traced to the present day.

There was a long gallery in the Historical Museum devoted to portraits of the Viceroys of Peru, and another to all its Presidents. They brought to mind the old taunt that in North America everyone can be president, in South America everyone has been president. Some of the portraits were allegorical. The soul of one assassinated nineteenth-century president was borne aloft by two angels, one simultaneously blowing a long trumpet, the other inscribing his name on a slab of black marble. His soul was still wearing a frock coat.

There was also a series of paintings depicting the War of the Pacific. It was Peru's second war against Chile, and the second it lost. The paintings obscured the fact of defeat, emphasising only the glory and ignoring the utterly prosaic origins of the war: a dispute over guano exports.

The President of Peru at the outbreak of hostilities, Mariano Ignacio Prado, was entrusted with a large sum of money to go to Europe to procure badly needed modern arms for the country; but neither Prado, nor the money, nor for that matter any arms, were ever seen in Peru again. The Prado family remains one of the richest in Peru, however.

> We laughed, knowing that better men would come,
> And greater wars; when each proud fighter brags
> He wars on Death – for Life; not men – for flags.

In the courtyard of the museum we met a group of young men in identical smart blazers, flannel trousers and striped ties.

Among them were two demure young ladies in suits and silk neckscarves. They were, they said, attending a diplomatic conference held in Lima between Argentina and Chile to avert war over two small islands in the Beagle Channel. People had come from all over Latin America, they said, to observe the conference.

'What, all in the same clothes?' asked Richard.

They explained that they were students in the Peruvian Diplomatic Academy, and that they attended such conferences by way of practical training, as medical students attend operations. The conference was taking place mainly in the Gran Hotel Bolívar.

Returning there, we bought the *Miami Herald*, the English language newspaper which, for geographical reasons, has the highest circulation of any in Latin America. We read of the riots, then convulsing many British cities from Bristol to Bradford. Our own subdued masses had emerged from their slums, better perhaps than the pueblos jóvenes of Lima, though more dismal. The news of the riots reduced our complacency vis à vis the tumults of the Peruvian capital.

To try to raise our sagging spirits, we decided on our last night in Lima to take dinner in the *Tambo de Oro*, one of the city's most expensive restaurants. The *tambos* were inns and hostels built at intervals along the Inca trails, where messengers of the emperor spent the night before continuing their journeys. The *Tambo de Oro* fulfilled no such utilitarian end, however. Furnished in luxurious colonial style, burning a fire in a magnificent fireplace completely disproportionate to Lima's climate, the restaurant was empty except for one other couple. The waiters almost fought over who should serve us. We drank pisco sours and Peruvian champagne, while a pasteurised trio of musicians in beautifully laundered ponchos serenaded us with sentimental Peruvian songs.

The musicians devoted much attention to us. We didn't know whether to listen intently and let the food go cold, or ignore them completely, so we veered between the two. At the end of a batch of songs something more tangible was required. The leader of the trio, with a brilliantined moustache, slipped a banknote under his poncho. Our banknote was smaller than the other couple's, and the trio turned its attention to them.

Back in my bedroom, slightly drunk, I tried to switch on the bedside lamp without success. No matter the number of times I pressed the button, the lamp remained in darkness. Suddenly there was a rap on my door. A man in blue and gold livery, still unbuttoned, stood panting before me; from the repeated clangs of his bell downstairs he had concluded there was something I needed very urgently, like a fire extinguisher or a crowbar with which to repel an intruder. I explained I had made a mistake; I had not wanted room service, only to switch on my bedside lamp. With great ceremony, though with the corner of one eye still upon me, he stepped over to the lamp and switched it on. He switched it off and on and off and on again, to make sure I had the hang of it. Then he bowed out warily backwards, still looking at me. I gave him two dollars before he disappeared. Back in his room, he no doubt reflected on the injustice of the world.

TWO

Iquitos, Peruvian Amazonia

NEXT MORNING the ministers of justice had departed, but not the water cannon. They now protected the military men from Argentina and Chile who were meeting in the hotel to avert war. They chatted amicably after breakfast, in a club-like atmosphere. They had probably attended the same academies in the North. If war was expedient, no doubt there would be war; if war was not expedient, there would be cocktails before dinner.

We left the Gran Hotel Bolívar's world of intrigue and high politics behind us. We were going to Iquitos, the city deep in the Peruvian Amazon. It can still only be reached by boat along the river or by air, for there are no roads connecting it with the rest of Peru.

The normal rules of air travel do not apply in Peru. A valid and reconfirmed ticket is not sufficient to board a flight. Cajolery, wheedling, displays of temper, tears and finally bribes are sometimes needed to secure a seat. Richard and Frances met an unfortunate American at a Peruvian airport who had spent fully three days trying to board a flight for which he had a ticket, before realising that ten dollars did the trick. Securing a seat at the airport counter is not, however, the end of the struggle by any means.

Peruvians are normally polite to the point of ceremoniousness. But when boarding an aircraft their character undergoes a change. Social inhibitions are cast aside. Venerable grandmothers with walking sticks are mercilessly pushed aside in the general *sauve qui peut* which follows the announcement that the aircraft is ready for boarding. Everyone takes as much with him as he can carry, using what he brings as a battering ram to destroy other people's baggage and impede their progress. It often, but not always, turns out that the number of passengers exactly equals the number of seats, and therefore the scramble was unnecessary. The successful outcome of a struggle, however, affords satisfactions that no more orderly method of allocation can rival.

In a few seconds we were high above the *garúa* which for the last few days had seemed to encompass our lives. We turned across the Andes, with plumes of powdery snow blown from their peaks. The eastern slopes of the cordillera were, by contrast with the western, covered in dense green, and soon, as far as the eye could see even from seven miles up, the jungle of the Amazon basin was stretched out before us. Great loops of muddy brown rivers snaked slowly through the flat green vastness, the largest rivers we had ever seen, though they were only tributaries of tributaries. Sometimes we would catch a glimpse of a river bigger than the rest, a river with a romantic name: the Huallaga, the Ucayali, the Santiago, the Pastaza, the Tigre, all tributaries of the Marañon, itself a tributary of the Amazon. The scale was stupendous, awing, numbing. We felt guilty that, as travellers, we were sitting in comfort seven miles high eating refrigerated tomato sandwiches rather than hacking our way through the jungle with machetes, à la Fawcett.

We landed as the sun became an angry red disk sinking quickly over the horizon of the tree canopy. The jungle grew up to the very edges of the runway, as though ready to reclaim its own should Man's vigilance for a moment be relaxed. We took a bus into the city, a vehicle without glass in its windows. This was as much a concession to the spitters of Iquitos as to its steamy climate. Iquitos is a frontier town, and frontiersmen everywhere, for some as yet unknown physiological reason, seem always to produce a great deal of phlegm, which they drag up and expel from the innermost core of their bodies. They have great expectorations. It is, I suppose, a sign of masculinity. The noise of it mingled with the more predictable night sounds of the jungle:

the croaking of frogs, the telegraph-wire hum of the cicadas, the chattering of monkeys. The driver, with one elbow resting on the bus's bonnet, was determined to finish his cigarette before starting out, in spite of the unfavourable comments of his passengers.

The bus was battery-powered, something of a paradox in a city whose growth and present relative prosperity depended entirely on the production of oil from the wells in the surrounding jungles. But Iquitos, though the centre of the Peruvian oil-extracting industry, suffered from occasional shortages of refined petroleum products. It illustrated in miniature the problems which countries with purely extractive industries often face.

When we reached the city, darkness had descended. We drove past rows of shacks, lit by hurricane lamps. Through cracks in the walls, amongst the flickering shadows cast by the lamps, we saw men collapsed fully-dressed on crumpled and untidy beds, while their women struggled to produce the evening meal on a hotplate made from the end of a forty-four gallon drum, placed over a dangerous-looking fire that threatened at any time to engulf the whole shack. The bus stuttered to a final halt in a potholed road deep in mud.

There was considerable life in the street, carried on in the brilliant but circumscribed white light of kerosene lamps. Women with small stalls at the side of the road were frying fish, while their children gutted fish by the stall and dogs scavenged the gutter for the remains. Customers relieved themselves at the side of the road, or carried on vehement arguments while waiting. Other men in dingy bars tried to forget their lives by gulping aguardiente. We struggled along with our baggage, avoiding wherever possible the light, and asking from time to time for the Plaza de Armas. 'Dos caudros más' came the answer like a refrain – two blocks more – however far it was.

As we approached the centre of Iquitos the lights became electric, though of low wattage. We found an hotel, reputedly decent and clean. As soon as she entered her room Frances was attacked by a mosquito the size of a British wasp, with a sting like a hypodermic needle. She took refuge in the bathroom, only to discover a column of giant ants marching up the wall. We tried to console her with the thought that we were, after all, in the jungle, but only pisco sours would comfort her.

In the roadside café we met a group of young Swedes, blond and tall and straight-limbed. They were going next day to a place called Leticia, a town on the confluence of the borders of Peru, Colombia and Brazil, in order to have their passports stamped with the stamps of all three countries.

After dinner we met a man, no longer young but reluctant to admit it, who exuded bonhomie like a sticky secretion. He had plastered his remaining hair with great care over his baldness, and squeezed his fat belly and thighs into Adidas shorts so tight that, when he thought we were not looking, he winced with discomfort. He owned a camp, he said, in the jungle. There were no washing facilities there, except for the largest river system in the world, and sometimes the food ran short. There was a young Frenchman there who had lived by himself in the jungle for six years who would look after us. He took us to his office, scarcely more than a hole in a wall, whose slowly revolving ceiling fan made no impression on the humid atmosphere. Behind his desk was a poster of the Place de la Concorde.

We asked him whether he would be coming with us to the jungle.

'Unfortunately not,' he said, implying that it was only by chance that we found him in Iquitos rather than the sixteenth arrondissement.

Even by day Iquitos did not look the boom town it was reputed to be. It resembled more Macondo, Gabriel García Márquez's mythopoeic town in the jungle. Iquitos had once known 'prosperity' before, in the days of the rubber boom that brought opera and high prices to Manaus (the Brazilian capital of the Amazon), incalculable wealth to a few and impossible dreams to a multitude. The destruction of Iquitos' first period of prosperity was entirely due to the British, who were determined to end South America's monopoly on rubber.

The story of the abduction from the Amazon of the rubber seeds that very soon brought about the ruin of the Amazon millionaires starts with Sir Clements Markham, an official in the India Office who was himself a Peruvianist of such distinction that Peru's only English public school is named after him. Among his other accomplishments he translated Bernal Díaz del Castillo's *True History of the Conquest of New Spain*, and Garcilaso de la Vega's *Royal Commentaries of the Incas* and *General History of Peru*. But, in the manner of Victorian gentleman scholars, he was also a man of action. In 1854 he made a dramatic journey across the Andes in record time, bearing with him specimens of the wild cinchona tree native to the forests of the eastern part of Peru. His specimens flourished in India and Ceylon, and the plantations there soon reduced the price of quinine to a sixteenth of its former level.

Markham realised that rubber was a vital component of all the modern machinery of his age. It was his opinion that if the wild rubber trees of South America continued to be exploited at their then current rate, they would soon be exhausted. If cinchona trees could be domesticated in plantations, why not rubber trees? Joseph Hooker, friend of Darwin and director of the Kew Gardens, was given this task by Markham. He employed an agent in Brazil, one Henry Alexander Wickham, whose career until then had been worse than merely undistinguished. However, he pursued the collection of rubber seeds with singleminded devotion, until he had seventy thousand of them. He smuggled them past Brazilian customs on a ship, declaring them to be only 'exceedingly delicate botanical specimens specially designate to Her Britannic Majesty's own Royal Gardens of Kew'. Britain had spent precisely £1505 4s 2d on destroying a South American industry worth millions. Wickham was later knighted for his exploit.

There were still a few architectural reminders of Iquitos' former glory. There were mansions faced with *azulejos*, the blue and yellow ceramic tiles imported from Portugal and Italy by rubber barons eager to outdo each other in the splendour of their homes. Elaborate cast iron balconies had been imported from England. The mansions were now divided into flats or, in one case, used as a police station. There was a curious building in the Calle Putumayo, constructed entirely of thick sheet iron, said to have been designed by Eiffel, the French engineer. Seldom in history can there have been a building less suited to its climate: the first owner was said to have abandoned it before his first night in it was through.

At one time, money was of so little account to the magnates of the rubber region that men lit cigars with banknotes worth fifty pounds; bought whole consignments of hats to find one which suited, chucking the rest in the river; or paid £400 (the pounds of 1900!) to hire a car to transport a mistress a few hundred yards.

But, as usual, great wealth has its seamy underside. Julio César Arana, the wealthiest rubber baron to live in Iquitos (or anywhere else, for that matter) was a man with an unusually puritanical aversion to ostentation and frivolity, devoted to the hard work in whose redemptive powers he evidently believed. He was the virtual dictator of the region at the turn of the century; when a man sold flysheets of Manaus attacking Arana and his methods, he was later found dead in a gutter with his eyes sewn up with cobblers' thread and his ears filled with beeswax. The message was clear.

Arana derived the greatest part of his wealth from a vast area adjacent to the Putumayo River, some twenty thousand square miles to which he had dubious title. The wild rubber was collected with the 'co-operation' of the jungle Indians. The area was divided into stations, each with its own overseer, to whom Arana paid commission but no salary. As a result, the methods used by such men as Miguel Loayza, overseer at el Encanto, and José Fonseca, overseer at Ultimo Retiro, were not scrupulously particular. At el Encanto the smell of dead Indians was so overpowering that the black guards, themselves no sissies, could not stomach their food. At a fiesta at La Chorrera a toast in champagne was drunk to the overseer who had killed most Indians in the past year. The palm was awarded to José Fonseca, who had gathered together hundreds of Indians from the Chontaduras, Ocainas and Utiguerres tribes, whose deliveries of wild rubber were deemed insufficient. With six men armed with machetes and carbines, he fell upon them, killing a hundred and fifty. Their blood lust temporarily sated, they told the survivors that any Indian not delivering his quota of rubber would be exterminated.

A torpor hung over Iquitos at breakfast time. Even an American oilman of the type who normally rises above the prevailing atmosphere of flyblown places, ate his roll and drank his coffee listlessly at the table next to us.

We awaited a boat by the river bank, watching the immense brown stream glide silently by, and contemplating with awe the opposite bank of an island that, even two thousand miles from the mouth of the river, was a mile across.

We went up river in a canoe that was larger than we had expected. It had a thatched canopy. What the owner of the camp had not told us was that other people, apart from the boatman, would be accompanying us. There was a half-caste from Aruba with a squint; his pale, anorexic Dutch wife who looked as though she were undertaking a painful cure for agoraphobia; and their anaemic daughter who asked for a bottle of Fanta as soon as the canoe left the bank. There was a Frenchman in platform shoes who was so intensely in conversation with his wife or lover that he scarcely had time to notice the Amazon; and a fat, jolly Austrian with a bird's nest beard, who had brought along a roly-poly Peruvian girl, reminding me of Boule de Suif. The Austrian had rescued her temporarily from the Aero Peru office in Cuzco where she worked.

We were a distinctly unimpressive party of jungle explorers. The canoe's outboard motor beat against the current – surprisingly strong – past the riverside slum of Belén, built on floating wooden platforms that rose and fell with the level of the river. Banana boats, laden until they almost sank, scudded by. The far bank of the river was two miles distant.

We were accompanied by two mestizo boatmen who had lived on the Amazon all their lives. One of them proudly showed us thin white scars on his fingers – piranha bites, he said. (I once knew a hospital administrator in England who kept a pet piranha. He dreamt, I think, of feeding doctors to it). As he showed us his scars, the canoe suddenly sprang a leak. The Dutch lady's shoes got wet and she shrieked; she knew she never should have come, and now she was going to drown; that is, if she weren't stripped to a skeleton first by the piranhas. One of the boatmen took off his shirt and stuffed it into the leak with the tip of his knife. The Dutch lady said she didn't like the look of that knife.

We kept close to the left bank – not more than a few hundred yards from it, which is close in the context of the Amazon. For some way out of Iquitos the jungle had been slashed and burned, and turned into banana plantations. The simple huts of the Indian workers looked not very different from the huts of the Gilbert Islanders.

Richard pointed to an emerald iguana, four feet long, on the bank.

The Dutch lady turned away in disgust. Reptiles! It was just as she had thought, the Amazon was full of them. The Austrian and Boule de Suif were so busy with their erotic explorations of each other that they had no time for the fauna; and the Frenchman, to judge from the heavy-lidded glance he bestowed on the iguana, considered lizards, unless they had read Jean-Paul Sartre, a bore. As for the Dutch girl, she did not look up from her electronic game, killing monsters from outer space with little blips.

The journey up river took six hours. After two hours on the Amazon itself we turned into a tributary, mightier than the Nile at Cairo. We were each given a banana to assuage our growing hunger, and the Dutch lady rummaged in her bag for a packet of Nestlé's chocolate for her daughter, who by now was engaged in drawing – appropriately enough, a jumbo jet. Soon everyone was asleep, Boule de Suif cradled in her Austrian's lap, probably dreaming of airconditioning and 'international cuisine'.

We turned into a tributary, no larger than the Thames at

Westminster. The water was of such glassy stillness that it was hard to credit it flowed. The tall and noble trees in the banks, and the blue sky above, were perfectly mirrored in the surface. When the engine stopped there was a profound and penetrating silence; not a leaf stirred, not a bird started.

We turned into streams yet smaller, reaching our destination called Tamashiyacu, after the tribe of Indians living thereabouts. The river there was narrow, not more than fifty yards: narrow enough, we all thought, for the arrows of hostile Indians to cross and fill us with arcane nerve poisons unknown to western science. The lodge, as it was called, consisted of a wooden mooring place; two thatched wooden structures, one for sleeping and one for eating; and a muddy yard leading to the kitchen, where a couple of shy Indian women moved about in the shadows, preparing food. A brightly coloured scarlet macaw called Aurora, and a green parrot called Edgar, sidled up and down a beam under the thatch of the dining hall, screeching and defaecating copiously. In the yard, near the kitchen, was a sleepy well-fed boa, the selvatic equivalent no doubt of a dustbin.

The Frenchman who had been living in the jungle for six years materialised from somewhere in the nearby trees. He was carrying an axe. He had survived the jungle, but it appeared not to have improved his health. He was emaciated, his ribs rachitic, his legs covered in sores at various stages of evolution; and his face had the vacant stare of a man who has indulged too much in marijuana. He was conscious, however, of a certain moral superiority over those who had not survived six years in the jungle.

He announced that lunch would be delayed, owing to trouble with the Indian cooks of an unspecified nature. The news was greeted less than joyfully, for we were by now very hungry. Instead of lunch, however, we were going on a two-hour walk through the jungle. Before we left, the Dutch lady inspected the premises for washing facilities. When she found there were none save the river, she berated her husband in public, who responded by squinting furiously in all directions until the storm was over.

She called Tamashiyacu the absolute back of beyond.

We set out, the French guide slinging an ancient shotgun over his cadaverous shoulder, and swinging at the clear path with his machete, just for effect. Later, it actually became necessary to hack at the undergrowth to clear a path. The party was dressed in costumes of varying degrees of unsuitability. The Frenchman's wife, for example, wore an elegant dress with a Suzie Wong slit up one side; the Dutch lady wore tree-frog green crimplene slacks; Boule de Suif had high-heeled shoes with delicate patent leather straps, between which bulged the ample flesh of her feet; and the Frenchman's platform shoes proved highly unsuitable for negotiating mud and undergrowth. When mud got in the Dutch woman's sensible shoes (sensible, that is, for Rotterdam) she squealed, blamed her husband for the mud, and cursed the Amazon.

Suddenly the guide put up his hand for us to freeze behind him. He raised his gun, aiming at the canopy far above us, and a shot rang out. We had not seen whatever he was aiming at, but it was clear from his face that he had missed. We expected a hue and cry from the startled birds of the jungle, as in the movies, but an eerie silence settled over the forest after the echoing of the shot died down. A rumour swept our little column that the guide had been aiming at nothing except impressing us.

A few minutes later the episode was repeated, again without success.

'Roast monkey,' said the guide sorrowfully. 'Delicious.'

Some of our party shuddered. The theory of evolution has been so deeply assimilated that eating a monkey appeared to them not far short of cannibalism.

Our walk through the jungle became strenuous, almost like a forced march. The guide hacked away furiously, as though it were a mortal enemy of his. I had conceived of the jungle as being perfectly flat, like a swamp, and was surprised to discover that the land was undulating, sometimes with hills steep enough to make us puff as we scrambled up the muddy sides. The astonishing profusion of plant life, of parasitic ferns and bromeliads growing on the trunks of trees, made the canopy above us a fantastic tracery of dark and light, an Islamic pattern without symmetry. The silence of the jungle at midday also surprised me – no Tarzan noises at all, only our heavy-footed snapping of twigs, Boule de Suif's giggles as her Austrian lunged erotically at her, and the Dutch lady's fresh complaints. By the time we returned to Tamashiyacu, most of our party had had quite enough of the jungle, an indication perhaps of the frailty of the town dweller's illusions about wild places.

Lunch was of river fish tasting of mud, and fried green bananas. A piranha had been caught in the morning, and the French guide asked us whether we wanted to see it. It was in a bowl in the kitchen (the Indian cooks scuttled away in fear as we entered), an unimpressive small silver fish seemingly of the type that English anglers stand all day in the rain to catch in industrial canals. So this was the fish of ill-repute, that every schoolboy knows can strip a horse to its skeleton within seconds of immersion! We opened the jaws of the harmless-looking creature, and saw two rows of needle-sharp teeth. The words of Colonel Fawcett came to mind.

> There was a splash in the river at night, and a sleepy workman woke up and asked, 'What's that?' Another replied, 'It's only Ladriguez fallen in the river.' The first grunted and went back to sleep. From the unfortunate Ladriguez there came not so much as a scream; he was literally torn to pieces by the piraña before he came to the surface!

After lunch we went out looking for Indians. Some of the party remained behind, the Austrian and Boule de Suif to pursue further their erotic adventures, the Dutch lady to sob on her hard bed. She heard that only twenty-five years before some Brazilian and American explorers had been killed by hostile Indians, and would not accept reassurances that by now the Indians of the region, and the Tamashiyacu in particular, had been thoroughly massacred and decimated by disease into submissiveness. All the same, the guide took his gun, though it was for game rather than

Indians, a less than clear distinction in some parts of the Amazon jungle.

A long forced march through the jungle brought us to a clearing in a gulley. There was a village, a few shelters made of logs and thatch, with platforms raised two feet above the muddy ground. There were embers still in the fires, but apart from one small and terrified girl leaning against the corner post of her house, the village was deserted, abandoned at our clumsy approach.

We knew the Tamashiyacu were well-disposed and peaceable, but we nevertheless felt exposed, standing in the middle of the village clearing in the knowledge that they must have been watching, while we had no idea at all where they were hiding. Unpredictable Indian uprisings were not after all unknown. The guide told us to behave normally, but in the circumstances it was difficult to know what normal was. Our conversation sounded tinny, our laughter nervous.

Eventually we heard a slight rustling, and an Indian in a grass skirt emerged from the nearby jungle, followed by a small pot-bellied boy in pink shorts. After a period of observation they had decided that we, too, were well-disposed and peaceable, their reasons for caution being historically a thousand times more justified than ours.

Christopher Columbus wrote to Ferdinand and Isabella of the Indians of Hispaniola: The inhabitants go naked . . . they have no iron or arms and are not capable of using them, not because they are not strong and well-built but because they are astonishingly shy . . . true, when they have been reassured and lost their fear, they are so naïve and so free with their possessions that no-one who had not witnessed them would believe it. When you ask for something they have, they never say no. To the contrary, they offer to share with anyone . . . I gave them a thousand pretty things in order to get their affection and make them want to become Christians. I hope to win them to love and service of your Highnesses and of the Spanish nation . . .

Within fifty years there was not a single Carib Indian left alive.

The Arawaks of Hispaniola committed suicide rather than fall into the hands of the Spanish; not one was converted to Catholicism. The process which Coulumbus started has not yet quite worked its way through: massacres still occur, where suitable material remains.

The Indian was the only member of his village who was not ashamed to appear before us in his traditional costume, donned especially for the occasion. The boy, his son, had all the false chubbiness of the severely malnourished. His distended belly was probably full of worms, contending for the small amount of nourishment that passed his lips. His father had brought a few bows and arrows with him, and some necklaces strung together from red beans, which he hoped to sell us, for money and its magical powers had penetrated even this far into the jungle. Some of us bought his wares, and I could hear already the conversations they would provoke at dinner parties.

'Wherever did you get that bow and arrow?'

'Oh, I bought it in the Amazon, from an Indian. And that necklace my wife is wearing . . .'

After the evening meal, our party went in canoes to some stagnant backwaters, in the hope of seeing the nocturnal animals with which we all felt the jungle must secretly be alive. A brilliant full moon cast eerie shadows among the creepers and overhung the narrow passages of water. We heard nothing but the plash of our oars, which stirred the phosphorescent bubbles in the silvered surface.

Alas, we saw no exotic creatures, nor heard them, nor even sensed their presence. All hopes of a sighting were dispelled when the trailer of a creeper unexpectedly swung into the face of the Dutch lady. She screamed and fought off the creeper as though it were a snake. Her shoulders heaved with not quite silent sobs for the rest of our nocturnal journey, and one could only feel sorrow for someone to whom the jungle had meant nothing but misery.

Night in the jungle was utterly silent, except for the giggles of Boule de Suif and her Austrian, to whose erotic fumblings the rickety building vibrated.

*   *   *

I woke before anyone else was stirring. A mist had descended in the night, bringing with it a softness to the landscape. The outlines of the trees on the opposite bank were blurred to a pastel green haze; fish leapt from the water and fell back in with a deep-sounding plop, perfect concentric circles radiating silently from the point at which they returned to the water, like the raked pebbles of a Japanese Zen garden. At such a time one achieved an almost mystical feeling of complete reconciliation with the world.

The rest of our party had had enough of the jungle and returned that morning to Iquitos. The French guide went with them, apparently for one of his periodic binges in civilisation – alcohol and prostitutes. He was replaced by one of those men who always have three days' growth of black beard whenever you see them, no more but never less. He said he was part-owner of Tamashiyacu, and immediately after imparting that information, climbed into a hammock and went to sleep.

The sun quickly dispersed the mist, and we spent two days quietly exploring the jungle, never going far, for even if the Indians were friendly, the jungle was still not a formal garden and it was possible to lose one's way in fifty yards. Frances fished for piranhas, eventually catching one small specimen; Richard swam in the river, surviving without the kind of mishap that befell Ladriguez. We canoed to a backwater where the river expanded to form a small lagoon. The Victoria lilies that grew there had pads six feet across on which it would have been possible to stand a small child. Wading birds with delicate feet and nervous tics hopped from lily pad to lily pad in search of food. We watched the myriad butterflies on their seemingly random flights, their wings tantalisingly gorgeous beyond anything we had ever seen, a pattern of incandescent yellows, electric blues and startling scarlets: 'the fearless children of the sun, the capricious tyrants of the flowers', as Joseph Conrad calls them. We watched the jewelled hummingbirds hover as they sucked the nectar from the orchids growing on the tree trunks towering above us. Everything was reflected perfectly in the still, still water.

Our only regret was that we saw no creature more dangerous to man than one small tarantula, and we proved far more dangerous to it than it to us. Above all, we wanted to see an anaconda. Here is Colonel Fawcett again, describing one he shot:

We stepped ashore and approached the reptile with caution. It was out of action, but shivers ran up and down the body like puffs of wind on a mountain tarn. As far as it was possible to measure, a length of forty-five feet lay out of the water, and seventeen in it, making a total length of sixty-two feet. Its body was not thick for such a colossal length – not more than twelve inches in diameter – but it had probably been long without food. I tried to cut a piece of the skin, but the beast was by no means dead and the sudden upheavals rather scared us. A penetrating foetid odour emanated from the snake, probably its breath, which is believed to have a stupefying effect, first attacking and later paralysing its prey. Everything about this snake is repulsive.

Such large specimens may not be common, but the trails in the swamp reach a width of six feet and support the statements of Indians and rubber pickers that the anaconda sometimes reaches an incredible size, altogether dwarfing that shot by me. The Brazilian Boundary Commission told me of one they killed in the Río Paraguay exceeding *eighty* feet in length! In the Araguaya and Toacantías basins there is a black variety known as the *dormidera*, or sleeper, from the loud snoring noise it makes. It is reputed to reach a huge size, but I never saw one . . . To venture into the haunts of the anaconda is to flirt with death.

Meanwhile, the *dormidera* of Tamashiyacu, its sleeping partner as it were, came to life and emerged from his hammock only as the sun went down, and the dinner hour approached. Having spent all day alone and asleep, he evidently felt a great need to talk. After dinner, eaten by the light of a hurricane lamp, he lit a cigarette with deliberation, and prepared for a long chat.

He told us we were extremely fortunate to have come to the jungle at this time of the year. At other times, the giant mosquitoes were so numerous that one dared not open one's mouth for fear of a cloud of them entering and biting the inside. Had we ever been bitten on the inside of our mouths? No; well then, we had experienced nothing.

Having established his moral superiority over us by virtue of his greater suffering, he told us of his past and opinions. He had spent seven years as a petroleum engineer in the jungles of Peru. Much of that time he was in the most inaccessible areas which, once entered, could not be left again for months at a time. There wasn't much he didn't know about the jungle, its terrain, its fauna, above all about the Indians who inhabited it. There was only one word of universal application to Indians: lazy. With the example of civilization before their very eyes (in the form of a petroleum camp, where civilization is *Playboy*, poker, beer and brawls) they persisted in clinging to their own savage and unreasonable way of life. As for those who bestirred themselves and took themselves off to the waterside slum of Belén, we should not waste our sympathy on them. Many of them had hoards of gold under their mats. In any case, they would not feel at home in a house with facilities like running water; an Indian is only happy when he is dirty. You have to live in the jungle for seven years to appreciate that.

His face was so contorted by hate as he spoke, the fasciculations of his facial muscles accentuated by the shadowy light, that we were shocked, though hatred was nothing new to us. But how could anyone hate the helpless, the powerless, the unfortunate, with such all-consuming, venomous hatred? La Rochefoucauld said that we forgive those who wrong us, but never those whom we have wronged. I believe that if there had been an Indian hunt the following day, this man would joyfully have joined it.

And yet he had a lively appreciation of the injustices under which he suffered. He told us about the Iquitos mafia, in whose profits he did not share. Iquitos, he said, was provisioned every day from outside. Vegetables and other fresh foodstuffs were flown in to feed (or half-feed) 150,000 people. Prices were high, profits enormous, and the monopoly tight. Any attempt to break it, however trivial, was met with force. There was ample opportunity for Iquitos to grow some of its own food in the district surrounding it. Prices would be driven down and everyone would benefit, except the monopolists. Nothing of the kind had been allowed to happen, though. When a friend of his had attempted to grow vegetables in his garden, only for himself and his family, the mafia moved in and destroyed it while he was away. He took the hint, and stuck to flowers.

Finding us sympathetic listeners, he told us about his private life. He was bored with the jungle, bored with life, and above all lonely. He decided to marry. He had found a beautiful mestiza in Iquitos, to which he was now engaged. But his mother, a pure European, was inordinately proud of her *limpieza de sangre* (literally, cleanliness of blood), and did not consider a mestiza good enough to marry her son. He banged the table with his fist and asked us what business it was of hers. At least the evenings and nights would not now seem so long.

Looking at his unshaven, sleep-ravaged face, already forming jowls, in the guttering light of the lamp, we all thought we saw his future clearly enough. His wife, so pretty now, would degenerate into a blowsy harridan, whom he would reproach for her racial origins. He would develop a belly, his thick wiry hair would recede (it had started in that direction already, though he was younger than us), he would have affairs and visit prostitutes. It was a depressing vision, and when the light extinguished itself we did not suggest it be rekindled.

On the day of our departure from Tamashiyacu we sat waiting for the thatched canoe to take us back to Iquitos. After his night-time revelations the part-owner resumed his station in his hammock, snoring or sometimes taking up a guitar which he strummed idly. He flicked away the flies that found his growth of beard endlessly fascinating or nutritious, and the hammock swayed with each movement. At last we heard the rhythmical chugging of the canoe's outboard.

Several people had come along on the canoe for a ride into the jungle: a quiet Peruvian family from Lima, making a pilgrimage to part of the national patrimony; two attractive and vivacious American ladies, dressed for a discotheque; and two German men, one about thirty and the other in late middle age, wearing identical outfits of beautifully cut battle fatigues, Rommel caps, new heavy boots fit for a long campaign, and each with a water bottle and a dagger slung on to his canvas belt. One would never have guessed they were returning to Iquitos that same afternoon.

The man with excessively tight Adidas shorts and carefully concealed bald patch whom we met in Iquitos had come along too, principally to dance attendance on the young American ladies, to whom he was attracted like a wasp to jam.

Our departure was delayed while they ate a leisurely lunch. We waited on the river bank, Frances attempting to wreak Man's vengeance on the piranha, while Richard and I composed limericks on South American themes. We set a South American name as the last word of the first line and gave ourselves five minutes to complete the verse.

> There was an old colonel of Lima,
> Whose nose was as long as his femur,
> The smells of the city
> Were not at all pretty,
> And thoroughly ruined his demeanour.

Richard's was best:

> There was a young lady of Lima
> Renowned as a terrible screamer.
> At the Opera, Manaus,
> She brought down the house,
> And sank the Amazon steamer.

During the return journey it grew quite chilly. For this, as for every other eventuality, the Germans were quite prepared. Unlike the rest of us, who had to huddle together for warmth, they had taken the trouble to find out the average minimum temperature in Iquitos at this time of year. From their identical, practical, well-designed and elegant kit bags they took identical warm capes, both useful and aesthetically pleasing, in which they wrapped themselves, thus provoking the ridicule and scorn of the rest of us, who belonged to less provident nations, especially the Americans who by now were blue with cold. Furthermore, the two Germans displayed great mutual tenderness as well as efficiency, thus setting off a train of speculation about their relationship to Ernst Röhm and the S.A.

We met them again in Iquitos. They were, in fact, father and son. They were exquisitely well-mannered and very charming. We vowed never to make such hasty judgements again.

On our last day in Iquitos we explored Belén, of which the *South American Handbook* says: '[it] is lively and colourful, and does not seem a dangerous place to visit, in daylight'. The height of the river varies by as much as thirty feet, taking most of the slum, perched on platforms, with it. The river was now low, however, and the passages between the houses were stagnant chasms of black mud, silt and litter, amongst which rooted small black pigs. A drunk fell out of a house at our feet, and addressed some kind of appeal to us, which my Spanish was not adequate to understand; fishwives harangued one another across passages. It was indescribably dirty, with filthy huts of blackened wood, and yet it was a place of laughter too. Children, playing stark naked, had converted a sloping flagstone into a kind of ski slope which, with a thin layer of moisture, became almost frictionless. If I had to live in a slum I should unhesitatingly choose Belén over Liverpool.

Not far from Iquitos is a beautiful lake with the sonorous name of Quistacocha. There is a menagerie there of the animals we had failed to see in the forest. We went to view them: no wonder the explorers of the seventeenth century reported marvels that never were! In spite of our relatively sophisticated zoological knowledge, fortified by the tales of Colonel Fawcett, many of the animals were entirely new to us, and unlike any we had seen before. In a menagerie one can stand and stare for a long time, and produce an accurate description at one's leisure; but a fleeting glimpse in the jungle must give rise to all kinds of imaginings.

Our favourite creature was a small animal about the size of a domestic cat, faintly striped, whose head tapered perfectly to a snout that almost doubled the creature's length. Its eyes were preternaturally round and bright as though, like mediaeval carbuncles, they emitted light rather then merely reflected it. At the end of its paws were long curled claws. What a creature of refinement! It sniffed the air with its snout vertical, like a debutante at a gas works. It broadcast a plaintive squeak, as if to beg for its release. Had we wire cutters to hand, we should have given it liberty.

We left Iquitos. Our last sight of it was something I shall never forget. We passed the city's rubbish tip, near which the trees were black and heavy with vultures, like some rotting, hellish fruit. Occasionally one of them flapped in an ungainly way from its perch to a particularly attractive pile of rubbish. The ground too, was thick with vultures. But there among them, as though they were brothers, were scores of small children, also sifting through the rubbish for tasty morsels. The children paid no attention to the vultures, nor the vultures to them. They were accustomed to each other's presence. The arch-priests of carrion had initiated the children into their rites.

THREE

The Altiplano, Peru and Bolivia

EIGHT HUNDRED AND FIFTY miles to the south we landed on the Altiplano at Juliaca, twelve and a half thousand feet above sea level. The Altiplano is a high tableland between two ranges of the Andes, the Cordillera Real and the Cordillera Oriental, seven-tenths of which lies in Bolivia, the rest in Peru.

The human body begins to adapt almost at once to the rarefied atmosphere of this extreme altitude. (No human community lives permanently at a greater height than the Altiplano.) Within a few minutes of arrival, extra blood cells are released into the blood stream and the body starts to manufacture more haemoglobin, the better to transport the reduced oxygen of the air. But our sudden arrival at high altitude from sea level was, as every textbook of physiology told us, the most hazardous and least comfortable way of making the adaptation. To reduce his chance of contracting the much-feared mountain sickness, the only cure for which is rapid descent to a lesser altitude, the traveller should take several days to reach his high destination.

We trusted to luck and our general robust good health. Our first breath of the air of the Altiplano was exhilarating. Its astringent purity seemed almost to scour our lungs. We experienced a euphoria, an exaltation, which was, no doubt, a physiological consequence of insufficient oxygen to the brain. Everything under the deep azure of the sky shimmered in the brilliant light. Distance hardly reduced our perception of detail. It was as though we had lived the rest of our lives with a filmy substance over our eyes, which the Altiplano had stripped away. The air was cold, but the sun's rays warmed what they struck. We were warm and cold at the same time.

An Indian with cheeks like polished apples drove us to Puno, on the shores of Lake Titicaca. He steered the car insouciantly, as though he too were in the grip of euphoria. I pointed to some white flecks by the side of the road and asked him whether they were snow. He laughed as the car veered from side to side.

'No, señor, it is salt.'

The short drive allowed us our first views of the Altiplano. The pessimistic Bolivian writer, Alcides Argüedas, described it thus:

> In the midst of this petrified quietude, of this grey and dusty plain where people, however numerous they may be, resemble groups of ants crawling across a vast surface, one feels so abandoned, such solitude, that one's spirit is quite unable to rise above it, or contemplate anything else. From this stems the absence of all poetic feeling in the people who live there. The beauty of the landscape, if uniformity of line and colour can be called beautiful, is strange. In the early hours of daylight, under a serene and limpid sky, the plain appears congealed in frost. The rivulets and springs are frozen, and from the hardened ground rise crystalline reflections of the sky, as well as little gusts of powdery snow. Calm reigns: the smoke of the native hearth spirals upwards towards the sky and nothing can be heard save the restless bleating of animals enclosed in their folds, the strident cry of birds of prey, the bark of a dog guarding an emaciated flock, or the sobbing, melancholy agony of the quena, the native flute . . .

A strange beauty – it is certainly that. I know of no landscape that so unmercifully exposes one's own insignificance. Unhappy the man who has to earn his livelihood from its unforgiving soil.

As we hurtled along we passed groups of Indian women sitting on their haunches, immobile as their fate, wearing the bowler hats that Charles III of Spain decreed their ancestors must wear after Tupac Amaru's rebellion. They were waiting for a bus, our driver said, and they might still be there tomorrow or the next day – it made no difference to anyone.

We arrived in Puno, the Peruvian port of Lake Titicaca. Our hotel was on an island in the lake connected to the shore by a causeway. The island, it was said, was the site of a temple of the pre-Inca. Tiahuanaco civilisation. The hotel was built with a magnificent view of the lake, into the side of a hill on the island in a style reminiscent of the Mediterranean; but regrettably the architect had failed to take account of Puno's climate, the temperature in winter sometimes declining to twenty-five degrees below zero. There was no heating, and the warming rays of the sun did not penetrate the frigid interior. It was the coldest building I have ever been in.

A few hours' rest is prescribed for people arriving suddenly at high altitude, but we were seized with a mania to be active. We took a cup of coca tea, the local remedy for the mild form of mountain sickness called *el soroche* which afflicts practically everyone. The tea was served by a waiter whose white jacket bulged with several layers of clothes underneath, including a bright red jumper with holes at the end of its sleeves for his numb, blue, spatulate fingers. Then we left the hotel to walk to the centre of Puno, about two miles away.

The road followed the lake shore. Ever since I had first heard of the lake, as a small boy, I had wanted to go there. Its very name, its remoteness, the story of how the first steamer was taken there, had all fired my imagination. And I was not disappointed. Its still, translucent and astonishingly sapphire waters, the bare brown silent hills surrounding it, the elegant tapered bulrushes that grew in it, enraptured us, and we stood gazing for a long time.

We watched an Indian silently paddle his *balsa*, the reed boat that has remained unchanged in design for thousands of years, through a passage cut in the thick beds of bulrushes. Towards us on the road came an Indian woman with a baby strapped to her back, driving a slightly reluctant llama before her. As she passed us her eyes flicked in our direction, but her bronze face was utterly devoid of expression. This inscrutability of the Indians, this apparent lack of any mental activity, has for centuries infuriated their oppressors, and inspired them to even greater

cruelties. In his dealings with outsiders, wrote the Peruvian
Nuñez del Prado, the Indian is 'suspicious, silent, withdrawn and
nearly inaccessible; he offers passive and systematic resistance.
He is humble, fearful, and inattentive; reticent and evasive in his
answers, indecisive in his attitudes. He suppresses and hides his
emotions and rarely conceals his disagreement even when he
finds himself in fundamental opposition.'

Further up the road we came across a group of men trying to
herd alpacas on to a truck, to take them to market. They were
using the ancient Inca method of herding, which appears in
illustrations to the early Spanish chronicles written after the
conquest. The men stand in a circle holding a rope between
them, except for an entrance to the circle. They try to surround
the alpacas with their rope, quickly closing the entrance. Once
enclosed, alpacas give up their struggle for freedom and can be
led meekly in any direction though their collective strength would
be quite sufficient to break out.

Surrounding them in the first place, however, is no easy task.
Alpacas are nervous, highly-strung beasts. They view the world
through melting brown eyes, their necks craning disdainfully,
until a sudden or unexpected movement alarms them and sets
them charging off in a herd, like wind blowing through a corn-
field.

The men had been trying to capture the alpacas for two hours.
Whenever they came close to success, the alapacas bolted at the
last moment, and the men were left to begin again. They asked
Richard and me to help them: an extra couple of stations in the
circle of rope might tip the balance against the timorous
creatures. When Frances – *la gringa* – joined in, the men were so
astonished they let fall the rope. Women on the Altiplano do not
herd alpacas.

It took another three-quarters of an hour to round them up.
The task absorbed us so completely that we forgot about soroche.
On the contrary, the rarefied air seemed to give us limitless
energy as we scrambled laughing over rocks. The owner of the
herd, a *cholo* with a face as weathered as Hemingway's, abused us

heartily when we made a mistake, encouraged us when we looked likely to succeed.

When at last the alpacas were safely herded into the truck, the owner came to us to thank us for our help. Frances was the object of general admiration and even awe. A blonde who herded alpacas! With rough good manners the owner offered her a cigarette, using his hat as a shelter from the wind to light it. He dressed no differently from his men, but his demeanour indicated that he was used both to command and obedience. He asked us where we were from.

'From England,' I said.

'Ah!' he replied. '*Completamente gringo!*'

He offered to take us in another of his trucks to Puno with his men. We climbed on board. As we did so the owner spotted a man who, for some reason should not have been there. The miscreant, a strong young fellow much bigger than the owner, got down from the truck like a chastised dog, and slunk away. The owner became equable and charming once more, but he was clearly not a man to be trifled with, an impression strengthened by the deferential greetings he received from pedestrians as we drove through the streets of Puno. We were in favour with him, however, for he placed the truck and its driver at our disposal – an offer we refused, as we had no particular place to go.

Puno was a hard, cold, bare little town. The eighteenth-century granite cathedral in the main square was a freezing sepulchre of a place, wherein a man's thoughts were more likely to turn to keeping warm than to God. The rest of the town was nondescript: streets of single-storey buildings in various states of disrepair where everyone walked on the sunny side to avoid the wintry shadows.

Indian men laboriously climbed the cobbled streets with baskets tied to their backs so heavy that they were bent at ninety degrees, and the men, facing downwards, were able to see only a yard or two in front of them as they walked. Their cheeks were pouched like hamsters': they were chewing the coca leaf that enabled them to work without eating. Peruvian landowners, at least before their haciendas were expropriated by the military government in 1969, used to say, The Indian is the animal that resembles Man.

There were llamas too in the streets. These animals that eat little, surviving on the coarse bristly grass called *paja brava* (wild straw), are able to carry burdens of only a hundred pounds, but they are very hardy and their hooves adhere to almost any surface. Of the llama Father José de Acosta, a Spanish priest of the seventeenth century, wrote in his *Historia natural y moral de las Indias*, 'God gave the Indians this animal because he knew they were poor'.

Sitting with their backs against the sunny walls were Indian women with a few vegetables for sale laid out in front of them. The women, whose multiple layers of clothes were stiff with dirt and cold, stared at the ground as though they expected to receive enlightenment from it.

There were a few young gringo tourists in the town, of the type that bring no money to the country they visit, and trouble to their consuls. They haggled in the market place over the price of ponchos. But the stallholders seemed to know well enough that the young bearded gringos had spent more on their fares to South America than a Peruvian earns in a year.

Quite suddenly, we felt exhausted. El soroche had caught up with us. We found a café for lunch – 'dirty, not recommended' said the *South American Handbook* – which was no more than a barn with tables. At one of the tables two Peruvians caroused, their heads slumping from time to time on to the table top with a crash. They roused themselves to take another gulp of aguardiente. A couple of young gringos, weakened by illness, filled their stomachs as cheaply as possible. The waiter was unspeakable. Fortunately, one of the symptoms of soroche is loss of appetite.

By morning, restored to whatever vigour we had ever possessed, we walked once more to Puno. We went to buy stamps at the adobe post office, outside which scribes did a small trade in writing letters of love for illiterates. The post office clerk, a cholo, took revenge for his humble status and low salary on his customers, poor *indios*, whom he treated with brusque contempt. It was ironic, therefore, that the stamps he sold us commemorated the bicentenary of Tupac Amaru's rebellion, after which the once-fasionable middle class guerrillas of Montevideo, the *tupamaros*, took their name.

We hired a boat to take us to the floating islands in the lake. Before we left, our small rickety craft was inspected by a soldier with deep but stupid suspicion. He had probably been told to maintain his vigilance at all times, and the only way he could manage it was to suspect everyone of everything. As he looked at our passports he tapped his gun. Eventually he let us go on our way.

We chugged slowly through the passages cut in the reed beds. The icy water was glassily calm. We saw the bottom of the lake clearly, a mermaid world with fields of dark green moss and forests of long weed, waving gently in unseen currents. The treeless hills around the lake bore scars of the ancient terracing that once supplied the Indians with a sufficiency of food, but had long since been abandoned. The beauty of the lake was cold, austere, and above all mysterious.

Titicaca exerts a powerful effect on the imagination of all who encounter it. The Incas believed it to be the birthplace of the sun. The Spanish, more prosaically, believed the Incas had thrown the priceless golden treasures from their temples into its depths to prevent them from falling into Spanish hands. They dredged the lake continually, but found nothing. The British, in the days when commerce was their glory, sent a steamer, the *Yaravi*, to Callao, where it was dismantled, transported across the Andes by mule train, and reassembled on the banks of the lake, whose waters it plied for eighty years.

We reached a floating island an hour after leaving the mole at Puno. There are many such in the 3,600 square mile lake, some of them inhabited by still-hostile tribes of Indians, others by tribes utterly dependent for their livelihood on visitors. The island we reached was inhabited by one of the latter, the Uru: as we arrived, tiny children gathered round us like mosquitoes at dusk, chanting 'Moneda! Moneda!' They learn their degradation young.

The island was a thick mat of reeds, on which reed houses were erected. On Titicaca, the reed is life, its *conditio sine qua non*. The reed is land, the reed is home, the reed is the means by which food is gathered.

The mat squelched under our feet. It was like walking on marshmallow. We treated it gingerly at first, half-expecting to fall through to the lake beneath. Our faith in its capacity to bear our weight increased, however, when we noticed a football pitch staked out with aluminium goal posts.

All the men were gone from the island except one, and he scurried off in his balsa at our approach. The women sat in a line, each with a baby strapped to her back. They hoped to sell us their brightly woven tapestries of Indian life. The small children had dirt ingrained on their rubicund cheeks. Their noses ran, and their protuberant bellies spoke of malnutrition. Their clothes were filthy. A little girl of four by my side urinated through her petticoats, the urine coursing down her leg and through the absorbent mat of reeds, leaving no trace.

We visited several more of the floating islands, all of them without their men. The largest of them had a missionary school with the inestimable Christian benefit of a tin roof. Once again we had the uneasy feeling of visiting an anthropological museum rather than a living community, whose destruction was assured by the idly curious like ourselves.

As the sun began to sink we left this Gulliverian world of floating islands. The lake, having been all day a deeper blue even than the sky, turned to blinding silver and then to gold. The sun slipped over the brow of a hill just as our old engine seized; we bobbed gently on the water, huddling together for warmth and anticipating an exceedingly uncomfortable night. Frantic activity by the boatman in semi-darkness restored some life to the engine, and with faint chugs like the last coughs of a tuberculous heroine, we edged slowly towards the faint light of Puno, where we warmed ourselves with pisco.

We left Puno for La Paz. The bus company was called Morales Moralitos which, in spite of its high-sounding name, possessed a well-earned reputation for leaving its passengers stranded by the roadside for days without assistance, for not honouring its own tickets, and for selling tickets for foreign bus companies without any validity whatever.

The bus was scheduled to leave at eight in the morning, but the ancient blue and white vehicle, covered inside and out with a layer of fine reddish dust, needed repairs before starting on the arduous journey. They took three hours to complete. The passengers waited patiently in a line, propping themselves up against adobe walls while Indian women with trays of dry bread rolls and small bars of prehistoric chocolate patrolled it in the hope that the delay would make us hungry enough to buy their wares. The sharp wind froze us, the sun burnt us.

A young Brazilian next to us looked desperately ill. His every movement required effort; his eyes, when he lifted his heavy lids, were glazed. His pale skin was pocked with sores, his emaciation was extreme. We debated at length – it helped pass the time – whether as doctors we were obliged to offer him our help, though he had not asked for it. We decided that we must.

Our offer was received with unflattering apathy. He just managed to tell us, before he lapsed into muteness, that he had been suffering from dysentery for two weeks. We gave him drugs to combat it, which he swallowed with no very lively expectation of cure. He had passed the stage of even caring whether he recovered or not. But, by the end of the journey, we had the mild gratification of seeing a marked improvement in his condition.

All the tyres were replaced before we departed – for others just as bald, without any remnant of tread. To the sarcastic cheers of a couple of Brazilians, a driver at long last swung himself into the driver's seat and started the engine. There was an immediate gush of liquid and steam, but the driver pronounced himself satisfied, and we started out.

As far as the small town of Juli the road was paved, following the lakeshore closely, and we rattled along at a pace which we should scarcely have thought possible. The town had four colonial churches and a military barracks. Our papers were checked at the barracks by a soldier who sat in a trance-like state behind a deal table, on which a cassette recorder played 'Saturday Night Fever' so loudly that all speech was drowned out. He scanned our documents by passing them up, down and across his motionless eyes.

After Juli the road became rough, surfaced only with rubble. The bus bounced us around in all directions and the power of the engine seemed insufficient to overcome the steep inclines. The gears ground horribly, the air was thick with dust and the smoke of fuel, all progress came to a halt, and it was only a matter of moments before the bus began to slip backwards, first slowly, then headlong. But the passengers gritted their teeth, urged the bus forward by jumping a little in their seats, and miraculously it summoned just enough power to reach the summit. The roads were littered with the skeletons of vehicles that had not been so fortunate.

Having passed through several more Peruvian military checks, we reached the border at a town called Desaguadero, which means, or can mean, 'drain': an appropriate enough name. We dragged our luggage down a street of adobe buildings to the Peruvian post. A brass band was playing somewhere in the town; an extraordinarily joyful and exuberant sound for such a place. The anarchic music was like a shout of life. The band was quite unable to agree as to the melody or the tempo, and yet the music had a strange, uplifting coherence.

The Peruvian official stamped our passports as though squashing a particularly repulsive insect. We moved on to the Bolivian side, where the red, yellow and green national flag fluttered over an adobe hut. Affixed to the walls was a notice in large lettering:

BOLIVIANOS!
EL MAR ES UN DERECHO
RECUPARLE ES UN DEBER

(Bolivians! The sea is a right, to recover it a duty.) Next to this notice was another, calling Bolivians to arms. It depicted soldiers in steel helmets rushing over rocky terrain, guns in hand, with old-fashioned jets flying overhead. In the background was a battleship, presumably on Lake Titicaca. They were all engaged, apparently, in recovering the lost Pacific coast from Chile, though for the last fifty years Bolivian troops have fought mainly Bolivian miners, and the territorial dispute with Chile was settled by treaty in 1904. Under the patriotic notices sat two Indian women, weaving cloth with their Inca looms.

We entered the adobe hut. The official sat at a desk with two portraits hung behind him, one of Simón Bolívar, the other a photograph of General García Meza, the President of Bolivia, whose *golpe* in July 1980 forestalled the inauguration of a democratically elected government. The official was explaining to some enraged Brazilians that their passports were not in order and they would therefore have to return to Lima. There was no bus back to Puno for two days, and the prospect of two days in Desaguadero was a powerful incentive to settle the matter by bribery. The official waved the Brazilians aside and stamped our passports with a grandiloquent flourish, as if to say, I can do what I like here. He told us to report to a security check in the hut next door, and resumed his haggling with the Brazilians.

The security guard wore a white shirt and a red baseball hat with *Boston Red Sox* printed across it. On his table was a silvery automatic weapon with a magazine of ammunition. He asked us to wait a moment while he went outside; he did not consider us much of a security risk, for he left the weapon behind. His security check, when he returned, consisted of looking in our passports to make sure they were stamped.

With the sound of haggling still issuing from next door, we awaited resolution of the crisis in the café of Desaguadero's only hotel. The counter was a graveyard of flies, while the owner, who was also the cook, the cleaner and the waiter, sat behind it in a reverie, watching the Desaguadero days go by. He made no pretence of hospitality, knowing that no-one came to his hotel through choice, and that no-one would return. We drank tea until the Brazilians emerged triumphant, objections to their passports' deficiencies overcome with pesos.

The road deteriorated further after Desaguadero and the country grew yet more desolate. Alcides Argüedas again: 'The barrenness of the plain seems almost evil. Speckled in places with ochre, in others with brown, in yet others with the colour of ashes, it stretches into the far distance, implacably bare, leaving a wide horizon that vibrates . . . The fauna is poor.' And yet the glittering white peaks of the distant cordillera lent the landscape a majesty not easily forgotten.

We stopped at several villages on the way to pay our respects to the Government representatives there, without whose permission it was not safe to progress further towards the capital. Each village was built around a dusty square, where dogs with rachitic ribs sniffed the ground, women waited in doorways for some event out of the ordinary, and children desultorily kicked a home-made ball about, raising dust. The walls were daubed with slogans:

¡VIVA BANZER!   ¡BANZER AL PODER!

General Hugo Banzer achieved the notable feat (in a country where there have been more revolutions than years of independent existence) of remaining in power for seven years, escaping not only with his life but also with his fortune. In all other respects his reign of terror was unremarkable, in the context.

Night fell and the villages were made out only by a few dim lamps which flickered in a darkness so intense it seemed not merely to be the absence of light but to have positive qualities of its own (city dwellers have rarely experienced true darkness). We reached the outskirts of La Paz still on unpaved road, a village on a large scale. Suddenly, a thousand feet below, in a hollow in the Altiplano selected by the Spaniards in 1548 to protect themselves against the biting winds of the plain, the lights of the city centre were spread out before us. Even the Brazilians, who have their Rio de Janeiro after all, applauded the sight.

FOUR

La Paz, Bolivia

THE STREETS of La Paz are all on steep hills. One's social position can be gauged by the altitude at which one lives. The Indians live at the highest altitudes; the generals in the Calacoto and La Florida suburbs, two thousand feet lower down. The people in the first streets through which we walked were mostly Indians, anxiously awaiting buses to take them back to their dusty high suburbs. We walked down a street in which every shop window drew a small crowd of onlookers and where, to our surprise, every shop was the establishment of a *director de pompas funebres* – an undertaker. There was no reticence in the window displays. Each had a de luxe coffin prominently on view, with rococo carving, twisted brass handles, and a crimson satin lining – the coffin of the week. Simpler coffins were stacked up behind, some of moulded plastic, others of pine. One shop seemed to specialise in coffins for infants. The crowds discussed their merits in the way cars are discussed elsewhere. But death is an important and familiar subject in Bolivia; its population has one of the shortest life expectancies in the world, and two out of every ten children die before their first birthday.

The Avenida Mariscal de Santa Cruz (a dictator who tried to unite Bolivia and Peru, and was defeated by the Chileans) leads from the Plaza San Francisco to the Avenida 16 de Julio, also known as the Prado (Meadow) on account of the carefully tended shrubs and flowers that run down its middle. The Avenida Mariscal de Santa Cruz is cleaved in two by yet another equestrian statue of Simón Bolívar, donated by 'the grateful nation' on the centenary of its independence. The European part of La Paz's population was performing arm in arm its nightly promenade up and down the Prado. Coloured lights suspended between the lampposts gave the street an air of gaiety.

We found a hotel on the Prado, and then looked for dinner. We found it in a precipitous side street. The restaurant was long and narrow, sparsely furnished, with old stoves in the corners trying, not very successfully, to heat the freezing air. Minor civil servants and office functionaries, all mestizos, wearing old suits shiny at the seats and elbows, with woollen cardigans under their jackets, were sitting over bottles of beer, discussing something with fierce and drunken earnestness. Our entrance produced a brief lull in their deliberations as they scanned us suspiciously, but they soon returned to their discussion.

A waiter in a white jacket approached our table, staring somewhat melodramatically at his watch. He slammed cutlery down on the table with more than ordinary brusqueness. There was fear in his eyes, which darted back and forth between the world and his watch.

Suddenly I had an idea.

'Is there a curfew?' I asked. The question being evidence of our ignorance and helplessness, produced a sea-change in the waiter's attitude, which became friendly and solicitous.

'Yes,' he said. 'At eleven o'clock.'

He asked us where we had come from today. Bringing us three bottles of beer he asked us whether Bolivian was not superior to Peruvian beer.

'Much,' we replied. 'No comparison.'

As indeed there was not. We had not tasted Peruvian beer. A beam of vindicated patriotism lit his face. He watched us drink the beer, foaming prodigiously, with crystals of ice suspended in it which failed to melt, since the temperature in the restaurant was below freezing. He regarded us complacently, like an accomplished murderer who has administered powdered glass to many victims.

He brought us a vast platter of food, on which there were sausages, pigeons, rabbits' legs, sheep's tripe, chicken livers and lamb cutlets. He also brought a plate of *chuño*, the compressed dried potatoes of the Altiplano. To make this dish, potato tubers are soaked in water for a week, then exposed to the heat of the sun and the frost of the night for ten days, then stamped with the feet to express any remaining moisture, and finally left out in the open for three or four weeks. The result is a hard and dry potato, the size of a walnut, which is said to keep forever, or as long as anyone is likely to want to preserve food.

The waiter watched us eat.

'Bolivian food is better than Peruvian, no?' he asked.

'Oh yes,' we said. 'Much.'

The waiter went to report our solicited testimonial to the occupants of another table.

Before we left the restaurant we asked him what happened to curfew-breakers. He told us that, if they were not shot, they were taken to the National Stadium, where they were made to run round the track until the curfew lifted, as six o'clock in the morning.

We gave him twenty pesos as a tip, two new green notes printed by Thomas de la Rue in London, bearing the portrait of Colonel Germán Busch. Busch was a young mestizo officer who was briefly president at the end of the thirties, whose 'military socialism' was much influenced by fascism, and who committed suicide on 23rd August 1939 in the hope that his dramatic gesture would somehow rejuvenate his decrepit and perpetually warring country.

We walked back to the Prado. It was not long to curfew. The promenaders had gone, and the coloured lights now looked melancholy and tawdry, like a funfair after the crowds have departed. There was no traffic except for occasional military vehicles with blinding headlights, and such pedestrians as there were kept close to the shadows of the buildings, scurrying like cockroaches to avoid the light.

Whatever slight inclination we had to test the efficacy of the curfew enforcement was driven out by the piercing cold and the absence of life on the streets. We re-entered our hotel, where an important-looking man in a military greatcoat and a peaked cap was holding court alcoholically, telling stories he considered amusing to a captive civilian audience who glanced nervously at their watches. For him, of course, the curfew did not exist. Surrounded by an alcoholic glow, aware that he was the centre of attraction thanks to the brilliance of his monologue, he exuded a kind of brittle bonhomie which, however, did not extend to the waiters. When he wanted something, either for himself or his friends of the moment, he rapped on the table top with a huge gold ring on his index finger, the resulting sound not unlike a machine-gun. He shouted at the waiters and cursed them for their slowness.

There was a television in the corner of the entrance lobby. No-one was watching it. A general was making a speech from a balcony. Behind him on the balcony was an array of officers, some in dark glasses, who interrupted the speech to applaud. The cameras panned to the square below, where the crowd applauded, though without conviction. General Luis García Meza – for it was he – was making a speech: he talked of order, progress and independence. We left him declaiming into an empty alcove.

The city next morning had recovered some of its gaiety. It was impossible to feel gloomy in such brilliant sunshine. International businessmen emerged from their hotels into the Prado with determination and purpose.

Though La Paz is not a small city, with a population of about a million, one can stand in its very centre and see out of it in all directions, thanks to the surrounding mountains in the shadows of which it shelters. This gives it an intimacy which not many cities its size possess. To the east towers the magnificent Illimani, one of the highest mountains of the Andes, though its exact height seems to be a matter of dispute among the authorities. This uncertainty is a characteristic of Bolivia, which is so little surveyed that even its size is a matter of conjecture. Harold Osborne, in his book on Bolivia, quotes the following figures:

United Nations Mission to Bolivia	411,127 square miles
Concise Oxford Atlas	415,000 square miles
South American Handbook	419,470 square miles
Encyclopaedia Britannica	424,127 square miles
Collins Graphic Atlas	507,000 square miles
Bartholomews Atlas	514,000 square miles

Clinging precariously to the lower slopes of the mountains are the hovels of the humbler citizens of La Paz, apparently ready to slip downwards into the city centre at the first rainstorm or tremor of the earth.

We went to the central square of the city, the Plaza Murillo, named not after the painter but the Bolivian patriot who raised the standard of criollo revolt against Spain in 1809, and was promptly hanged for his trouble. His defiant last words on the scaffold were: 'The torch I have lit will never be extinguished.' He was right; but Bolivia, the first country in South America to claim independence, was the last to achieve it. His statue now stands in the square named after him, surrounded by four ancient Greek ladies with pigeons on their heads.

On one side of the plaza stands the Palacio de Gobierno, known also as the Palacio Quemado – the Burnt Palace – twice gutted by fire. That morning the grey stucco building was firmly shuttered against prying civilian eyes. There were ceremonial guards in early nineteenty-century costume standing stiffly to attention outside black and white sentry boxes. The real palace guards, however, were soldiers in steel helmets who, having propped up their weapons against the walls, slouched until the arrival of a general, when they snapped to and saluted. The ceremonial guard banged the ground with the butts of their muskets, and the great grey doors of the palace swung open to swallow the general, and swung shut behind him.

The Palacio Quemado has witnessed some remarkable men and events. In its first century Bolivia ran through 40 presidents, 6 of them assassinated in office, and experienced 187 armed uprisings. One of the first to occupy the palace was Manuel

Belzu, a man of Spanish descent who nevertheless took the part of the Indians, a rare thing in the republic's early days. Historians in general have excoriated him for his policies, and designated him a violent despot; but he tried to redistribute the land to the Indians, he reduced their tribute tax (which at the time constituted forty per cent of government revenue), and appreciated that free trade worked only to the advantage of strongly industrialised nations. He was given to making demagogic speeches from the balcony of the palace, in which he revealed himself a Marxist before Marx:

> Companions, private property is the principal source of most offences and crimes in Bolivia; it is the cause of the permanent struggle among Bolivians; it is the basis of our present selfishness . . . No more property! No more inheritances! Land for everyone; enough of the exploitation of man . . . Aren't you also Bolivians? Haven't you been born to equality in this privileged land?

It was Belzu who sent the British minister-plenipotentiary packing (on a donkey), to the wild acclamation of his countrymen. Queen Victoria was less impressed: she wanted to send a warship to Bolivia, until someone tactfully pointed out where it was, whereupon she is supposed to have taken out her map, put a line through the name of Bolivia, and said: 'From now on, there is no Bolivia.'

Belzu resigned – the first president to do so – after having put down the fortieth armed revolt of his seven-year term of office. He declared Bolivia to be ungovernable, and retired temporarily to Europe. He was succeeded by a series of military dictators of varying degrees of barbarism. The most colourful if least attractive of them was undoubtedly General Melgarejo, a man of titanic strength and courage, who was passionate and barbarous, at times generous to the point of mawkishness, completely uncontrolled in his temper, a drunkard, chivalrous and cruel at the same time, and a complete boor. Abysmally ignorant (he stoutly maintained that Napoleon was a better general than Bonaparte), he was supported by the silver mining and landowning families. His policy, insofar as he had one, was the reverse of Belzu's. He sold the rights to the guano in the Atacama to the Chileans, and took such a liking to the Chilean negotiator that he offered him the post of Bolivian minister of finance. He passed a decree demanding that Indians purchase the title to the land they occupied within sixty days, or forfeit the land to the state (i.e. Melgarejo), after which it was sold to the highest bidder.

Melgarejo was not a man to disguise his meanings. Replying to several toasts at a banquet in which the word 'constitution' was mentioned, he said: 'I'm going to rule Bolivia as long as I feel like it, and I'll have anyone who disagrees strung up in the nearest square.' When a speaker in Congress suggested that Bolivia should return to constitutional government, Melgarejo said: 'I want the gentleman who has just spoken to know that I have put the Constitution of 1861, which was very good, in one pocket, and that of 1868, which is even better in the opinion of these gentlemen, in another pocket, and no-one is going to rule in Bolivia but me.'

In order to impress a visiting foreign dignitary with the loyalty and obedience of his troops, Melgarejo once ordered a platoon of soldiers to march up the stairs of the palace, through a saloon, and straight over the balcony into the street below.

History does not record the fate of the unfortunate soldiers, but it does record the fate of Belzu, who returned to Bolivia to lead a popular uprising against Melgarejo. At first his revolt was successful, for Belzu was supported by the great mass of the population. He installed himself in the palace, and all seemed lost for Melgarejo, most of whose forces deserted him. Resourceful and brave if nothing else, Melgarejo hit upon the ruse of pretending to be taken prisoner, with some of the few men remaining loyal to him acting as his supposed captors on Belzu's behalf. They marched up to the palace, where Belzu prepared to receive Melgarejo's surrender. Belzu greeted his opponent with a salute. Melgarejo greeted Belzu with a bullet. He then calmly walked to the balcony and addressed the crowd below. 'Belzu is dead!' he said. 'Now who are you shouting for?' And the crowd – or some of them – shouted 'Long live Melgarejo!'

Not surprisingly, Melgarejo himself came to a sticky end. He was overthrown and exiled to Peru, where he led an impecunious life, for though corrupt beyond measure he had failed to set aside foreign funds (an error not since repeated by many Bolivian dictators). He tried one day to collect a debt in Lima from the brother of his lover, Juana Sánchez. The debt was cancelled with a fatal bullet.

Melgarejo was not the last of the ignorant caudillos; when Enrique Peñaranda became president by coup in 1940, his mother is reported to have said, 'If I'd known Enrique was going to be president I would have sent him to school.' Lack of educational qualifications, however, did not prevent New York's Columbia University from conferring on him an honorary doctorate of laws; the Allies needed Bolivian tin at the time.

Not far from the Palacio Quemado is another of Bolivia's national monuments, the lamppost from which President Gualberto Villarroel was hanged by an enraged mob in 1946. He headed a coalition government of revolutionary army officers and the *Movimiento Nacionalista Revolucionario*, which at the time was strongly fascist in its sympathies, though these later changed as it became clear that Germany would be defeated. A bust of the hanged president now stands near the fateful lamppost, with a plaque on which are inscribed some of his words: 'I am not an enemy of the rich, but I am more a friend of the poor.'

We explored the streets round the Plaza Murillo, catching views of Mount Illimani. We sat for a time in the Plaza Obispo, a small square with a colonial church and a neo-Palladian villa at right angles to it. This was the police headquarters. On one of its balconies stood several men in dark glasses, endlessly picking their teeth as they idly watched the square below. On another balcony three men in dark suits conferred conspiratorially. Two uniformed men propped up the lintels of the main entrance, chatting lazily. This idyllic scene underwent a sudden transformation. The men disappeared from the balconies into the unobservable darkness beyond, and the uniformed men at the entrance slipped quietly inside. The windows closed by invisible hands. A tall man in military greatcoat was striding towards the headquarters. A small mestizo policeman came rushing out to meet him, with steps that were both urgent and obsequious, and stamped his foot on the ground as he turned sideways on to the commander to salute him. The man in the greatcoat swept past him without any acknowledgement of his existence, and the mestizo policeman trotted after him, like a dog that wants to be stroked but fears to be kicked. As the commander passed the church and entered the hallowed portals of the police head-quarters, he crossed himself.

Much of the surrounding area of La Paz is a carefully pre-served and very well-maintained colonial quarter, including Murillo's house, whose upstairs rooms allegedly have been left undisturbed since his death. (As there was a fifteen-year gap between his death and Bolivian independence, this is not easy to believe.) There is a collection in the house of paintings depicting Murillo's life, or rather his death, his execution being what gave his life significance, and the event that captured the imagination of successive generations of Bolivian painters. The represent-ations of his martyrdom range from the lofty allegorical to socialist realism. One portrait from the 1890s has him, torch in hand, flying heavenwards as the apotheosis of the Spanish waiter about to set light to crêpes suzettes. Only the gibbet in the background and a line of soldiers beating a drum roll precludes this interpretation. Another portrait, from the 1930s, has him square-jawed and resolute, a real proletarian hero (but not yet an Indian).

That afternoon, we read the Bolivian newspapers. García Meza's speech was widely reported and extensively quoted. It was a sustained diatribe against the United States which, becoming sanctimonious about human rights in Bolivia, had cut off aid to the regime, there being no prospect in view of a left-wing over-throw of the military. In the first place, replied the General, the Bolivian Government would not dream of harming any of its own poeple, not so much as a hair of a head. The several hundred people killed resisting his *golpe* were not true Bolivians. Second, though redundant in view of his first point, since when had the United States concerned itself with brutality in Latin America, except to promote it? Bolivia, he said, would stick firmly to its chosen course, achieving development and national independence at the same time.

We spent the evening in the cinema. The performance started with a propaganda film, provided by the German-Bolivian Chamber of Trade, about how splendidly paraplegics lived in West Germany. The main feature was called *Canibales*, the translation of the English title of *Eaten Alive*. The audience of mestizo office workers and their families settled into their seats, bags of nuts at the ready. The film soon reduced their appetite for nuts, however. Its story was founded on the events at Jonestown in Guyana, where a charismatic religious leader persuaded nine hundred of his followers to commit mass suicide in the jungle. But the director of the film, finding these events insufficiently dramatic, populated his jungle with cannibals, who ate the survivors live and raw. At first the audience tittered, but everyone left the cinema pale, weak and nauseated. For them, there was no need of a curfew that night.

The gringo prisoners of San Pedro gaol, says the *South American Handbook* in small print, would appreciate a visit from anyone with a few moments to spare. We found the Plaza San Pedro, of which the implacably featureless wall of the gaol formed one side. The gate was heavily guarded. I explained that we had come to visit the prisoners 'de habla inglés'. They signalled by a slight inclination of the head and a wave of the gun for us to enter. Richard and I filed off to the left to be searched, while Frances filed off to the right, to join a queue of prisoners' wives. We were frisked, but not very thoroughly, and given a plastic card on which was printed a warning: any visitor who lost the card would not be allowed out of the gaol.

The English-speaking prisoners were already in the prison courtyard to greet us as we emerged from our frisking. News travels fast in prisons. They crowded round us, laughing and expostulating like puppets controlled by a demented puppeteer: they had so much to say that it all came out in an excited, unintelligible babble. Though there were only four of them the noise they created reverberated round the prison. When their initial excitement had died down a little, they asked us whether we would take them to the prison restaurant to buy them a meal. We agreed, and one of them said: 'Boy, this is our lucky day!'

On the way there, they explained the prison system. Everything, they said, could be bought in San Pedro gaol. For prisoners with money, the prison was like a luxury hotel with a few minor restrictions, which could usually be circumvented by judicious bribery. Colour televisions, guns, carpets, prostitutes – all were available in San Pedro, but especially cocaine, whose quality was said by aficionados to be amongst the finest in the world. All four gringo prisoners were in prison, of course, for trying to smuggle cocaine, as were six out of ten of the Bolivian prisoners: but the prison authorities winked at its use in the prison, since they were frequently the vendors, and had other means of making money out of the practice.

Not only *might* everything be bought in San Pedro, but virtually everything *must* be bought there. Food and accommodation of a sort were provided, but the food barely staved off starvation, while the accommodation amounted to little more than a pest hole where only rats prospered. Better food could be purchased within the prison walls at a subcontracted canteen, or from stalls run by Indian women, who paid the warders a commission. The warders also rented out accommodation, each taking a cut according to his rank and dignity. This accommodation varied from luxury suites of rooms with fitted carpets to mere holes in the wall from which the bricks had been removed. The warders were stern and exacting landlords: eviction occurred at the first sign of nonpayment of rent.

When the Canadian consul visited the prison out of tender concern for the welfare of his nationals (three of the four were Canadian), he was shown round by the Governor, who naturally exhibited only the best rooms.

'And is it true,' asked the consul, 'that the prisoners have to rent these?'

'No, they are free, your excellency,' said the Governor unctuously.

The three Canadians laughed bitterly at their recollection of their consul's visit.

'Our consul's a prick,' said one of them.

The 'restaurant' comprised a few tables near a greasy serving hatch. They ordered their food with eager anticipation. We heard the saliva in their mouths. When it came, the meal was an overflowing plate of greasy dishwater in whose centre was a large chunk of grey meat on a bone.

I had never seen people eat more voraciously. All social inhibitions and pretences were abandoned. A spoon proved too slow for one of them: he picked up the plate and poured the liquid down his gullet, spilling half of it. But the grey meat was the real prize, and they tore at it like hyenas.

The meal was over in a few seconds. They all sat back and patted their stomachs contentedly.

'Boy, was that good!'

After cigarettes provided by Frances, they told us a little of themselves.

'We're not exactly innocents in here,' said one of the Canadians.

'We hadn't supposed you were,' said Richard.

The first of them was a twenty-one year old Norwegian who learnt his English working in the Australian outback. He was tall and lean, with a slightly effeminate face. His hair was already beginning to thin, and later, when we happened to pass a mirror, he saw a reflection of himself, and tears came to his eyes.

'Christ, I've aged!' he said.

His mood was otherwise buoyant, though tinged with hysteria. Officially, he had only a month to serve of his sentence of three years (but the others shook their heads at his naivety; they had seen such hopes of timely release dashed before many times). He claimed to have made his fortune from several cocaine-smuggling trips completed successfully before he was caught.

'I've made my money,' he said. 'I used to live in the best rooms in the prison, with carpets, colour television, everything.'

We did not ask him the painful question of why he lives there no longer, or why he had to beg cigarettes of Frances.

Unlike the others who, he maintained, had been caught through their own bungling, his capture was a matter of mere bad luck. He had all but boarded the plane out of Bolivia when he was pulled back. Several kilos of white powder were found on his person when he was searched.

'What is this white powder?' asked the men who had searched him.

'You know what it is, you bastards,' he replied.

He was taken to another room where a big crowd of policemen gathered.

Their chief smiled.

'Is this cocaine, gringo?'

'You know it is.'

'We had better make sure.'

He took out a chemical kit for testing for the presence of cocaine.

'If this test tube turns blue, gringo, it's cocaine.'

'I know it's cocaine, you bastard, there's no need to test it.'

The policemen enjoyed the mock-suspense. It suited their sense of humour. When the test tube turned blue they crowed in triumph.

'It's cocaine, gringo. Tut-tut.'

The chief put some on his palm and took a deep sniff.

'It's good cocaine, gringo. Very good. Where did you get it?'

'I'm not telling you, you bastard.'

All the policemen took a turn at sniffing the cocaine, and then the chief dismissed them from the room. He wanted to talk confidentially to the Norwegian.

'You're in trouble, gringo. You could go to prison for fifteen years. That's a long time.' He smiled. 'Unless you pay me twenty thousand dollars.'

'I don't have twenty thousand dollars.'

'Come on, gringo, cocaine like this is worth a lot of money.'

'I don't have twenty thousand dollars.'

The chief lowered his demand to ten thousand, but the Norwegian did not have that much, either, in spite of his alleged fortune. But even if he could have raised it, bribes in Bolivia do not always secure their ends. The policeman, having taken the money, would not have felt obliged to release his prisoner. Bribes work often enough only to keep the institution alive, no more.

Nevertheless, the chief was relatively well-disposed towards the Norwegian, though he did not realise it at the time. The chief gave him some of his own cocaine to sniff, which at first he refused. The chief was so insistent, however, that in the end he decided he had little to lose by complying. The two of them sniffed away to their hearts' content, the chief in raptures about the quality. And it transpired that the chief had done him a great service by his insistence; the Norwegian was able to claim in court, with the chief as a witness, that he was an addict who was smuggling the cocaine for his own use, an offence carrying a much lighter sentence.

We asked him whether he would ever smuggle cocaine again, and he said no; but he added wistfully that one really successful smuggling trip would set a man up for life. The Conquistadors, it seems, live on, but now they are smuggling drugs.

The second gringo prisoner was a young blond Canadian who would have been handsome had he not been so obviously racked by disease. His hands shook ominously, and the others whispered that he was an alcoholic. If he didn't find alcohol by ten o'clock, they said, he grew desperate, and was quite likely to fall down in fits. He was probably the most intelligent of the four. He freely admitted to having been a professional drug smuggler. He was caught not by the Bolivian police, but by the American Drug Enforcement Agency. Having received a tip-off, the Bolivian police searched his hotel room (the same hotel as ours), but found nothing. The day before he was to leave Bolivia three Americans from the Agency broke into his room and hustled him into the bathroom, where they held a gun to his head.

'We have no authority here in this country,' they said. 'But you're going to tell us everything you know.'

Before long, the men from the Drug Enforcement Agency had found the cocaine: stuffed into a set of aqualungs, odd equipment to possess in a landlocked country (he had told the Bolivian police they were for diving in Lake Titicaca).

He was in prison for three years before knowing the full extent of his sentence. He had paid lawyer after lawyer, each of whom said, 'Don't worry, it'll be all right, but we have to wait until the case comes up in Sucre' (where the Supreme Court of Bolivia sits). In three years he appeared in court thirty-five times and was never once allowed to speak. Even when his lawyer failed to show, he was not allowed to say anything in his own defence. Some of the lawyers made no pretence of doing anything; they just pocketed the money.

The only purpose in having a lawyer in Bolivia is to have a conduit to the judge for one's bribe. But there is no guarantee that the bribe will ever reach the judge; nor that the judge at the beginning of a case will be the judge at the end of it, for appointments to the bench are political and change with each coup; nor finally, if the bribe reaches the judge and he remains a judge, that he will take any notice of it. Indeed, there are good reasons why he should not; the Drug Enforcement Agency pays the authorities in Bolivia several thousand dollars for each conviction secured in a cocaine-smuggling case, and a conviction always leads to appeals, and hence more bribes for everyone. In addition, of course, the authorities get the cocaine, which they then sell.

The Canadian had exhausted his money on fruitless attempts to secure his release. His father was a wealthy man who could easily have afforded to overwhelm Bolivian resistance with money, but his official position as a judge in Canada precluded him from doing so, even had he wanted to (his son was unsure on this point). As it was, the young Canadian had nine more years to serve, his sentence being twelve years with no chance of remission. After his release, he was to pay a $20,000 fine before being allowed to leave the country. Fortunately, the Bolivian-Chilean border was not difficult to cross, and the two countries did not exchange criminals except at ambassadorial level.

The third of the prisoners looked physically at the end of his tether. His hair was unkempt, his beard too weak to grow. His spindly arms were covered with sores, and the scars of countless injections with old needles. He told us, not without a certain gallows pride, that he now weighed less than seventy pounds. He claimed to have given up cocaine, but his appearancce belied his claim. He said he could no longer afford the hush money of $300 each time the warders caught him, without the payment of which they informed the prison governor, the dignity of whose position demanded a bigger bribe, without the payment of which he informed the Minister of Justice, who demanded the biggest payment of all, without which he would increase the prison sentence by several years.

A confirmed and violent criminal, the third of the prisoners was first convicted for armed robbery in Montreal at the age of sixteen. Once he discovered we did not wish to buy from him the crude stone pipe bulbs he had carved in the shape of heads of various prisoners, he slunk away. The three others said he was secretive and shifty, under no circumstances to be trusted.

The fourth of the men had good reason to hate the third. He was a French-Canadian from a small and economically depressed village in Quebec, where his father had died many years ago in an alcoholic stupor. His only employment there had been as a casual labourer. Eventually, he moved to Montreal to seek his fortune, or at least regular employment. But no-one wanted unskilled labour, and he lived as best he could until one day somebody offered him $5000 to go to Bolivia and return with some cocaine. The job was presented to him in such a way that there seemed no possibility of being caught, and $5000 was a tempting sum. His partner in the journey was the violent and drug-addicted criminal we had just met. All went smoothly until Bolivian customs on the return journey. The French-Canadian passed through safely, but his colleague was caught. As he did not much care for the prospect of languishing alone in a Bolivian gaol while the French-Canadian enjoyed freedom and $5000, he informed on him without any pressure to do so from the Bolivian police. Each of them received a ten-year sentence, with an $8000 fine to pay at the end of it.

We asked him whether he had not at times felt like killing the Judas who betrayed him. To have to live in such close proximity to him must have been agonising; and, after all, he looked as though the life would easily enough be wrung out of him.

He replied that at first he *was* subject to such murderous impulses, but his Catholic faith overcame them, and the events were now so long ago that he had forgiven. He saw his betrayer now as pitiful, rather than evil.

For some reason, we talked of death. With the exception of the Norwegian, the gringo prisoners half-expected to die in San Pedro. Not long ago, an unpopular prison warder was found upside down with his head in a latrine. A Colombian prisoner killed another Colombian prisoner in a feud, and hanged himself rather than face his thirty years additional sentence. Two well-known troublemakers in the prison had required operations, one for a broken ankle, the other for appendicitis, and both had died under the anaesthetic.

They agreed that conditions in San Pedro, while physically hard, were preferable to those encountered in most prisons else-where. There was considerable freedom within the walls. After roll call in the morning, the day was theirs to spend as they pleased. There were workshops, but attendance was avoided by the payment of a few centavos each day. Ill-treatment in the prison was rare, the system being one of benign neglect. Every prisoner was beaten up on arrival, but rarely thereafter, if he kept his nose clean. Bolivian prison was preferable to Peruvian, they said, where torture was systematic and continuous, whatever government was in power: the tradition did not yield to mere political ideology.

We asked them whether they had ever thought of escape. They told us of an Australian who painstakingly forged a visitor's card, and walked out of the prison one day at the end of visiting time, dressed in women's clothes. He made it across the Chilean border. Another prisoner, a Bolivian, learnt tailoring in the prison workshops, and gradually made himself a fine suit. San Pedro was visited one day by an international commission of jurists. Donning his fine suit, he tagged himself on to the commission and the authorities, anxious to make a good impression, failed to count them on their way out. The escapee was at liberty for nine months before his capture and return to San Pedro, where he was received with a hero's welcome.

But for every successful escape there were a hundred failures: the risk was too great.

We sat and talked. San Pedro was the finest place, they said, from which to observe Bolivian political events. The prisoners were intimate with the innermost secrets of the government, and invariably knew when a coup was imminent. They also knew about General Luis García Meza Tejada. In his year as president he had salted away $40 million from the cocaine trade. After his coup, the saying went, 'it began to rain cocaine in Bogotá.'

García Meza was not alone, of course. The Minister of the Interior, Colonel Luis Arce Gomez, and the Bolivian military attaché in Caracas, Colonel Norberto 'Bobby' Salomon, ran an airfreight company with weekly flights for contraband between Santa Cruz in Bolivia and Columbia. The Minister of Education, appropriately named Colonel Ariel Coca, was formerly air force chief in Santa Cruz, where he ran a large operation with his brother, who was arrested in Panama in possession of a hundred kilos of cocaine.

But best of all was Colonel Natusch Busch. He was a contemporary of García Meza's at the Colegio Militar, and was reported to have been somewhat put out when García Meza but not he was promoted general. He attempted a golpe, which was so unpopular that after initial success he was forced to step down. Before he did so, however, he ordered six trucks to the Banco Central, where they were loaded with whatever gold bullion was contained in its vaults, which was then flown out and deposited in his own name in a country whose bank accounts are much favoured by insecure dictators. The colonel was promoted general for this exploit, in the hope that he would return the gold. Instead, he had attempted three golpes in the last three weeks, with another attempt expected shortly.

They reminisced about the various coups and coup attempts they had witnessed from the vantage point of the prison. During one of them, the *golpistas* decided, for some reason, that the key to success lay with pacifying the prisoners in San Pedro. They lobbed CS gas canisters into the prison and sprayed the walls with machine-gun bullets.

On another occasion, the golpistas were so certain of success that they persuaded the newspapers of La Paz to print a proclamation of the new government on the night preceding the day of the projected coup. The newspapers were distributed as usual early next morning, but the coup failed, and a new edition was printed while a frantic search for all the copies of the old edition was conducted. The drama was enacted before La Paz was properly awake.

We walked through the prison to their rooms. We saw the kitchen where the gruel for the prisoners who could not afford to buy their own food was prepared. In the centre of the kitchen stood two boiling black cauldrons, sufficiently large for a man comfortably to drown in. The walls and floor were caked in thick dried gruel, which had oxidised to a jet black. The 'cook' stirred the contents of the cauldrons with a crowbar, and gave us a sweaty grin that could only be described as evil.

The main courtyard of the prison was where the prisoners spent most of their time, day after day, year after year. Old lags stood about, exchanging stale prison gossip. As we passed through, various prison characters were pointed out to us; notorious homosexuals, the controller of the illicit still, a prostitute who claimed to have had intercourse with every prisoner, including the eighty-year-old doyen of them all.

We saw the prison mascot, a mongrel bitch.

'That bitch has pups every six months', said the Canadian.

'I suppose they're half-human,' I said.

'Don't joke,' he said. 'That bitch is the most fucked bitch in Bolivia.'

He told me the Quechua word for one who finds dogs sexually exciting.

'That's the kind of Quechua I speak,' he said.

He asked for some money to buy alcohol. He returned to us in triumph, with a bottle filled with a transparent oily fluid.

'You've made me happy for a day.'

We went through the least affluent part of the prison. It was like the catacombs of hell. There were people in dark holes, like maggots in a cheese. We emerged into another courtyard, where stood an eroded limestone statue of St Peter, his arms extended in a gesture of compassion towards the world.

The blond Canadian took us to his room, eight feet by six, up a rickety ladder under a neglected part of the prison roof. Even at midday it was dark up there. He switched on the light. The electricity was metered by the warders, who collected payment for it. He sat down on his thin mattress on the floor and offered us a drink from his bottle. It tasted industrial, like paint-remover. The trick, he said, was to gulp it quickly, to bypass the mouth; a trick which he then performed, half-emptying the bottle.

He showed us his drawings, portraits of other prisoners. He had considerable talent as a draughtsman, but he had run out of pencils and paper. He hoped his mother would send him some for Christmas in six months' time. Six months! The mention of time beyond tomorrow stirred his emotions. His voice cracked. He would be more than forty when he left San Pedro, he said: his youth gone, his life ruined. He emptied his bottle and was soon drunk.

The French-Canadian insisted that we visit his cell too. It was the prison penthouse, he said: no cell was higher up. We were surprised to see a crucifix hanging above his bed. Noticing that we noticed, he said:

'I still say my prayers.'

Suddenly embarrassed by his abandonment of the tough-guy

pose in front of his companions, he added:

'My prayer says: God, get me out of here!'

He laughed. But there was also a plaster statuette of the Virgin Mary by his bed.

He told us he would go straight when he left prison. He would work as a labourer in the Canadian North, where the work was hard, wages were high, and temptations few. After four years of existence at the outer edges of human experience, his ambitions were entirely conventional; to be married, to have a son, to own a house.

'I'm just about keeping it together,' he said, talking of his sanity.

Before we left, he showed us his especial treasure, which he kept folded in a tobacco tin under his bed. It was a doggerel epic of prison life, bequeathed by a former inmate of San Pedro. Ceremonial had attached itself to the reading of the epic, which was performed only on special occasions. The three gringo prisoners greeted each line as an old friend. They laughed in anticipation of its jokes; they were mournful when it was over.

We returned to the prison gates via a catwalk from which there was a view of Illimani, unimpaired by any urban sprawl. The mountain was calm, silent and majestic. They looked at it almost with reverence, as though it symbolised all they had lost. They said they never failed to watch it as the sun went down.

'It must be the best view from any prison in the world,' said the judge's son.

'If they really wanted to punish us,' said the French-Canadian, 'they could build a wall and blot it out.'

The three of them strained at the barred gates to catch a last glimpse of us. Two of them were in tears.

'Boy, this was our lucky day.'

We hired a taxi to take us the seventy-two kilometres from La Paz to Tiahuanaco, the site of the famous pre-Inca ruins. The driver protested our price: the road was rough, the taxi big, fuel expensive, his wife sick, his family large, he would have to wash the car afterwards, there was no profit in it for him, besides which I was a rich man. He took us all the same.

The road *was* rough. We passed through the dusty slums high above the city, and thence into the harsh landscape of the Altiplano, where we saw Indian women scratching the rocky surface of the land with implements of wood. It was a backbreaking and thankless task, whose yield at best would be a meagre crop of potatoes.

We reached the ruins. They were once on the shores of Titicaca, but the lake shrinks every year. The River Desaguadero, from which the border town takes its name, drains into the lake and is its main source of water. 'A lazy, thirsty, shallow river that looks as if it had never had a good drink', it was once called. It fails to make up for Titicaca's losses by evaporation.

A village with a colonial church stands near the ruins. They themselves are thought to date from AD 800, when Tiahuanaco was the centre of an empire the size (whatever it is) of present-day Bolivia. Tiahuanaco was already in ruins by the time of its incorporation into the Inca empire, when the local inhabitants were at a loss to explain the vast hewn stones in their midst.

We bought our entrance tickets from a man who sheltered from the climate in an upright wooden box the size of a coffin. We wandered in an area of enormous stone slabs cut into geometrical shapes. A French lady in a mauve cape was supervising four adults who appeared to be searching for something among the slabs on their hands and knees. They called out to her whenever they found it, and she took notes in a little notebook.

'Excuse me,' I said, 'What are you doing?'

'It's the winter solstice,' she replied, writing urgently in her notebook. Evidently, she considered her explanation sufficient.

'I'm sorry,' I persisted, 'but I don't quite understand . . .'

'They're throwing coins to determine hexagrams of the I-Ching,' she said, a little irritably.

A man who had just thrown the coins and crawled after them announced the results, which the others found exciting. There was a gentle ripple of applause.

'Isn't it mixing your mythologies, rather?' I asked. 'I mean, throwing coins, the temple of the sun, the I-Ching, winter solstices, and all that?'

'They're all part of the Great Rhythm,' she said, as though the Great Rhythm were as much a fact of everyday experience as the 7.24 to Waterloo. 'The I-Ching can tell you everything, if you ask it in the right way – everything.'

'Including what will happen on the stock exchange?'

'The I-Ching cannot be bought,' she said primly. 'It tells you only what you need to know.'

Like a third-world dictator, I thought. We left the lady in mauve cape and her followers (they were all Belgian computer programmers), scrabbling over the rocks, divining what they needed to know.

We entered a square sunk beneath the level of the ground, whose facing walls were lined with perfectly-fitting blocks of grey stone. Near their base was a line of protruding faces carved in relief, quite unlike anything produced by the Incas, who were master masons rather than sculptors.

A central stairway led from this mysterious, deserted square to ground level, where an arch of three gigantic blocks of stone (the true arch was never discovered in pre-columbian America) framed a view of a monolithic statue, carved elaborately with the symbols of a defunct pantheon.

Pre-columbian ruins have always attracted cranks with bizarre theories to expound, usually strongly influenced by consider-ations of race. Such is the depravity of present-day Indians, their slowness and mental incapacity – so the argument goes – that no ancestors of theirs could conceivably have summoned the intellectual or physical energy to create the pre-columbian monuments, which must therefore have been built by another race, or even by extraterrestrial beings. Amongst others, the Hebrews, Phoenicians and ancient Egyptians have been cast in this role. A man called Ranking published a book in London in 1827 entitled *Historical Researches on the Conquest of Peru by the Monguls*, in which he asserted that the first Inca was almost certainly a younger son of Kublai Khan. In 1867 a German called Frenzel published a book in Leipzig proving to his own satisfaction at least that the Aztecs were Irish. A Peruvian called Vincente Fidel Lopez published a book in Paris in 1871 entitled *Les Races aryennes du Pérou*, in which he proved, by means of etymological coincidences, that the ancient civilisations of Peru were offshoots of ancient Greece. It remained for the twentieth century, however, to discover that in reality the ancient Peruvians descended from outer space.

We tried to buy a lunch in the village but it was deserted, apart from a blind man sitting on a bench in the plaza, a small girl and a dog. The inhabitants had removed themselves in their entirety to the next village, where the annual fiesta was taking place. They would return in the morning, we were told by our driver, exhausted by dancing and drink. We noticed as we left the village an elegant and beautiful woman standing by the side of the road. We stopped and asked whether we could be of any assistance. She said she should be glad of a lift back to La Paz. She had been waiting at the roadside for two hours. She had come by bus to see the ruins, thinking to return to La Paz by the same means. While waiting, she had been approached by a drunken Indian who made sexual advances to her.

'What did you do?' we asked.

'I ignored him,' she replied.

The Indian had retired in drunken confusion. An Italian of aristocratic mien, she was dressed casually, but coolly and in the utmost taste. There was an inviolable penumbra about her: alone of all the objects on the Altiplano, dust had not settled on her. We admired her slightly chilling beauty in the taxi. Her skin had a natural marmoreal smoothness; her nose was faintly aquiline and her brown eyes had a liquid clarity. Her every movement was performed with a fastidious grace.

Her husband worked for a large international company in Lima. She had a degree in economics, and had registered for a doctorate at the University of San Marcos. Her thesis was going to trace the development of the Peruvian economy, but she had not so far started her researches because of other commitments: attendance at a lecture course on pre-columbian art and entertaining her husband's business guests.

She found Lima dull. It had no cultural life to speak of. There were only three theatres, one of them amateur, for seven million people. Social life consisted largely of vulgar displays of wealth. Everyone had so much money.

Everyone? Surely she was using the word in some highly technical sense.

In spite of her theoretical left-wing economic views, she was a victim of the servant problem. When she first arrived in Lima she had been warned that her Indian servants would work only under direct compulsion. Nevertheless, she treated them initially with all consideration, asking them whether they wouldn't mind doing this, whether they had a moment to do that. But under the polite dispensation nothing whatever was done: clothes went unwashed for weeks, dust accumulated, food rotted, and everything was stolen. Before long, she had resorted to the *ancien régime* of screams, docked wages, and indomitable suspicion. The servants seemed relieved; here was a system they understood and expected. The household economy improved at once. She concluded that the Indians were lazy and stupid.

We journeyed to La Paz to the continuous accompaniment of a football commentary on the radio. The local heroes, Bolívar, were playing a team called Always Ready (who were nevertheless near the bottom of the league). Scarcely pausing for breath, the commentator found every goal kick, every throw-in, unbearably exciting. He broke down into incoherent sobs, like a nun at a papal audience. When a goal was scored he announced the fact with an exclamation of the word 'goal' so long that we seemed to travel between two villages before he completed it.

That afternoon in La Paz was our last together. Richard and Frances had to fly back to Britain. We walked through the steep and narrow streets behind the church of San Francisco, through a market of Indian herbal remedies. The herbs were laid out in little piles on the ground, with small explanatory notices beside them: 'Buen para el hígado', good for the liver, or 'Buen para los pulmones', good for the lungs. The purchasers, for the most part, looked beyond remedy. Aperients sold best.

There were stalls of magical prescriptions which the owners, old women in shawls and hats, hurriedly covered over with blankets, lest our unbelieving and sceptical eyes deprive the dried llama foetuses – their stock-in-trade – of their magical powers. The foetuses are used widely as ritual abortifacients, among other purposes, though without much effect. Bolivian women continue to have many more children than they want, though their faith in this method is undiminished. Asked by an anthropologist whether she had wanted her children, a woman from Oruro said: 'Children are in the world because God sends them. It isn't the women. If it were up to the women, there wouldn't be any more. A woman alone cannot have children. But the men are pigs and they get the girls in trouble when they walk in the street.'

The hostility towards us in this quarter was so manifest that we decided to return to the more European parts of the city. We sat out the wait for the flight drinking pisco sours, and then went to the airport. El Alto is the highest commercial airport in the world, at 13,100 feet, requiring heavy fuel loads and exceptionally long runways. The airport was busy with flights by battered old military transports, ferrying in essential military supplies like Scotch whisky and video sets, for sale to officers at concessionary prices.

We parted there, and I returned to the city, alone once more in a vast and alien continent. The taxi driver warned me to beware of all Peruvians – they were thieves. He also warned me that I should stay indoors – a coup was imminent.

The next day, Saturday, the sun shone with its winter brilliance. The young cadets of the armed forces were out in strength, promenading in the Avenida 16 de Julio. They strolled, stiff-backed but arm-in-arm, their faces as highly polished as their brass buttons, their calf-length boots clicking on the pavements, aware that everyone was admiring them. The naval cadets had short swords on which to rest a hand; but epaulettes were an even

greater asset in the struggle for the glances of the señoritas. I
passed a future president or two, no doubt. When they saw a
senior officer, out taking the air in civilian clothes, they dis-
engaged their arms, puffed out their chests, and saluted smartly. I
thought I detected vague and cynical smiles play upon the faces of
officers saluted thus.

I went to the Plaza Murillo to read the newspaper. People were
gathered there to feed the pigeons, eat ice-creams, and gossip.
There were urgent comings and goings at the Palacio Quemado,
but no-one took notice of them. According to the newspaper,
General García Meza had been making one of his flatulent
speeches again. One can sample his style in a speech he made
three months before he came to power:

> The Armed Forces . . . interpreters of the true wishes and aspira-
> tions of the real people of Bolivia . . . adhere to a rigid organic
> political régime, with a Bolivian ideology and social conscience
> which is derived from our rôle as the guiding force of the nation's
> existence . . .
>
> We make it an article of faith to safeguard and build a sovereign
> and great fatherland in the context of a new conception of the
> Republic.

A man of about thirty sat next to me. He was dressed in a
sheepskin jacket and carried a child wrapped up like a parcel.

'Where are you from?' he asked in English.

He was a Bolivian engineer who had spent a year studying in a
Rolls-Royce factory in Coventry. His wife was out at work and,
uncharacteristically for South America, had left her husband to
dress, feed and amuse the baby.

We went to the Parque Central and sat with a magnificent view
of the city before us. I asked him whether a coup was on its way.

'In Bolivia,' he said, 'a coup is always on its way. But coups have
nothing to do with us. We are only the people: *they* are the Army.
Who cares which general is president? They all have a turn in the
end.'

Sometimes, of course, the coups are violent. After Natusch

Busch's temporarily successful coup, barricades were set up in the streets, and before long the small river of La Paz, the Río Choqueyapu, flowed red with blood. When General Ovando ousted the reforming Paz Estenssoro, he said to him: 'I am taking you to the airport or the cemetery. Which do you prefer?' (He chose the airport.) But mostly the coups are peaceful, pre-arranged affairs between brother officers. On one famous occasion in Ecuador the incumbent general asked for the imminent coup to be postponed until after the wedding of his daughter. The plotters obliged.

The engineer's father lived in the province of Mendoza in Argentina, surrounded by the estancias of Nazis who had fled from the Nuremberg Trials, or survived the sinking of the *Graf Spee*. These refugees had brought up their children to be 'good' Nazis, and their homes were shrines to the memory of Adolf Hitler. They still got themselves up in Nazi uniforms and stomped round their estancias. One of them raised the Nazi flag every morning, to the accompaniment of 'Deutschland, Deutschland Uber Alles' played on a trumpet.

The baby needed feeding and we returned to the engineer's flat, which was small but in a clean and modern block for what he called 'the technical middle class'. Each room had its bouquet of plastic flowers and a plaster virgin. While he prepared the baby's food in the kitchen – something of a phenomenon in a continent of *machismo* – he played Argentinian music on his stereo. He had been a student in Buenos Aires, and he said the music of Argentina was full of the wild poetry of the pampas and the hotheaded revolutionary fervour of the student cafés. Every time he heard it, he wanted to rush out into the street and hurl a brick at a tank.

I looked at the books on his shelves. There were a few American textbooks of electronics, an engineering work or two, Albert Camus' *Myth of Sisyphus* in Spanish, Marshall McLuhan's *The Gutenberg Galaxy* and (also in Spanish) *The Protocols of the Elders of Zion*. I left the engineer, puzzled as to the nature of his beliefs.

The same evening I had arranged to meet a contact at the British Embassy. I stood waiting in the lobby of my hotel, holding a bunch of flowers for his wife, while the television in the corner relayed a football match. When one of the players missed an open goal a viewer spat at the screen and then banged the television top with his fist, as though it were to blame.

I recognised the diplomat as soon as he entered. His shabby clothes proclaimed him an Englishman enjoying a weekend. Although our eyes met, and we knew at once we were waiting for each other, it was several minutes before we spoke. He was balding and putting on weight. He was an attaché: he used to be culture, but now he was commerce. He had spent the afternoon washing his car.

We drove to his home, in an exclusive suburb of La Paz which was built in the last days of General Banzer. The president sold the houses at knockdown prices to his senior officers in a last-ditch effort to keep them loyal. They bought the houses, but betrayed Banzer all the same. Now they rented them out to foreign companies and legations at high rents.

His wife greeted us at the door. She was wearing apple green trousers of synthetic fibre. She declared at once how bored she was. Servants relieved her of even the lightest domestic duties. She passed her time playing bridge and mah-jong with other diplomatic wives. Occasionally she got together with the Protestant Ladies of La Paz to distribute secondhand clothes to the poor of the city. Her previous posting had been in a Saharan republic: life had been no different there.

We talked only of Bolivian politics. Trouble was on the way, of that there was no possible doubt. American diplomats had been warned not to leave La Paz because of an impending coup (admittedly a warning they received every other weekend). García Meza had come to power on an understanding between himself and his fellow-conspirators that he would stand down after a year in office, on August 4th, to give another general a turn at the presidency. A rumour was circulating to the effect that García Meza himself wanted to retire to enjoy a prosperous retirement, but his wife so enjoyed being Mrs President that she would not let him retire. In any case, he had hired a crowd in Cochabamba to cheer a speech he made from a balcony there, and he was so moved by their cheers that, after several requests to do so, he finally agreed to stay on as their president. The other generals were not impressed by this manoeuvre, and were now plotting to remove their former partner.

The present government of Bolivia was so repulsive, said the diplomat as he poured half a glass of sherry, that even the French would not sell arms to it. The British government, in one of its fits of morality which are seldom commercially very damaging, had decided to suspend all loans to Bolivia and reduce the scale of its diplomatic representation. To have been consistent, of course, it should have done the same to Chile, Uruguay and Argentina; but trade with those countries was too profitable to allow of any fine gestures. García Meza had been able demagogically to exploit this hypocrisy for his own dubious ends, citing it as an example of foreign interference in the internal affairs of Bolivia, thus gaining sympathy which he did not deserve.

The diplomat told me that if I wished to see the old Nazis who were widely believed to be behind both the cocaine trade and the present government in Bolivia, I should go to the German Club for lunch on Sunday. The food was the best in La Paz; but on no account should I take a camera.

We parted, wondering why we had met.

I went to the German Club. It was not a hundred yards from my hotel, down a street running parallel to the Avenida 16 de Julio. A man was sweeping the floor of the entrance hall, in the corner of which was a bust of Bismarck atop a marble pedestal. I was the first customer in the restaurant, which was simply but comfortably furnished. I sat at a table from which I could observe all the other tables. The menu said 'Wilkommen'. I chose South American dishes. People began to arrive. Some of them were just Bolivian families out for lunch. Others were silver-haired Germans in their seventies or eighties, with Spanish-speaking ladies on their arms. One of these men, with a pronounced limp, arrived as the funeral march from the *Eroica* struck up over the loud-speakers. He received the acknowledgements of the other Germans, bowing slightly as he limped between the tables.

He might have been a perfectly respectable man or a monster of evil. In our enlightened age a mass murderer can look like a bibliophile, a lover of Schubert *lieder* can supervise a gas chamber.

FIVE

Cuzco, Peruvian Andes

As SOON AS the curfew lifted next morning, I went to catch the
bus to Cuzco. Other folk were up early, too. Three military
jets screamed back and forth over the city, and desultory gunfire
could be heard from the heights above it and the suburbs below it.
A *golpe* had started. Indian women went on arranging their wares
on the pavements as though nothing unusual were happening –
perhaps nothing unusual for La Paz was happening. In the city of
Santa Cruz de la Sierra, General Busch had also (once more)
raised the standard of revolt: he had set up a provisional government – it turned out to be very provisional indeed – which he
named *el Gobierno de Dignidad Nacional*, the Government of
National Dignity. The justification for the golpe was the same as
that used in the first golpe of all. 'The tyrant is dead! The laws are
restored!' cried the assassins of Francisco Pizarro in 1541.

The bus departed late. Punctuality, something very rare in
South America, used to be known in Peru as *hora británica*, British
time, on account of the strange, punctual habits, long since
abandoned, of British businessmen and merchants. The road was
distinctly rough. We travelled along the eastern shore of Lake
Titicaca, even more beautiful than the western shore. The
serenity of the landscape did not, however, exert a calming effect
on the driver. Until we reached the tortuous mountain passes he
gave every indication of wishing to remain alive, but the sight of
the hairpin bends unhinged him completely. They were a flagrant
challenge to his masculinity, and one he accepted joyfully. He

accelerated wildly, especially at blind corners on precipices plunging several hundred feet. It must have been the plastic Virgin that preserved us.

We stopped for lunch at a small town, and four gringos on board coalesced like drops of mercury. There was a woman artist from Los Angeles, recently divorced of course, who was travelling through South America, 'to find out who I really am and to get my head together'; an English professor of oceanography, working at a university in New York, who had gone as a guest lecturer to an institute in the south of Chile, only to discover that the students spoke no English and the journey as a consequence was futile; a North American Maryknoll father, a professor of ecclesiastical history, with a complexion like a plucked chicken; and myself.

We milled around after lunch, waiting for the driver to finish his siesta. I fell into conversation with the professor of ecclesiastical history. The Maryknollers are a Catholic order from North America with a reputation for extreme radicalism. The professor was a short man who looked as though his growth had been stunted in youth by malnourishment and ill-usage. He had a small moustache and wore round horn-rimmed glasses which flashed disconcertingly in the sunlight. He looked strangely familiar, and I struggled to remember as he spoke where I had seen him before.

'Have I ever met you?' I asked.

'I don't think so. Why?'

Then it came to me where I had seen his face: Heinrich Himmler! He was the very spit and image.

'Are you now,' I asked, 'or have you ever been, a chicken farmer?'

'No. Why?' he asked again, a little bemused by my question.

'Oh, no reason.'

I looked at his sandals and crumpled beige trousers which barely reached his ankles. They were not so much a sign of otherworldliness as an advertisement of it.

He was anxious to explain his philosophy of ecclesiastical history to me. He wanted, he said, to put it at the service of the people; if necessary, at the service of the Revolution. I said I found it hard to conceive how ecclesiastical history could do either of these things. He admitted it had only a small part to play in the final, inevitable victory. But he hoped that his researches in the archdiocesan archives of La Paz into the history of the Church in the province of Puno, which the Maryknollers were to publish as a book, would help stir the peasants to righteous revolutionary anger. I said I thought it unlikely the peasants would ever get to see his book, especially as it was to be in two volumes and in English; but, warming to his subject, he seemed not to hear me.

'We will use the book to pressurise the Church authorities into changing direction,' he said. 'The Church has always been the handmaiden of the ruling classes, the landowners, the caudillos, and the generals. It has been their ideological prop.'

I asked him what he wanted the Church to be like instead.

'We want to modernise the Church,' he said. 'Democratise it. Clear away all the accretions that have nothing to do with Christ and His Gospel . . .'

I saw in his eyes and in his professorial spectacles the gleam of a new orthodoxy, and I recalled the lines of the Chilean poet, Nicanor Parra:

> Independientemente
> De los designios de la Iglesia Católica
> Me declaro país independiente.
>
> Que me perdone el Comité Central.

(Independently of the designs of the Catholic Church I declare myself an independent country. May the Central Committee forgive me.)

'I think,' I said, 'that you have mistaken the part religion plays in the lives of poor people. Their lives are monotonous, humdrum, and without beauty. They go to church for the mystery, the beauty, and the ceremony. Religion, remember, is the opium of the people, the sigh of the oppressed, the heart of a heartless world. Without the accretions, as you call them, people could do without it altogether.'

'I admit,' he replied, 'that Andean religion has always had

strong elements of pagan superstition grafted on to it. The Inca Earth Mother, Pachamama, was incorporated into the Catholic Church as the cult of Mary. After the Conquest the church was more concerned with numerical and financial strength than doctrinal purity. But change is coming.'

'You see,' I continued, also warming to the subject, about which I knew little, 'what the peasants want is a solid silver altar and golden reliquary to which they can crawl on their knees from half a mile away to ask for the saint's heavenly intercession for the recovery of their pig that has just been run over by a bus.'

'Things are changing now,' he said. 'Even the Indians are getting more educated.'

'Education is another thing the Church should set its face firmly against,' I said, 'if it wants to retain its influence. Education equals secularism.'

He looked at me as though he were not sure whether I really believed what I said.

'Everything is changing already,' he said. 'Villages without priests are administering the sacraments to themselves. Think of it: laymen taking the sacraments into their own hands! The Church is becoming the community, and the community is becoming the Church.'

'It's institutional suicide,' I said.

'Especially in Chile,' he continued. 'The Church in Chile is a power in the land. That's because the Church in Chile's got balls. But the Church in Bolivia's different. It's in the pocket of the generals. It's got no balls at all.'

I said I thought it was a very odd choice of metaphor for a celibate organisation. My remark was so frivolous that it brought our discussion to an end. In any case, the driver had finished his siesta and we climbed back aboard the bus.

We reached the border, where there was the same stirring exhortation to Bolivian patriotism: ¡*Bolivianos*! *El Mar es un Derecho. Recuparle es un Deber*. We stayed on board while our passports were collected up and taken inside the adobe post. At length, a man whose revolver was half out of its holster came to the bus and called for the professor of oceanography and me to follow him. Another official was sitting at a table, waiting for us.

He looked up and asked us our names. Then he told us we must pay fifty pesos for each day we had been in Bolivia.

'What's he saying?' asked the professor, a blunt Yorkshireman with not a word of Spanish, or much time for foreigners. He had suspected immediately that the official was up to no good.

'He says we must pay fifty pesos for each day we were in Bolivia.'

'Why?' asked the professor, going red in the face.

'¿Por qué?' I asked.

The official shrugged his shoulders. Because he felt like it. Because his salary was not big enough to live on without supplementing it. Because we wouldn't leave Bolivia without paying it – that was why.

'Cincuenta pesos por día,' he repeated bleakly, while a picture of the Liberator scowled at us.

'But why us?' asked the professor.

I said I thought it might be something to do with the titles on our passports. I turned to the official, and told him we no longer had fifty pesos for each day we were in Bolivia, having changed our money in La Paz.

'How much do you have?' he asked, evidently willing to negotiate.

He settled for a hundred and fity pesos between us, which he stuffed straight into his pocket, and stamped our passports.

'It's sheer bloody extortion, that's what it is,' murmured the professor as he climbed back on to the bus.

By chance, he was one of the few people who had visited the Gilbert Islands, where I now worked. He went there to study the ocean currents.

'It were a grand piss-up,' he said. 'Never did any work, mind.'

In Peru every house – even the meanest hovel – was flying the red, white and red flag of the country, for the anniversary of independence from Spain was approaching. The flags fluttered brightly in an otherwise monochrome landscape, symbolising a bedrock of patriotism that no amount of political jobbery, broken promises, landowner oppression, or exacting officialdom could ever quite erode.

We crossed Titicaca on a ferry that looked far from water-worthy. Most of the hundreds of passengers found the instability of the boat highly amusing. The situation had the makings of a small paragraph in the bottom right hand corner of the *Sunday Times*, opposite an advertisement offering a cure for baldness. *Titicaca Ferry Sinks* 320 *Drown*. Nevertheless, we reached the other side safely, and by virtue of further demoniac driving approached Puno at dusk. The lights of the cold, grim town glimmered feebly, and homeless migrant Indians huddled in the doorways for warmth, or at least shelter from the cold.

The artist from Los Angeles and I searched for somewhere to have dinner. She recalled having read – in *The Vegetarian Guide to South America*, she thought it was – that there was a good vegetarian restaurant in Puno. I said I thought it unlikely there was a good restaurant in Puno of any description, but she insisted we try to find it. She searched as assiduously as for her True Self, but we failed. Down a pitch-dark disused railway siding, I said: 'Are there many restaurants down unlit railway sidings in Los Angeles?'

We settled for a small café, stifling with the airless heat of kerosene stoves, and very overcrowded. We sat at a table with a Peace Corps worker and his wife. They soon learnt I was a doctor.

'My wife has a cold,' said the Peace Corps worker. 'Is it true that Vitamin C prevents colds?'

'I don't know,' I replied. 'But it's too late now in any case. And given the choice between swallowing Vitamin C every day in large doses and having a cold once a year, I should unhesitatingly choose the cold.'

'And what about Vitamin E? Do you think she could be short on Vitamin E?'

I looked at his wife. Her eyes were circled with red and her nose was sore from rubbing. Her hair looked as though birds had nested in it.

'I was reading an article the other day,' said the Peace Corps worker, 'about all the things caused by Vitamin E lack.'

'Such as?'

'Oh, I don't know. Just about everything, I guess.'

Plates of lake fish were brought to us.

'Maybe I'll give her Vitamin E anyway,' he said. 'It can't do any harm, I guess.'

Two years on the Altiplano had sapped their natural North American ebullience and optimism. The avoidance of suffering, rather than the pursuit of happiness, was now their aim.

I took the train from Puno to Cuzco. It was supposed to leave at seven in the morning, but by eight it still had not made its appearance in the station, and the passengers, all of whom supposedly had reservations, were herded into two small waiting rooms. Rumours swept through the waiting rooms like wind through grass. One stated that the passengers in the other waiting room were to be allowed on to the train first when finally it came. This rumour swept both waiting rooms simultaneously and caused mass migrations from one to the other, two tides of passengers struggling to pass each other.

When at last the train arrived, the passengers fought like panic-stricken refugees to get aboard. No-one seemed merely to be travelling between Puno and Cuzco: they were moving house. There were mattresses and stoves, cooking utensils and bathtubs, chickens and goats, and vast numbers of suitcases. By the time everything was stored there was hardly room for the passengers themselves. I had to sit with my bag on my knees, my feet eking out a bloodless existence between two steel trunks. If the train jolted, my feet would have been crushed like cloves of garlic. Half an hour after the train arrived in the station, it looked as though it had been home to hundreds of people for several weeks.

As soon as the train started to move, the fat lady opposite me dragged her provisions from her baggage and put them on the table between us. The journey to Cuzco takes ten hours under favourable conditions, and she clearly had no intention of going hungry in that time. There was a bunch of bananas, a packet of potato crisps (economy size), several bars of chocolate, and a bag of popcorn two feet high and one in diameter. She shook the popcorn out of the bag until it covered the whole table, and then started to pick at it one piece at a time, like doing a jig-saw puzzle in reverse. Her slim young daughter sat next to her reading one of Lima's lurid crime magazines. The cover had a photograph of a flabby white body with multiple stab wounds. She read with furious concentration. One could tell when she reached a particularly gruesome and satisfying passage by the rate at which she chewed her gum: it slackened, and at the climax ceased altogether.

We stopped at every settlement on the line. The Peruvian flag fluttered everywhere, usually at the end of a long, thin pole that bent in the wind. At one of the settlements, a gnarled old man was led on to the train by a small boy of about ten. The old man was blind and sang on the trains for a living, his young guide holding out a battered tin plate for alms. Everyone was moved by their plight as they picked their way tortuously through a minefield of luggage, and though not rich, all gave something.

The train, an express, was agonisingly slow. I felt at times I wanted to climb down and run alongside it. The relentless munching across the table began to unnerve me. The woman had the body and soul of a ruminant. Her daughter, the devoted follower of the Lima police department, fell asleep with her head lolling to one side, her mouth wide open, and the crime magazine clutched open to her chest. At a place known as Aguascalientes because of several hot springs that bubble through the ground there, the train broke down. The scenery was magnificent, but tempers were short. A replacement locomotive had to be brought from further down the line, and we considered ourselves lucky in the end to be delayed by only two hours.

We arrived in Cuzco well past nightfall. I deposited my luggage in an hotel in the Calle San Agustín, a converted colonial mansion, and went for a walk in the former capital of the Inca Empire.

No description of the Inca masonry that still lines Cuzco's streets, and was the foundation on which the Spanish built all their monuments, could begin to convey its majesty and splendour. The awesome walls slope inwards from the ground at an angle perhaps of twenty degrees and are made of massive, irregular, but perfectly fitting blocks of smooth stone, between which it would not be possible to insinuate so much as a sheet of paper, though no cement or mortar of any kind was used in their construction. In the Calle Hatun Rumioc is the famous stone block with twelve angles, all of which are perfectly met by its surrounding blocks, the weights of which are measured in tons. It is doubtful whether anywhere in the world today such walls could be constructed, though the Incas had no iron tools and no draught animals save man himself; nor had they discovered the wheel.

My footfall echoed in the deserted streets of the Pachacutec and Huáscar. The carved wooden balconies of the Spanish above remained shuttered and barred. The street lights, projecting from the houses, cast long and inconstant shadows on the cobbles, and it was possible to imagine oneself back in the seventeenth century (with the odours removed).

I emerged into the Plaza de Armas, the main square of Cuzco. After the semi-darkness of the streets around, it was brilliantly illuminated, and my eyes took time to adjust to the light. The Cathedral and the magnificent church of la Compañía de Jesús (the Jesuits) were floodlit. On the southern side of the square was a charming colonial arcade, where tourists picked their way through piles of shoddy handicrafts.

I found a restaurant where all the customers were Peruvian. I was shown to the last free table where before long I was joined by a man of about my own age. He asked me politely – with ceremony, almost – whether I objected if he disturbed me. After sitting down, he eyed me closely for a few moments.

'Where are you from?' he asked in almost accentless English.

'England,' I replied.

'Do you mind if we talk? I know you English are very reserved.' He said it with a slight smile.

Before long he had told me a lot about himself. His father was an Italian immigrant to Peru in the time of Mussolini. He started a business, prospered, and married into the Peruvian landowning class. His mother had owned a hacienda of more than ten thousand hectares before General Velasco's coup in 1968, after which it had been confiscated, with compensation, in the land reform, one of the four thousand laws the military regime decreed in nine years. The loss of the hacienda hardly mattered to the family, who rarely went there anyway, and whose main business interests were elsewhere. Though they had controlled the lives of thousands of Indians living on the hacienda as competely as any Inca emperor, the hacienda was not even a hobby with them. Like all Peruvian landowners, they called the Indian 'the animal that resembles man'. After the military coup, Velasco decreed that henceforth the Indians should be known as *campesinos* – that is, peasants – a name they considered more dignified than the *indio* of old, with its pejorative connotations.

The hacienda was vast, sprawling, and inefficient. The will of the *hacendado's* family was sovereign. The Indians, though legally free, were effectively serfs, or even slaves. They spoke little Spanish and were all illiterate; they had no recourse to law, for all the officers of the law were in the pocket of the hacendado. Jorge, my interlocutor, remembered the days when his grandfather, having risen from bed in a bad mood, would call an Indian into the house from the fields outside and pummel him with his fists and kick him to the ground merely to relieve his feelings, at the end of which the Indian, picking himself up bruised and bleeding from the ground, would, to avoid a further beating for insolence, bow low, murmur 'Muchas gracias, señor,' and return to work in the fields. And yet it was his grandfather, not the Indian, who felt aggrieved and cursed his fate; to the Indian, it was merely another inevitable hazard of life.

Jorge recalled that when he was at the University of San Marcos, he and his university friends would get drunk, drive out to the hacienda, and beat up a few Indians, the next morning scarcely even remembering what they had done.

'There's no doubt we deserved to lose our lands,' he said. 'And for myself, I don't ever want them back.'

But there were still former landowners who wanted to reverse the flow of time and history, and undo the land reform. At the time of the coup, one in five thousand people who owned land – to say nothing of the totally landless population – owned more than two thirds of all the land. Land in South America has not merely economic value: it has an almost mystical ability to confer status and membership of the tiny upper class, which money alone could never do.

'Of course,' continued Jorge, 'the reform was an economic disaster. The generals hoped that the former landowners would use their compensation for starting industries, but they just bought apartments in Miami instead. And agricultural production reached almost zero. The Indians just weren't used to making decisions for themselves – they were used to being given orders about everything – so that the fields just rotted and food became scarce.'

Inefficient as the haciendas had undoubtedly been, between 1972 (when half the land was distributed) and 1978, the average consumption of calories in Lima, always well below a proper subsistence, had declined by a further quarter; and the consumption of protein dropped further below the minimum for health.

'But you can't turn an animal into a man overnight,' Jorge said. His lack of feeling – or was it cant? – startled me. But he approved of the reforms in spite of their economic failure, because no social progress would have been possible without them. The task now, he said, was to transform the mass of apathetic, coca-chewing automata into rational economic men. Nothing less than a reversal of the past four hundred and fifty years of history – or more, if the Inca period were included – was required.

Jorge was trained as an engineer. Until recently he worked in an Ecuadorian jungle oilfield. But Peru and Ecuador had just had a brief border skirmish over some uninhabited but possible oil-bearing land (they fought a war in 1943, which Peru won), and he was arrested as a Peruvian spy, and tortured. The Ecuadorians believed he was sending messages to the Peruvian air force, disclosing the location of vital oil installations. The house which he owned in Ecuador was confiscated. At the end of hostilities he was released and sent back to Peru.

'Now things are back to normal again, I could go back and claim my house,' he said. 'But I don't want to go back to Ecuador. They really took the whole thing seriously there.'

I mentioned that I had seen war propaganda posters in Peru, with pictures of President Belaúnde inspecting· a captured Ecuadorian gun in the jungle, with the Army Chief of Staff and the Minister of Defence at his side.

'We didn't take it seriously in Peru,' Jorge replied dismissively. 'Everybody in Lima went down to the beach as usual. We know we can march into Quito any time we feel like it, and the Ecuadorians know it too.'

After a brief pause, he continued: 'Actually, I would like there to be a real war. You know, a proper war with battles and thousands of people killed.'

'A war against whom?' I asked.

'Oh that doesn't matter, anyone would do. Chile, perhaps, or Colombia.'

'But why?' It was an odd attitude for someone who had been tortured.

'Because life is so boring without war. Because the country needs discipline.'

I suppose I looked shocked.

'Listen,' he said. 'I don't care too much about democracy. So long as my party wins, that's all. Basta. You see, I'm a Peruvian patriot. I love my country. But there are two Perus. There are the Indians and us. How can I call them my countrymen? There are two cultures, and there's only Catholicism in common. I know nothing about them and they know nothing about us. I don't believe in God, but I support the Church and I'd always bring up my son as a Catholic, for the sake of Peru.'

I found his credo somewhat incoherent, to say the least.

'You see, we South Americans are used to death by violence. We expect to die violently. My grandfather was the first man to fly an aeroplane to Cuzco. He wanted to be the first man to fly to Puno as well, so he flew to Puno. But when he arrived there, the landing field was completely full of Indians waiting to see the iron bird. So he crashed into a mountain instead and killed himself.'

'I'm not sure I understand the moral of that story,' I said.

'Listen: my best friend and I were drunk one evening in Lima. There were riots all the time then, and there was a curfew. We broke the curfew and the soldiers shot my friend in the back. Death is not so terrible.'

'Yes,' I said, 'but it's rather final.'

We left the restaurant and went to a bar he knew up a narrow flight of dark stairs, suitable for the forcible ejection of drunk ruffians. It was crowded and very smoky. In the corner a black band played Peruvian jazz, raucous and loud. People were having the kind of good time that often ends up in a brawl.

I took a beer while Jorge drank Scotch – a sign of sophisticated taste in Peru. He looked round the bar.

'I can always tell the tourists,' he said. 'They dress like Indians.'

After a couple of drinks I told Jorge I was tired and we walked back through the deserted streets to my hotel.

'You English are very reserved,' he said.

'Yes, I suppose we are,' I replied.

Cuzco was the capital of the Inca Empire, Tahuantinsuyo. Cuzco means navel and Tahuantinsuyo means Four Quarters of the Earth. When the Spanish entered the city for the first time they were astonished at its magnificence. By comparison with any Spanish city of the time, it was clean, comfortable, and well-ordered.

The Spanish erected a splendid city of their own on the foundations of Inca masonry, though it was never their capital. It was, however, one of the centres of their religious endeavour. The churches and monasteries of Cuzco attained an unsurpassed glory.

The church and monastery of La Merced is perhaps the most magnificent of all. It was founded in the year after the conquest, but rebuilt a century and a half later, when the missionary impulse had entirely given way to the desire for a rich and luxurious life. The cloister is exquisitely ornate and sumptuous: no-one who took a vow of poverty there could possibly have meant it.

I had lunch in a café in the Plaza de Armas. Through the cool arcade I could see the Peruvian flag, a splash of brilliant red against the green and brown, drooping gently on a flagpole in the centre of the square. A television in the corner broadcast the Independence Day parade from Lima. President Fernando Belaúnde Terry took the salute, wearing the red, white and red sash of the Presidency. The tanks that rolled past the dais, further worsening the surfaces of Lima's thoroughfares, dipped their guns in respectful homage to the man whom only a dozen years before they had helped to oust and drive into exile. The crowd cheered wildly, as though tanks were Man's best friend. An excited voice called out the names of the regiments as they goose-stepped to martial music. The parade seemed endless: I began to suspect that the troops were merely marching round the block and appearing again before the dais.

In the afternoon I went up to the fortress of Sacsahuamán, several hundred feet above the city. It was from here in 1536 that the Indians, led by Manco Capac, a half-brother of Atahuallpa's whom the Spaniards had set up on the Inca throne as a malleable puppet, directed their siege of Cuzco in a last, desperate attempt to preserve Inca independence. According to Pedro Pizarro, who was at the siege, in his *Relaciones de Descubrimiento y Conquista de los Reynos del Peru*, 200,000 Indian warriors besieged the city, which was defended by only 200 Spaniards and 1000 Cañaris, an Indian tribe which had only recently been incorporated into the Inca Empire. Atahuallpa had killed 60,000 of them so they bore the Incas no love. The Cañaris were rewarded for their assistance to the Spaniards by a privileged position (for Indians) in colonial Peru, being exempt for ever from the *mita* and other exactions. The siege lasted several months and was a desperate affair. The

Indians hurled rocks into the city below, and the sky was some-times dark with arrrows, according to the chroniclers. The Indians sent down firebrands to set the thatched roofs of the city alight, but all to no avail. The provisioning of such hordes proved impossible, and eventually they melted away. The story is told of how, when the Spanish retook the fortress, an Indian chief, rather than fall captive to the Spanish and seeing that further resistance was useless, cast down his war club, drew his feathered cape around him, and threw himself down from the heights.

But now the fortress was calm, with only the giggles of a mestizo couple rolling in the grass to disturb the peace. The city below, with its narrow streets, orange-red tiled roofs, and church-dominated squares, could have been in Spain. The valley of Cuzco looked Mediterranean, except that the surrounding mountains were too grand.

In the hotel, everyone gathered round the television. The Indian waiters rushed from the dining room between courses to watch; a Dutch lady, as large and healthy as she was ugly, settled on a sofa and began to sob into a lace-frilled handkerchief. It was, the announcer said, *la boda del siglo*, the wedding of the century, *directo de San Pablo en Londres*, direct from St Paul's in London, courtesy of a famous brand of toothpaste. Advertisements, which interrupted the Archbishop of Canterbury as he droned on and on, implied that what Peruvians needed for economic and social success was white teeth and the confidence that their breath did not smell. Kiri te Kanawa sang Handel in a hat that looked like a Martian's helmet. There were admirals without fleets, field marshals without armies, kings without kingdoms, and emperors without empires. Their uniforms were gorgeous: from the other side of the world it looked like the purest Ruritania.

As the Dutch lady burst into tears, I had never felt so humiliated by my own country, or so fearful for its future.

No visitor to Cuzco escapes Macchu Picchu, nor should he. Though visited by all, like the Taj Mahal, that is because it is worth the seeing.

In my carriage on the train was a small group of elderly American tourists, led by a domineering Peruvian guide with many gold teeth, who wore a loud Prince-of-Wales check jacket and a yellow paisley cravat. He soon licked his group into shape. When he told them to look out of the left-hand window, they looked out of the left-hand window; when he told them to look out of the right-hand window, they did that too. While the train was still in the station he gave them a few practice commands. Later, he told them when to look out of neither window when there was nothing spectacular to see, and they obeyed him by looking straight ahead. He gave them a few more rules: they must stick together, they must follow him, they must have lunch when they arrived, they must ask him questions at any time, and they must have a good day.

'Now, are there any questions?' he asked.

'Can we buy camera film in Macchu Picchu?' asked a man in a stetson.

'Sure,' replied Carlos, the guide. He had told them they must call him Carlos. 'You can also send postcards from Macchu Picchu post office to the folks back home.'

'Gee, that'd be real cute,' murmured someone appreciatively.

A small Peruvian boy sat next to me, and I gave him a prophylactic glare against misbehaviour. In fact, he was as well behaved as his father was charming and generous, giving me a newspaper to read. I felt slightly ashamed of my misanthropy.

The journey lasted five hours. At first the valleys were broad and green and cool, with cypress trees that seem always to lend a landscape tranquillity. But then the train entered gorges of uninhabitable steepness. Mountains rose to 20,000 feet, their peaks glistening inviolably white, awe-inspiring and intimidating.

I met a man called Rudi on the train. He was no longer quite as young as he dressed. Originally Swiss, he had decided to leave for the United States when one day the police called on him at the request of his neighbour because, contrary to cantonal by-law, he had hung his washing out on a Sunday. He sought a less ordered but less bigoted atmosphere.

He was caught up in the Vietnam war, and trained as a reconnaissance pilot. His most vivid memory of the war was of the beauty of napalm bursts seen from five miles above the ground. He had crossed the Sahara, climbed in the Himalayas, descended in a bathyscape. He was now a professional fashion and wildlife photographer, though he qualified as an engineer; he was a scuba diver, he programmed his own office computer, and was licensed to fly jets. I was uncertain whether I was listening to Renaissance Man or Baron von Munchausen.

He pointed to one of the mountains from whose white crest a plume of snow was whipped by winds the very imagination of whose force caused me to avert my gaze and shudder.

'Six Italian climbers were killed there last week,' he said. 'But I've been higher up in the Himalayas.'

There seemed nothing Rudi had not experienced. Wherever he went, events of the most extreme kind happened. Recently, for example, while in Honduras on an assignment for a magazine, he had entered a police station to ask the way. Through a window to the back courtyard he saw a line of hooded men against a wall. A volley of shots rang out, and the bodies crumpled like brown paper bags. They were brought through the police station and dumped unceremoniously in a waiting truck outside, which drove away. No attempt was made at concealment, and the policeman of whom Rudi had asked the way continued throughout the episode to give his directions as though nothing untoward were happening.

I discreetly asked his wife, a surprisingly mousy creature with a brace on her upper teeth and a lisp, whether the story was true.

'Oh yeth,' she said. 'I wath there.'

Towards Macchu Picchu the landscape changed once more. The mountains were less high, perfectly conical, and covered with a thick green jungle. It was one of the most mysterious and beautiful landscapes I had ever seen, but it was not one with which I could ever feel entirely at ease or inhabit. Nor far from the railway track were valleys still unexplored, with who knows what secrets still to divulge.

'Once you've looked at scenery,' said Rudi, 'what do you do with it?'

I understood what he meant. Mere looking was unsatisfactory. Having been bred in the city, the countryside never quite enters my soul. The Cuban poet Julián del Casal wrote a poem mockingly entitled *En el Campo*, In the Country:

> Másque el raudal que baja de la cumbre
> quiero oír a la humana muchedumbre
> gimiendo en su perpetua servidumbre.

(More than the torrent that cascades from the mountain peak I long to hear the human crowd, groaning in its perpetual servitude.)

The ruins of Macchu Picchu are several thousand feet above the railway station. They have no name other than that of the mountain, to whose side they cling, for no-one knows what the lost city of the Incas was called by its inhabitants. As one climbs dizzily upwards, one begins to appreciate the mere feat of rediscovering them after they had been hidden for four centuries. Hiram Bingham III, later a senator of the United States and author of a book declaring the obsolescence of the Monroe Doctrine, led the Yale University expedition of 1911 that rediscovered them. (His father, Hiram Bingham II, was the first Christian missionary to the Gilbert Islands. A puritan from New England who wore a frock coat and a top hat among the coconut palms, he was not notably successful in his endeavours. After several years of residence, he had converted precisely seven nonbacksliding Christians. Those who heard him preach frequently went to sleep, or used bad language during his sermons.) A brass plaque expresses the gratitude of Peru to Hiram Bingham III for having so stimulated the Peruvian tourist industry.

The desperation of the South American Continent, however, does not allow the ruins to be merely the object of idle wonderment. They are, rather, the touchstone of political belief, a kind of archaeological shibboleth testing one's stance to the Continent's social, economic and racial problems. Pablo Neruda visited Macchu Picchu in 1943, and extracted politics from stone:

> Déjame olividar, ancha piedra, la proporción poderosa,
> la transcendente medida, las piedras del panal,
> y de la escuadra déjame hoy resbalar
> la mano sobre la hipotenusa de áspera sangre y cilicio . . .

(Let me forget, wide stone, the powerful proportion, the transcendental measure, the honeycomb's stones, and from the setsquare let my hand today slide down the hypotenuse of bitter blood and hairshirt . . .)

> . . . veo el antiguo ser, servidor, el dormido
> en los campos, veo un cuerpo, mil cuerpos, un hombre, mil mujeres,
> bajo la racha negra, negros de lluvia y noche . . .
> sube a nacer conmigo, hermano.

(I see the ancient being, the servant, the sleeper, in the fields, I see a body, a thousand bodies, a man, a thousand women, under the black gust of wind, black with rain and night . . . rise to be born with me, as my brother.)

Despite its rhetorical power, there is in this simple message of brotherhood something false, electioneering and hectoring almost; a desperate determination to show that, when it comes to the poor and downtrodden, of whom guiltily he is not one, his heart is in the right place. He need never have been to the ruins of Macchu Piccchu to have written his poems about them, since his mind was already made up about what message they conveyed. The Macchu Picchu poems can ring hollow, like the tinny populism of one of Belaúnde's speeches:

> Once more the expressive and eloquent answer rings in my ears with the burden of a triumphal march, I feel within me Peru's whole history, its today and yesterday and the promise of tomorrow. 'The people made it, the people made everything here. The people made the road, the church, the school; they made the terraces where crops grow on our mountain slopes, and the embankments which control the floods . . .'

But the centuries-old gulf between peoples and cultures is not to be bridged by fine sentiment, however powerfully or poetically expressed, or else it would have been a long time ago. The fate of the Indians, the builders of Cuzco and Macchu Picchu, has been a European axe to grind for nearly half a millennium. The motives have usually been ulterior. In 1656 John Phillips, a nephew of Milton, translated Las Casas' *Brevísima Relación de la Destrucción de las Indias* (Very Brief Account of the Destruction of the Indies). But Phillips' concern was not so much with the welfare of the Indians as with finding a *casus belli* with Spain, as his dedication to Oliver Cromwell makes clear:

> May it please your Highness
> I have here laid prostrate before the Throne of Your Justice, above Twenty Millions of the Souls of the slaughter'd Indians; whose forc'd departure from their Bodies, Cruelty it self Compassionates . . . there is no man, who opposes not himself against Heaven, but doth extol Your just Anger against the Bloudy and Popish Nation of the Spaniards . . .
> Pardon me, Great Sir, if next my zeal to Heaven, the loud cry of so many Bloody Massacres . . . hath induced me . . . to publish this Relation of the Spanish Cruelties; whereby all good men may see and applaud the Justness of Your Proceedings . . .

Every time for the next hundred years that English relations with Spain deteriorated Phillips' tract was reprinted. In the times between, the souls of twenty million Indians could look after themselves.

So is it with Neruda. When he speaks of what he hates, rather than of what he feels he ought to love, his poetry reaches heights of passion and scorn and power:

> Cuando sonó la trompeta, estuvo
> todo preparado en la tierra,
> y Jehová repartió el mundo
> a Coca-Cola Inc., Anaconda,
> Ford Motors, y otras entidades:
> la Compañía Frutera Inc.

> se reservó lo más jugoso,
> la costa central de mi tierra,
> la dulce cintura de América.

(When the trumpet sounded, everything was prepared on earth, and Jehovah shared out the world between Coca-Cola Inc., Anaconda, Ford Motors and other entities: the Fruit Company Inc. reserved to itself the juiciest portion, the central coast of my land, the sweet waist of America.)

But in the last analysis it is not the admirers and defenders of the Indian architects of Macchu Picchu – the line from Las Casas to Neruda – who have triumphed; nor even the reasoned detractors like Prescott, who saw in the Inca Empire 'the most oppressive, though the mildest, of despotisms'; it is rather the followers of Fray Tomás Ortiz, writing in the early sixteenth century, who have had the most practical influence:

> The men on the mainland of the Indies eat human flesh and are more sodomistic than any generation. There is no justice among them, they go about naked, they feel neither love nor shame, they are asses, stupid, mad, insane; to kill or be killed is all the same to them; they have no truth in them unless it be to their advantage; they are inconstant ... In short, I say that God never created people so steeped in vices and bestiality, with no leaven of goodness or politeness.

*   *   *

I had mentioned to Rudi that I had never taken cocaine. He said I must try it. Back in Lima, sitting at my desk in the hotel, the phone rang.

'Hello,' said Rudi. 'I've got the stuff.'

He and his wife came to my room and drawing the curtains we began to snort cocaine up a silver tube.

'Where did you get it?' I asked.

'Oh, someone I know,' he replied.

His answer was less than reassuring. Supposing he were an *agent provocateur* employed by the Drug Enforcement Agency? How would I stand up to fifteen years in a Peruvian gaol, worse by reputation than San Pedro in La Paz?

The cocaine – very pure, not cut at all, Rudi assured me – began to take effect. At first I felt more alert, and then jumpy, my mind not able to fix on anything for long. The teeth at the back of my mouth felt heavy, as though a dentist had overdone the local anaesthetic. Though I had not eaten that day, I was not merely not hungry: hunger passed my comprehension. Speaking of the leaf, Garcilaso de la Vega Inca said, 'It satisfies the hungry, gives new strength to the weary, and makes the unhappy forget their sorrows.'

The hotel room was too small for the energies the drug had released, and we hired a taxi to take us to Pachacamac, a few miles along the coast from Lima. A battered specimen arrived.

'Are you sure this'll get us to Pachacamac?' asked Rudi.

The driver was shocked. Only last week it had taken a gringo all the way to Trujillo.

The seats were covered with a kind of plastic that went sticky in the sun. Had it been invented during the Inquisition, it might have had a use in removing the skin of heretics slowly and bit by bit. But, as we took further doses of cocaine in the back of the taxi, everything appeared hilariously amusing.

We reached Pachacamac after a bumpy ride through industrial suburbs. The same colour as the surrounding desert, the temple there was built before the coming of the Incas. It was devoted to the worship of Pachacamac, also known as Viracocha, the Supreme Being, the Creator and Ruler of the Universe, who was so ethereal that his attributes were unknown and unknowable, like the Brahma of the Hindus. He was therefore a much less popular object of obeisance than the tangible Sun. But the Spaniards, hearing of a temple devoted to the Supreme Being, concluded that it must contain the greatest treasure of all. When in 1533 Hernando Pizarro, the only legitimate half-brother of Francisco, sacked the temple, he and his followers were disgusted to find it bereft of the expected gold and jewels. Instead, at its summit they found a closed sanctum. As they approached it there was a violent tremor, a sure sign, thought the Indians, that

Pachacamac would exact revenge for the desecration about to be committed. But Pizarro and his men were not to be deterred: they broke into the sanctum, to discover only the blood and feathers of minor sacrifice and an evil-looking wooden idol with the head of a man, which they promptly destroyed and replaced with a cross. When no dire consequences followed, the Indians switched their religious allegiance.

The driver waited by his taxi below as we clambered laughing over the ruins, stopping sometimes to watch the surf of the Pacific break on the shore. We took more cocaine, the sacred drug of the Incas (who of course knew only the leaf). I was uncertain which were the pharmacological effects, which the effects of expectation and example, and which of fear. It seemed to me that even the desirable effects – increased alertness, a certain euphoria, and loss of appetite – were scarcely worth the effort and risks to obtain them. As for the dangers in taking the drug in the long-term, they are not known for certain. But Carlos Guttiérrez-Noriega (a distinguished Peruvian pharmacologist who was dismissed from his university post and driven into exile when he attacked the cocaine planters and distributors for profiting from human misery) and Zapata Ortiz found that coca-chewers were dull and torpid, sat silent and motionless for hours, had dry skin and bad posture, lacked sexual interest, answered questions vaguely, made contradictory statements, and could not abstract logically; though these might all have been their characteristics before they started to chew.

We returned to Lima. Rudi and his wife were flying that afternoon to Paraguay. Before they left, they made me a gift of the rest of their cocaine which, Rudi said, was worth a thousand dollars on the open market, after adulteration with scouring powder, chalk, and other white substances. Walking along the streets of Lima with the forbidden and dangerous chemical in my pocket, I began to understand how paranoia felt. Every person on every street corner looked at me suspiciously; every policeman was coming towards me.

I flushed the cocaine down my well-appointed sink.

SIX

Quito, Ecuador

CARACAS, said Bolívar, is an armed camp, Bogotá a university, and Quito a convent.

Guayaquil, on the other hand, is a city which no-one conceivably could mistake for a convent, for it has some of the worst slums in the world, and the visitor is well-advised to look as poor as possible, though he is unlikely even thus to evade the thieves. On the tarmac apron of its airport I came across a young American called Clara, searching for something under the wing of our aircraft. She was evidently in considerable distress.

'This is a disaster!' she cried. 'A catastrophe!'

I asked what the matter was and whether I could help.

'Oh it's too awful, it's too awful! What am I going to do? Tell me, what am I going to do?'

I said that rather depended on what the matter was. She pointed to her shoes.

'It's awful, it's terrible. What am I going to do? Look at my shoes. Ruined. Completely ruined.'

'They look all right to me.'

'Men, what do they know? Can't you see one of the bobbles is missing?'

Trying to bring some comfort, I said: 'Well, at least you can still walk in them.'

But this only fuelled the flames of her misery.

'But they're my best shoes! And they're ruined. Oh god, what am I going to do?'

We searched the tarmac for the bobble. She was certain it had still been attached to her shoe at Lima Airport, which meant it must have fallen off somewhere between Lima and Guayaquil transit lounge.

We crawled on the ground, but without success. The security guards grew suspicious, but they did not stop us.

'Don't you think it would be easier just to take the bobble off the other shoe? Then you'd have a matching pair again.'

We continued our search until the aircraft left for Quito. We sat together on the way there.

Clara was the director of a small museum on Staten Island. For the past three months she had been travelling round South America on a fellowship to study collections of pre-columbian art and their rôle in the cultural life of the continent. By the time we met, she was tired of museums, bored by pre-columbian art (her speciality), and sick of Latin America. She couldn't wait to get back to Brooklyn, where there was no Moche pottery. Fortunately, Quito was her last stop before returning home. All of a sudden, she recalled the terrible loss of her bobble, and started to lament it in the most extravagant fashion. I told her I was slightly puzzled by her grief. If she felt its loss as a disaster, a catastrophe, what words did she retain for a train crash, an earthquake, a famine, the third World War?

Only an Englishman could ask my question, she said. The English found all expression of emotion strange and even pathological; whereas, in fact, it was they who were pathological.

Soon after we landed at Quito an Ecuadorian who had been watching us for some time approached me, attracted apparently by the volume of Edgar Allan Poe I had been reading in a desultory manner in the lulls in our conversation.

'Excuse me, sir,' he said with an exquisite bow, 'I see you are reading a book of Edgar Poe.'

I could not deny it, nor had I any reason to, except that it was once said that an excessive interest in Poe is the mark of a second-rate mind.

'Would you allow me to purchase it from you? It is a great

treasure for me, and you can easily buy another one.'

What he said was perfectly correct, and it would have been churlish to refuse. And yet his request did not please me: a book once started bears the indefinable imprint of one's own personality, and becomes quite unlike any other copy, even of the same edition.

'But of course,' I replied, and was about to add that, as he was clearly a lover of literature, it would be my pleasure to give him the book, when he pulled out a ten dollar bill from his pocket.

'Will that suffice?' he asked.

'I owe you a dollar and five cents,' I replied, searching in my pockets for change I knew to be non-existent.

'No, no please. It is a great bargain for me. I am in your debt.'

He bowed exquisitely again, and looked at the book with admiring, even loving eyes.

Ecuador seemed better organised than Peru, less down at heel. It, too, had just returned to democracy after eight years of military dictatorship. The first president in the renewed cycle of democracy, anarchy and military despotism that has bedevilled Ecuador for much of the twentieth century, Señor Jaime Roldós, had recently been killed in an air crash in what were popularly believed to be mysterious circumstances. His vice-president and successor, Señor Osvaldo Hurtado, was a young and eminently reasonable political scientist who, however, had publicly expressed doubts in his well-known book on the development of Ecuador that the era of absurd and brutal military regimes had fully passed. But in the clear sunshine, nine thousand feet above sea level, it was difficult to imagine that Quito, with its freshly whitewashed walls and eighty remaining colonial churches, had ever been other than the tranquil convent of Bolívar's description.

We stayed at a guest house with a courtyard, run by a friendly, plump young woman. Her two children played in the courtyard, the elder a little girl with long plaits tied by coloured ribbons, the younger a boy with the blue-eyed face of an angel, but the character of a devil. He pulled his sister's plaits when he thought no-one was looking and then, to pre-empt any retaliation or retribution, sat on the ground and howled piteously. His mama, misled completely by the glistening tears on his cherubic face, chastised his sister with considerable vigour. As soon as his sister's punishment was complete his tears cleared like showers in April, and he turned on the family dog, a snow-white mongrel of great patience, to whose tail he gave a vicious jerk. We tried to encourage the dog to bite the boy, but to no avail.

After lunch Clara had an appointment at the Instituto del Patrimonio Nacional. They would tell her where all the best private collections of pre-columbian art were situated, and give her introductions to their owners. The institute was in the old part of Quito, one of the best-preserved of all colonial cities, in a renovated house overlooking a square. The skyline was dominated totally by the belfries of churches.

The guardians of the national patrimony were mostly asleep with their feet up on their desks and newspapers over their faces when we arrived. We created a small stir, first of interest, then of annoyance, when it became clear that Clara was dynamic and determined to have her way in the typical gringo fashion. She wanted answers, and she wanted them today, now! How tiresome! Slowly, reluctantly, the feet dropped from the desks, the newspapers were withdrawn from the faces, and the whole bureaucracy of the culture woke up after its lunchtime nap.

While Clara spoke to the Director, I explored some of the surrounding churches. It was easy to see how Bolívar formed his opinion of the city. For three centuries the wealth of the entire country had been poured into the construction and decoration of the churches of Quito. Until comparatively recently, the Church had been by far the largest landowner in Ecuador, its holdings swelled by the donations of dying *hacendados* wishing to smooth their passage to Heaven after a less than innocent life. And the churches of Quito are still full of pious old ladies dressed in black, praying on their knees for hours at a time before a saint's reliquary or in a sidechapel.

The churches are decorated with a sumptuousness which defies belief. At first, as one enters the darkness from the bright sunshine outside, only the gold and silver of the screens and gilded wood are visible in the flickering candlelight. But as one's eyes grow accustomed to the gloom, the whole church fills with a seemingly anarchic riot of religious art and statuary. There is so much of it that one is inclined to discount its quality; but Quito was the greatest artistic centre of colonial America, and everything is of the highest quality. The artists of Quito were not mere craftsmen, content to be imitative or derivative, though that is the judgement often passed on them. They undertook their art with the same passion and seriousness as the artists of Europe. Miguel de Santiago, a famous mestizo painter, wanted to give his Christ on the Cross an authentic expression of agony, with which model after model was unable to provide him. In frustrated exasperation, he picked up a spear and thrust it through a model. The tortured expression of the dying man impressed itself for ever on the memory of the painter, who spent the rest of his days doing penance in an Augustinian convent.

I found when I returned to the Institute that Clara was still engaged with the Director. I bought a newspaper and read it in the courtyard. The headlines reported the coup – 'yet again' said the newspaper, a little smugly, considering Ecuador's history – in Bolivia. According to some reports, García Meza has resigned and gone quietly; according to others, he was still struggling to retain power. The most eloquent comment came from the government's press secretary: Everything, he said, is as usual in Bolivia.

The rest of the news ranged from the absurd to the terrifying.

It was reported that General Romero, the Panamanian president and friend of Graham Greene had a presentiment of death shortly before he died in a helicopter crash. The editor evidently found this remarkable; it struck me as the minimum of actuarial common sense.

The Argentinian writer Borges had stated in Buenos Aires that if he were named dictator of Argentina, he would resign at once.

In Italy the Red Brigades had shot the brother of one of their former colleagues who had turned informer. The spirit of Nechaev lives on.

In Iran, the Ayatollah Khomeini warned the newly elected president, Ali Rajai, that if he made a mistake or betrayed the Islamic Revolution, the thirteen millions who voted for him would call for his blood.

The son of Fulgencio Batista, the former dictator of Cuba, said on his return to the United States from Europe that he wanted personally to overthrow Castro. His statement continued modestly: 'I would be a great leader for Cuba, not only because I am the son of my father, but also because of my foreign contacts and experiences, and my personal charisma.

'If I came to power,' he added, 'I would make things in the North American style.' (By North America he no doubt meant Las Vegas).

'I don't have as much money as people think,' he said. 'But I have enough to go shooting.'

Clara emerged from her meeting with the Director with a list of important collections. The first of them was in a church school called *el Cebollar* – the Onion Patch. We struggled our way up some of the steepest cobbled streets of the old city and eventually reached a crumbling edifice, deserted except for a tiny Indian girl with red apple cheeks and a running nose. She ran away to alert her mother, who extracted herself from a small hidden alcove in the wall to ask us what we wanted. She took us to see an elderly man of European ancestry in an old-fashioned green tweed suit which he appeared to have worn every day for the last forty years. He greeted us with the kind of courteous formality that no longer exists in Europe; alas, grief-stricken though he was by his inability to oblige us, the museum was closed and he had no key. However, if we should care to see the rest of the Onion Patch he would be only too delighted to show us . . .

Clara betrayed some impatience; her schedule was tight and she had come only to see the pre-columbian collection. But it would have been rude to refuse. The highlight of the tour, over which our elderly guide lingered lovingly, was an arcade with murals depicting the life and work of the Beatified Brother Miguel, who taught at the Onion Patch school in the nineteenth century. Brother Miguel was shown patting children benignly on the head, while the children turned their eyes up to him in adoration.

'One day,' said our guide, his voice trembling with emotion, 'they will make a Brother Miguel a saint. They are working on it now.'

He asked us to return in two weeks when the museum would be open again. We told him we should not then be in Quito, and he shook his head uncomprehendingly at the hurry people were always in nowadays.

We walked back through the narrow streets with the crushed remains of the morning's market strewn across them. We were looking for another collection, this time in the Municipal Museum. It turned out to be one of those strange little museums with a bit of everything, all displayed in dusty glass cases: the kind of place children go on a rainy Sunday afternoon before they are old enough to resort to delinquency. There were stuffed birds, old swords, tablets of Sumerian cuneiform script and multiple portraits of Mariscal Sucre, the national hero after whom Ecuador's currency was named. Clara examined the cases containing Inca and pre-Inca potsherds, all arranged with economies of space and lighting in mind. A few children ran around playing a noisy game of tag, which annoyed the attendant not because of the danger to the exhibits, but because it interrupted his doze.

'Fascinating,' murmured Clara as she peered through the gloomy glass at the small brown bits of pottery. 'Fascinating, don't you think? It shows the influence of meso-America. I mean, this pottery is amazingly similar to some of the stuff found in Mexico. Maybe there was more contact between them than we thought. It's very exciting.'

I was more interested in the sepia photographs on the walls of García Moreno, the most remarkable of all Ecuador's many presidents. They showed him marching through the streets of

Quito carrying a heavy wooden cross on his shoulders, followed by his entire cabinet. García Moreno always dressed in black and uncovered his head in the presence of a priest. He was a religious enthusiast, to put it mildly. He performed frequent acts of physical self-humiliation, and made his family say the rosary every afternoon. His ideal republic was theocratic, he always recognised the superiority of church over state, and no non-catholic was considered a citizen. He personally supervised the catechism in schools. Harsh and violent to opponents, he re-named the best regiments in the army 'Guardians of the Virgin', 'Volunteers of the Cross' and 'Soldiers of the Infant Jesus'. His religion was utterly sincere, terrifyingly consistent.

And yet García Moreno was far from being the merely reactionary bigot all this might suggest. He had studied natural sciences as well as canon law, and before he was president he was a professor of chemistry. He started the first railway in Ecuador, from Quito to Guayaquil. He had roads, hospitals and schools built. Having decided that the country suffered from a surfeit of lawyers amounting to a plague, he encouraged education along more modern and technical lines. He closed down the university and started a polytechnical institute to teach engineering, geology, agronomy, and other useful sciences. During his term of office he succeeded in reducing the bureaucracy's share of the national budget from 37 to 17 per cent; he reduced also the military budget, while expenditure on education and public works rose from 7 to 23 per cent. He was unimpeachably honest.

It was this strange dual aspect of his rule – on the one hand religious obscurantism and intolerance, on the other a belief in the modernising power of technology and an upright administra-tion – that has divided Ecuadorians on the subject of García Moreno ever since. No-one speaks or writes of him except with passion, either for or against. He was not a democrat, for he believed that in Ecuador's social conditions, democracy was bound to be illusory (a view still shared by many, both of the right and the left); but he undoubtedly worked for what he saw as the good of his people. Even his strongest opponents recognised that he was no ordinary South American caudillo. The liberal journalist Juan Montalvo wrote in exile: 'You have shown yourself to be excessively violent, Señor García Moreno . . . How much more meritorious to dominate oneself than to dominate others! Let me speak to you frankly; there are in you elements of the great hero and, to soften the word, of the tyrant. You have valour and audacity, but you lack political virtue.'

In 1875, the year in which he stood for election as president for the third time, García Moreno was brutally assassinated on the steps of Quito cathedral as he left after mass. A man approached to speak to him, drew a machete from under his cape, and struck him with it. Three accomplices fired point blank into him, his bodyguard having fled. A group of pious women, also leaving mass, gathered round him to protect him, but he was struck once more with the machete. On learning of García Moreno's fate, Juan Montalvo exclaimed exultantly: 'My pen killed him!'

García Moreno's spirit lived on after his death, however. As late as 1958 the bishops of Ecuador issued an Instruction of the Episcopate on the Obligation to Vote: 'Only a sincere Catholic who believes, confesses and practises the Religion of Christ, who has faith in God, reveres His authority and yields to His laws, can offer genuine guarantees to the Catholic church that its divine origins will be recognised . . . Ecuadorian Catholics, men and women, go to the polls; vote and vote well; vote for truly Catholic citizens, upright and fit to hold high office.' And the favoured candidate duly won. In 1966, Ecuador's legislature spent many hours – more than it spent on economic matters – debating whether to include or exclude the name of God in the new constitution (the twelfth since 1821).

Clara wanted to take photographs in the Municipal Museum. At the first flash the attendant slid wearily off his chair and shuffled towards her.

'Es prohibido,' he said.

'Why?' asked Clara, disinclined like all Americans to accept limitations on her freedom of action.

But the attendant was stating a fact, not inviting dialogue. He shuffled back to his chair, his duty done, and when Clara continued to take photgraphs he merely shook his head and murmured, 'Tut tut.'

Driving ever onwards, Clara decided we must see the collection of an old retired colonel before nightfall. We sought out his apartment in a dilapidated quarter of the old city, built around courtyards now containing wheelless bicycles, dogs with three legs, rachitic children and a lifetime of washing. We asked for the colonel's residence, and the children pointed to the top left hand corner, up some rickety stairs and along a collapsing wooden gallery to an open door. Inside the dark entrance we dimly viewed the chaos: furniture, ornaments, packing cases, all arranged without any evident design. It was not what we had expected of a retired colonel.

The colonel's maid came to greet us, wiping her hands on her apron.

The colonel, she informed us, was – most unfortunately – away in the country, and she did not have the authority to show us his collection. We should contact him when he returned.

'When would that be?' asked Clara suspiciously.

It was impossible to say, but soon, very soon.

'Tomorrow, perhaps?'

'Perhaps tomorrow.'

'Or next week, maybe?'

'Maybe next week.'

'God,' said Clara as we picked our way back carefully over the worm-eaten boards of the gallery, 'I'm sick of South Americans. They have no sense of time.'

In the days that followed I became an expert, if not in precolumbian art, at least in Quito's private collections of precolumbian art. We crisscrossed the city in search of them. First we visited Señora ——, widow of a conservative president of Ecuador during the 1950s. Her house was unremarkable from the outside, situated in a quiet street, its high, small windows barred and shuttered. The garden was neglected, with only a climbing plant that would soon cease to climb. The door was opened slowly, reluctantly, by an old servant, who ushered us in after discovering that the Señora was expecting us. We waited in a sepulchral hallway, heavy Victorian crimson plush sofas with gilt legs piled one on top of another, and other furniture covered in white sheets as though someone had just died.

The servant returned and showed us upstairs, into a remarkable room. It was cluttered with furniture of every style since the seventeenth century, though the Victorian era predominated by sheer bulk. I sat on a small Empire chair whose seat was so low that it was difficult to rise from it, except by a clumsy struggle, Clara on one whose seat was full of horsehair lumps.

Along one side of the room were bookshelves, with a heavy emphasis on Plato and Sir Walter Scott. There were also Victorian art books, of the kind that contain the whole of Piero della Francesca in sepia plates. Along the shelves, partially obscuring the long-unread books, were rows of pre-columbian pottery figures: terrible gods, fierce warriors, curse-uttering shamans, and small pregnant women. Many of the figures were of surprising size: two feet high, and perfectly preserved. There were myriads of tiny clay figurines too, which Clara identified as belonging to the oldest civilisations of South America, five thousand years old.

The other walls were lined with escritoires, desks and chests of drawers, some gilded, others purely utilitarian. Bric-à-brac filled the room in suffocating quantities, from Meissen porcelain to plastic flowers. The most conspicuous ornament was a white china infant Jesus in a glass box, His hands and feet prematurely bearing the stigmata of His martyrdom, His head already encircled with the crown of thorns. The walls were covered with portraits, presumably of ancestors, from the sixteenth century onwards. There was not an Indian face among them. (The descendants of the conquistadors Diego de Sandoval and Rodrigo Nuñez de Bonilla are to this day the greatest landholders in the provinces of Pichincha and Chimborazo.) During the nineteenth century, the portraits became photographic, self-confident men in satin-lapelled frock coats tailored in Paris, peering farsightedly into the future, in which they believed they and their kind had a majority shareholding.

At last the Señora arrived. She was in her early sixties, dressed in a bright red trouser suit with lipstick to match. I noticed at once that she was an asthmatic, as she issued breathless orders to the servants outside. Clara explained that she was the director of a small museum in New York, and would very much like to see the Señora's famous collection. The Señora said her collection was nothing, there were far better in Quito than hers. Nevertheless, she was clearly flattered by this emissary of the Imperial Power. With great pride she handed us some of her most prized pieces, extolling their beauty. She had made an amateur study of archaeology and was able to discourse on the ritual significance of each piece. Many of them had been found by Indians working on her hacienda. I doubted whether she made any connection in her mind between the finders and makers of the pieces.

Alas, she said, her children were not in the slightest interested in archaeology. They thought it a waste of time and space to store these pagan idols of clay. To whom should she leave her collection when she died? (I thought I saw Clara's eyes glistening.) If she left it to the Instituto del Patrimonio Nacional, it would be plundered mercilessly. The Director would take the biggest share, of course, and everyone under him would purloin according to his rank. If she left it to the university department of archaeology, on the other hand, it would remain intact, but fall into the clutches of communists. Unfortunately, she lamented, only the communists studied archaeology these days: not for the pure love of the past, but to prove their theories and incite the Indians by recalling their past glories.

'My husband was not interested in archaeology either,' she said, tears welling in her eyes at the mention of him, though he had been dead five years. 'He lived only for politics.'

She took down another figure to show us, to stem her flow of tears.

'I don't know the meaning of this one,' she said.

It was a grotesque man holding a long tubular object about his own size in front of him.

'I think it's a fertility god,' said Clara. 'That's his penis he's holding.'

The Señora looked at the figure. She had owned it for thirty years but it had never struck her in that light before.

'Possibly,' she said a little tartly, returning the figure to its shelf. She pulled out a drawer. It was packed with old chocolate boxes and tins of toffee – Mackintosh's Quality Street, amongst others. She took one of the boxes, covered in faded maroon plush, with worn golden tassels, and opened it. We gasped.

Inca gold! Even now, after four hundred years, the words were capable of producing a *frisson*. Nestling in the box was a necklace of considerable size and weight. All the other boxes were full of Inca gold too. There were armbands and amulets, collars and rings, bangles and breastplates. There were long, open tubes of beaten gold which, as the Señora explained to us, the Inca nobles used to cover the shafts of their spears. We handled them with awe: perhaps they had seen action in the wars of the conquest.

'You would not believe it,' said the Señora, who appeared genuinely amazed at this further evidence of human malfeasance, 'but sometimes when I show my collection to people, they steal things from it.'

Her words made me feel guilty, as though I were responsible for some crime; Clara expressed shock. Fortunately, the Señora did not doubt our honesty.

'I shall give you a small gift,' she said, and gave Clara one of the tiny clay figures from the earliest South American civilisation. Clara was suitably overwhelmed.

'It is from my hacienda, like the gold,' said the Señora.

We began to suspect that her hacienda covered half Ecuador. We went to the next room. On the way, the Señora wheezed sharply at two Indian servants carrying feather dusters. We caught a glimpse down a corridor of the Señora's bedroom, of a size that would not disgrace Versailles. Eighteenth-century furniture lined the walls, which two further servants dusted with feathers. There was an ornate four-poster bed at the far end of the room.

The next room was impassable because the whole floor was two feet deep in pre-columbian potsherds, again all from her hacienda. The Señora had not had time to catalogue everything in this room, and now she doubted whether she ever would.

We went to the conservatory. Religious paintings, marble-topped tables, bouquets of plastic sunflowers gathering dust, pots of tropical ferns, chaises longues, were all lost in the vastness of the room. The Señora drew our attention to a portrait on the far wall: a somewhat rectangular-headed man, the remains of his hair greased firmly to the sides of his balding head, his grey eyes merciless in their rectitude, his double-breasted suit the height of fashion in 1947. He stared out from a background of mono-chromatic yellow.

'That is my husband,' she said, 'painted by Guayasamín.'

We stood before the portrait respectfully, our hands clasped in front of us.

'You have heard of Guayasamín?' asked the Seōra, as though the question were really superfluous.

We confessed that we hadn't.

'He was very famous all over the world. He is the most famous Ecuadorian painter. Now he charges forty thousand dollars for a portrait.'

'I don't know much about modern art,' said Clara, trying to explain why we had never heard of him.

'He exhibits in New York, Dallas, Miami, everywhere. He has a whole gallery to himself in Miami. He is a millionaire many times over.'

Although the Señora did not appear to be short of money herself, she spoke the word with distaste – the old Spanish disdain of anything that is earned rather than inherited.

'Guayasamín painted my husband before he was so famous. I think the portrait is horrible but it is of my husband. That is why I keep it.'

'It *is* pretty ghastly,' whispered Clara in my ear.

The Señora recalled her husband, again with tears in her eyes. 'He was a good man,' she said. 'Completely honest. Not like that rabble-rouser, that charlatan, Velasco.'

She spoke with surprising bitterness. Her own husband had completed his term having respected the constitution, almost an unprecedented feat, whatever his other achievements or failures in office. But Dr Velasco Ibarra was five times president, and four times removed by coup. He was, for forty years, the dominant figure of Ecuadorian politics. An unashamed demagogue, he was known by his supporters as 'the National Personification'. His inflammatory speeches from a balcony in the Plaza San Francisco were famous: once, when he was removed yet again by coup, he remarked, 'Give me a balcony, and I will be president again.' He flattered the mob with unblinking cynicism; once in power, he merely awarded contracts and disbursed lucrative posts to his friends and followers.

'Would you like to meet Guayasamín?' asked the Señora, drying her eyes. 'He has a very good collection.'

We agreed eagerly. The Señora clapped her hands to summon a servant to fetch the telephone directory, which was lying on a chair ten feet away from where we were standing. After the directory, she asked for her glasses.

'Guayasamín is very rich,' she said as we waited. 'But he is a communist. I don't understand it. If the communists come, who will pay forty thousand dollars for a portrait? But Ecuador,' she said, shaking her head sadly, 'is full of communists now.'

When she spoke to Guayasamín on the phone, however, it was with respect and even deference. She fixed an appointment at four o'clock that afternoon. We thanked her profusely for her kindness, and a servant with a limp showed us to the street below.

We took a taxi to Bella Vista, the suburb to the north of the city where Señor Guayasamín lived. The old city was laid out a thousand feet below. The only people walking in the quiet streets of the rich suburb were Indian servants, out on errands. Our requests for directions met with the blank looks of the habitually intimidated.

As we were early for our appointment, we went to the gallery in Bella Vista where Guayasamín exhibited his work to the public. This was his former residence in which his own work mingled with that of the Quitan school of the seventeenth and eighteenth centuries, thus implying of a kind of continuity with it. Everything was elegant and in the best taste: the gardens of the gallery, with dark green lawns and cypress trees, soothed nerves and put one in the buying mood. But there was also an unmistakably commercial atmosphere, despite all attempts at muting it. Well-dressed sales ladies of the purest blood clung to prospective purchasers, and every corner of the premises was swept by the relentless gaze of security cameras.

One of the sales ladies, having quickly come to the conclusion from our appearance that we were unlikely to buy paintings for forty thousand dollars, asked us whether we had yet been to the gallery's shop. Giving us a leaflet to read, she led us there, where less expensive items of Guayasamín's work were available. According to the leaflet, Guayasamín did not believe that Art should be divorced from Life, an elegant trapping in the homes of the rich. He believed it should be part of normal life for everyone, woven into its fabric, as it were. For this reason, Guayasamín had designed jewellery, toys, cutlery, furniture and crockery, all of which might be purchased at reasonable prices and all of which were guaranteed designed by him. Also available in the shop was a glossy book devoted to Guayasamín and his work. Its title was 'Guayasamín – the Ecuadorian Artist Who Berates Human Oppression Throughout the World.'

His work certainly has an expressionist style of its own, and the depiction of suffering plays a large part in it. One of his most famous motifs is a pair of gnarled and calloused hands, clasped together in a paroxysm of suffering. Another Ecuadorian artist, less famous than Guayasamín and jealous of his success, claimed to have used the motif as a symbol of Indian oppression before Guayasamín, whom he therefore accused of plagiarism. But such claims were out of place in the garden of art, replied Guayasamín. The first artist who painted the Crucifixion had no copyright on the subject, and it would have been the worse for art if he had.

It was time now for our visit. We made our way to Señor Guayasamín's new home, further up the mountain side, several hundred yards along a dusty road. It was a large white building standing almost on its own. The rest of Bella Vista had petered out long before and only a handful of humble shacks spoilt its splendid isolation. Its extensive grounds were surrounded by a high white wall. At the electronically controlled gate, another security camera maintained its vigil.

'How can this guy be a communist?' asked Clara. 'He lives in a palace.'

'Well,' I replied, 'if he has a strong enough telescope he can see how the poor live.'

It must be admitted we were approaching our host in a hostile spirit. Having decided in his gallery that he was a monster of egoism, we now decided he was a hypocrite as well. We enjoyed our righteous anger against him.

'But if the communists came to power,' said Clara, 'he couldn't live like this.'

'Oh yes he could,' I retorted. 'They would use him as an example of how tenderly communists treasure culture and the arts. They would make him a Hero of Ecuadorian Labour and give him a huge pension to live in his house until he died. He'll be all right whatever happens.'

We rang the bell at the gate.

'Who is it?' asked a suspicious female voice over a microphone.

We told the female voice that we had an appointment with Señor Guayasamín. The gate clicked and opened automatically. We entered sheepishly. The house was even larger than we first thought, in what property developers might describe as 'Spanish Colonial' style. It was, however, completely without vulgarity, and the cloister-like walkways gave it an atmosphere of studious calm. A yellow Mercedes was parked under a shelter.

A servant came out to greet us and showed us to a small waiting room where we sat facing two paintings by Guayasamín. The first was a view of Quito, the second a deposition from the Cross. As we looked at these paintings our attitude to the artist changed rapidly and radically. The deposition could only have been painted by a man with a deep feeling for his subject. No Stalinist could have done it. As we continued to look, the beauty of these paintings struck us more and more forcibly.

Guayasamín entered. His appearance surprised us. He was short and rather fat, smoking a cigarette which, I could tell from the way he breathed, had been his constant companion for thirty years. He was dressed a little shabbily and, having come straight from his studio, was splashed with paint.

'What can I do for you?' he asked, with perfect simplicity.

He was obviously not a monster of egoism. It suddenly occurred to me that it was we who were behaving egocentrically, disturbing him at work in this casual way.

Clara explained why we had come, and from her faltering manner I gathered that she, too, felt abashed. She told Señor Guayasamín how much we admired his painting of the deposition. It was, he said, a rendering of a Flemish painting of the same subject in the Louvre. He had removed all the extraneous details so that the heart of the drama was laid bare. He stood proudly, reverently almost, in front of his own work, as though he had merely been an instrument rather than a creator. He used no high-flown language to describe his work – only words that anyone could understand.

He took us to his huge dining room, one wall of which, being completely of glass, overlooked the city a thousand feet below. The room was as large as a baronial hall. He had designed the house himself, for he was once an architect. It was in the dining room that he kept his treasures. The pre-columbian pieces were displayed on a ledge raised from the floor, sufficiently separated from one another (unlike the other collections we had seen) to enable us to appreciate their individual merits. It was an artist's, rather than an archaeologist's, collection.

Guayasamín told us about each of his pieces, but his chronology was so bad that even I was able to fault it. In his opinion, each piece was an unimaginable number of millennia old. We did not think it right to correct him. Instead, when he had finished, Clara asked him whether Indians and mestizos, as well as Europeans, appreciated pre-columbian art.

'I am mestizo myself, señora,' he replied, and he looked it too. Clara was embarrassed.

When he showed us his religious paintings from the Quito school, it was clear he was on firmer and more congenial ground. Whatever his ideological commitment to devalue the colonial and commend the Inca eras, he looked upon the paintings with the besotted eye of the lover.

'Es muy bonito, muy bonito' (it's very pretty, very pretty), he said, standing in front of them, tears in his eyes.

We were interrupted by a man in a business suit carrying an attaché case. He engaged Guayasamín in earnest conversation at the far end of the room: Guayasamín gave his orders without hesitation or anxiety, and the man strode out to execute them.

'My lawyer,' said Guayasamín, returning to us. He led us round his furniture, mainly Spanish colonial, but with some Italian renaissance. His greatest treasure of all was in an alcove off the main hall. It was a series of prints illustrating the horrors of war.

'Goya,' he said.

He had bought them in Spain while he was working on a mural for the new airport terminal in Madrid. He smuggled them out of Spain, and chuckled at the recollection of this exploit.

'Colonial despoliation in reverse,' he said.

He took us to his studio, where he was working on another view of Quito from the same vantage point. He had painted the same view several times before, but in different lights. Quito was his Rouen Cathedral. He showed us his other work in progress, and then accompanied us to the gate. A spotted dog leapt joyfully around his master, and Guayasamín patted him affectionately on the head, telling him to behave.

We walked back down the dusty hill, the poor people staring at us from their shacks. They knew we had been to see Guayasamín, and some of his importance rubbed off on to us. We hurried back to the centre of Quito, for we had a dinner appointment with the cultural attaché of the American embassy. She was a woman in her early spinsterhood who wore woollens and sensible shoes. She gave the impression of being a sad and lonely person, a little bewildered by life. She was the kind of loyal employee who gives forty years' devoted service, and is forgotten the day after her retirement. It was her job to meet and have dinner with any passing American who had the vaguest connection with 'culture'. She also arranged scholarships to American universities for Ecuadorian students, and tours by third-rate dance companies to foster American-Ecuadorian relations.

She took us to a small restaurant run by Italian immigrants, where we asked her about life in Quito. It was quiet, she said, which seemed to be something of an understatement, for we had noticed that by eight o'clock the streets were deserted, and such people as there were looked destined for bed. It was the altitude, she said. It played funny tricks with the human body and tired it out, for it was not designed for life at nine thousand feet (or any other altitude, one felt she almost added). Ever since she had arrived in Quito, for example, her memory had been poor. As a doctor, I was expected to provide some clue to this mysterious phenomenon, and I muttered something about the low oxygen pressure in the atmosphere. The main advantage of life in Quito as compared with Washington DC, she continued, was the much smaller chance of being raped in the street. Fear seemed to condition her life. But Quito had been exciting for one brief week during the border skirmish with Peru, when air-raid practices were held (in the war in 1943 between the two countries Quito was bombed) and war fever gripped the city. It was believed that, had President Roldós not been killed, the skirmish would have developed into a full-scale war, for he had staked his prestige on the outcome of the dispute. The intelligence community (meaning the CIA) believed that the crash in which he died was engineered by an anti-war party which realised that war would have been disastrous for Ecuador. But with the exception of this one short interlude, life in Quito had a timeless quality, as though everything would be much the same two or three centuries hence. It was an atmosphere to which the attaché, with her manner of refined hopelessness, seemed well-adapted.

She provided us with an introduction to a famous old lady of the city, said to possess a fine pre-columbian collection, who had for many years run a shop selling the folk arts of Ecuador. We parted at the late, late hour of ten o'clock.

We took up our introduction and visited the old lady. She walked with a stick and spoke English with a strong German accent. She had long since reached the age at which old people take a pride in their advanced years, and always ask visitors, 'How old do you think I am?' The deliberate underestimate, followed by protestations of disbelief when the real age is revealed, never ceases to delight them, and so it was Señora Olga Fisch – whose clarity of mind was, in plain truth, remarkable.

She had been born in Budapest in 1900, into a wealthy *haut bourgeois* Jewish family. She went to Germany to study art, and set up in Berlin as a designer and painter. With the advent of Hitler, however, she left Europe and went to New York, where she was offered a job on the staff of *Vogue*. She had so much difficulty obtaining a residence permit that, despairing of ever being granted one, she boarded a ship bound for Ecuador, which at the time, and to its eternal credit, was one of the few countries still open to refugees from the Nazis. As the ship prepared to sail her American residence permit came through, but she decided to continue to Ecuador, and she had never regretted it.

Her residence was above her shop, and the balcony of her living room overlooked the magnificent extinct volcano of Pichincha. It was a view, she said, that almost made up for the disappointments of her life. Her shop was full of ethnic ornaments, amended to the taste of the mid-western states of North America. There were rugs and puppets, dolls and ponchos, necklaces and shawls: all of them recognisably South American, but at the same time not quite genuine either. We mentioned to Señora Fisch that we had been to see Guayasamín. She did not approve of this:

she pursed her lips and shook her head.

'He is very commercial,' she said, tapping Clara on the arm. 'He paints for money, my dears.'

Surrounded as we were by objects for sale of dubious taste, it seemed an odd complaint to make. In it was the contempt of the metropolitan for the provincial; and the resentment of the aspirant towards the man who has actually achieved. We felt it sad that after a long, eventful and not unsuccessful life she should still harbour such sentiments.

An American from Arizona in a stetson and his wife interrupted us. She was vastly fat, tented in a jet black poncho with tassels. Her cheeks were so bloated that they almost closed her eyes, while rolls of fat rippled under her poncho like the body of a queen termite. Her husband wanted to show Señora Fisch a Navajo ring with supposedly magical and aphrodisiac powers, bought from a member of the tribe.

The ring was crudely worked in silver with a pink stone an inch in diameter, worn like a knuckleduster.

Señora Fisch praised the ring, though with words of ambiguous connotation. It was both hideous and a complete fake; she wanted simultaneously not to offend the Arizonan, who was likely to spend a lot of money, and to let us know that she recognised it as such.

'It is most interesting,' she said. 'Such an unusual colour.'

Señora Fisch showed us round her house which, in addition to her precolumbian collections, contained a large scattered library in three languages, and a collection of genuine folk art from all over South America. Finally, she took us into her warehouse where she stored a vast stock of craft work.

'I try to teach the Indians what is saleable,' she said. 'I don't direct them, but I give them advice.' As sole purchaser of their output, it is advice they were well-advised to accept. She showed us traditional Indian drums, used in village fiestas north of Quito. The drums were covered with simple, primitive pictures in primary colours of Ecuadorian village life. They were not unlike the paintings of Lowry, transposed to a more colourful environment.

'No-one wanted to buy the drums,' she said. 'So I told the Indians to paint exactly the same pictures, but on canvas. Now they are sold all over the world.'

We saw the canvases. The figures, the colours, and the composition were the same, but the effect was different: what looked fresh, vigorous, naive and charming on the drums looked self-conscious, gaudy and crude on the canvas.

'I prefer the drums,' said Clara.

'Of course they are better,' sighed Señora Fisch. 'But the Indians have to eat. I teach them how to make money. They have no initiative of their own and without encouragement their crafts would die out.'

She talked of the Indians as though they were a nearly extinct species of flightless bird, or small mammals of retiring habits.

'But in changing traditions by teaching them to work for money,' I objected, 'aren't you destroying the traditions you are trying to preserve?'

'But how else is it to be done, my dears?'

How else, indeed?

We said goodbye to Señora Fisch, who delivered up her small and slightly withered cheek for us to kiss. She gave Clara a small basket woven from reeds as a gift.

'What am I going to do with this goddamned basket?' she asked out in the street.

I told her not to be so ungrateful. In another fifty years, such baskets would cease to exist.

My time in South America was drawing to a close. On my last day we drove to Latacunga, a town of thirty thousand inhabitants recommended by Señora Fisch on account of the attractive light grey lava rock from which it was built.

We soon left Quito behind, the city still being of manageable size, by modern standards. We drove south on *el Panamericano*, the Panamerican Highway, a grand-sounding name for a road of uncertain surface, driven on by men with no thought of safety. We passed the grim slopes of Pichincha on which, in 1822, Mariscal

Sucre defeated a Spanish army in one of the decisive battles of the era, and secured the independence of Gran Colombia.

We reached Latacunga in the middle of the day, as the sun beat down on the dry, grey streets. It was deserted, a Mary Celeste of a town. The main square, the Parque Vincente Léon, was a surprising and luxuriant botanical garden – a strange oasis – in which the shrubs had been carefully sculpted into bizarre shapes, from fans to wedding cakes. By contrast, the grey lava cathedral looked stark and bare. Only a dog or two stirred, and then not for long: as the shadows moved, they sought new shelter from the sun.

We did not wait for Latacunga to awaken, but went instead to the village of Telpulí which Señora Fisch had recommended as 'typical', and possessing a famous monastery. There was only a dirt track to the village, with several unmarked turnings to confuse the unwary. We breathed the dust and bumped our heads on the roof of the car. Clara, who was not feeling well, said she was dying; I said she was uncomfortable. After half an hour we came across an avenue of cypresses, a sure sign of nearby habitation. The road ended at a long and low white building forming three sides of a rectangle. An old plough stood in the middle, and a solitary hen pecked at the ground. The silence was dense, except for the desultory buzzing of a few bees. I got out of the car and stood in the yard next to the plough, the sun's rays seeming to throb in the air. Although I stood silent and still, my presence somehow made itself felt inside the building and eventually a small girl emerged, dressed like an Edwardian rag doll. She did not speak; I asked her the way to the monastery. She pointed the way, but again did not speak. I returned to the car, feeling I had been in a dream.

The monastery was another fifteen minutes away, along a ridged track that Clara believed had been specially potholed for her discomfort. We arrived in a flurry of dust. I peered over the wall at a point where it had crumbled into a pile of rubble. The old red-tiled buildings were surrounded by a shady, half-wild garden of old trees and shrubs, radiating from a lily pond. In the distance were the geometric cones of several extinct volcanoes, including Cotopaxi, the finest of them all. Here, if anywhere, might a man's thoughts have turned to spiritual matters.

I walked round the perimeter of the monastery, and thought I caught a glimpse of the monks at prayer in the chapel. They wore white habits. But they were either ghosts, or my imagination was feverish; for, as I discovered when I spoke to two dishevelled gardeners through an old wrought iron gate who were dragging a hose after them like a prisoner's fetters, there had been no monks here for many years. (The haciendas of religious communities were confiscated in 1908.) A family had bought the confiscated hacienda and then, two years ago, sold it to the State. The State gave it to the community of Telipulí on condition that it turned it into a tourist attraction within two years, which is what the two gardeners, amongst others, were doing. So far, there had not been a single tourist.

'Well,' I said, 'we are tourists. May we see round the hacienda?'

The two gardeners looked at one another: such a thing had never been heard of, it was unprecedented.

'You must have permission,' one of them said at last.

'From whom?' I asked.

'From the mayor of Telipulí'

The village was two miles down a very rough road. Clara was all for giving up, but I was more determined than ever. Like Latacunga, it was asleep. It was a wretched place, a few houses gathered round a large, unpaved square, full of dust and flinty stones. The walls of the houses were stained, as though with faeces. A black dog with well-developed ribs scavenged in the dust. I went to the far end of the square, where I found a building more official than the rest, with the words 'Political Agent' over the door. The first room was empty, except for a chair. I noticed that the smearer of faeces had been active indoors as well as out. Through a courtyard with the same forlorn surface as the square outside I found a room in which the political agent was having a game of cards with two other men of unsavoury and ferocious appearance.

The welcome I received was not warm. The approach of a stranger could only mean trouble or, even worse, work.

I explained that I was a foreigner, not just to the village but to the country – sufficiently obvious in any case – and that I should very much like to see the hacienda and monastery.

Only the mayor could give permission, said the political agent.

'Where is the mayor?' I asked.

'He lives in Latacunga.'

'The Mayor of Telipulí lives in Latacunga?'

'Of course,' said the political agent, and I saw his meaning. No-one would live in Telipulí if he had an alternative.

I explained that we had been to Latacunga, and that we did not wish to return there just to seek the mayor's permission. We had come all the way from Quito to see the monastery.

The three men conferred amongst themselves.

'All right,' said the political agent. '*I* will give you permission to enter the monastery. I will write a note.'

'Thank you very much, señor.'

We looked at one another for a few moments.

'Do you have a pen?' he asked.

'No.'

'Do you have paper?'

'No.'

He shrugged his shoulders.

'Then I cannot give you permisssion to visit, señor. I'm sorry.'

The political agent of Telipulí had a pack of cards, but no pen and no paper. I turned to go, defeated by the crushing inertia of these men. Had I stayed in the room with them much longer, I should not have summoned the will power to leave at all.

'Wait,' said the political agent suddenly, as though struck by a brilliant path out of the impasse. 'These two men will come with you see in the monastery, if you promise to bring them back again.'

The two men sprang to life, smiled gaily, and started chattering. The prospect of a four-mile ride in the back of our car broke the monotony of their day, their week, perhaps even their month.

Clara, who did not wish to see the monastery anyway, did not trust the two men who clambered joyfully into the back of our vehicle, like children on an outing.

'I suppose you promised to bring them back,' she said.

'They wouldn't have come otherwise.'

But the two men proved quite knowledgeable about the monastery and its hacienda. It was built in the sixteenth century, to withstand every category of disaster, from volcano and earthquake to political irruption. The walls were two feet thick, giving the interior a mossy coolness.

The monks' cells were to be converted one day into hotel bedrooms, and in good anticlerical style, the chapel was used to store cement (whose sacks had appeared to me as monks earlier in the day). The two men were particularly pleased by this profane use of the chapel. They forgot that where anticlericalism was strong, the Church was still a force.

'And this,' they said, leading us into a large dank cellar, 'was the prison in which lazy Indians were held.'

They spoke as of ancient history, though the last prisoners for laziness were incarcerated only ten or fifteen years ago, and they were personally known to the two men. But in a sense, what happened in Ecuador fifteen years ago *is* almost ancient history. The country has changed more in the last two decades than in the previous four centuries, thanks above all to oil. The value of Ecuador's exports in 1975 alone exceeded those of all the years between 1821 and 1950. Ecuador's tax revenue in 1975 was equal to that of the entire 1950s. The quantity of electricity generated in 1975 was 1,666 times greater than in 1949. The unchanging appearance of Quito and the countryside were illusions.

We returned to Quito on the Panamericano. On the way back Clara told me more of her life story, while I declined to tell mine. We debated the virtues of candour and secrecy: she taking the part of candour, I of secrecy. Concealment, she said, turned life into an abscess, waiting to burst. Candour, I replied, made for self-absorption and triviality. Without enigma to decipher, life had no meaning.

I went directly from Quito to San Francisco. Accustomed now to altitudes of 10,000 feet, I ran up and down the city's famous hills, laughing. The bookshops of the city seemed to devote more space to books about cocaine and how to gain the most pleasure from it than to books about the whole history of the world, let alone so insignificant a portion of it as South America.

I listened to conversations on my right and on my left in the restaurant of my hotel. (I had to borrow a tie from a waiter to gain admittance.) On my right was a family group, the newly-married son expatiating on the vanity of wealth.

'Oh yeah,' said his mother, pushing some soufflé into her predatory mouth. 'What are you doing here, then, eating in this expensive restaurant?'

The *ad hominem* argument pained her sensitive son.

'I can do without this kind of food,' he said.

'Oh yeah?'

'Yeah.'

There was tension in the air. The father smirked and ate in silence. His wife wanted to draw him into the discussion, in which all the grievances of domestic life would be obliquely aired.

I turned to my left. A businessman was dining his personal assistant. The young beautiful woman was expressing her gratitude.

'You know, until I met you . . .'

His hand slithered across the table, past the silver vase containing a pink rose, and united with hers.

'My . . . my Therapist said my biggest problem is I don't take myself seriously as a person.'

I nearly choked, and put my glass down on the table with a crash. His hand closed round hers.

'You've taught me how to take myself seriously as a person.'

Another squeeze of her hand.

'I've discovered in Therapy that I'm not such a terrible person after all. I've changed from a Negative Self-Image to a Positive Self-Image.'

I turned from what Life and Therapy had taught her – candour without revelation – to my bowl of raspberries, and longed for the Altiplano.

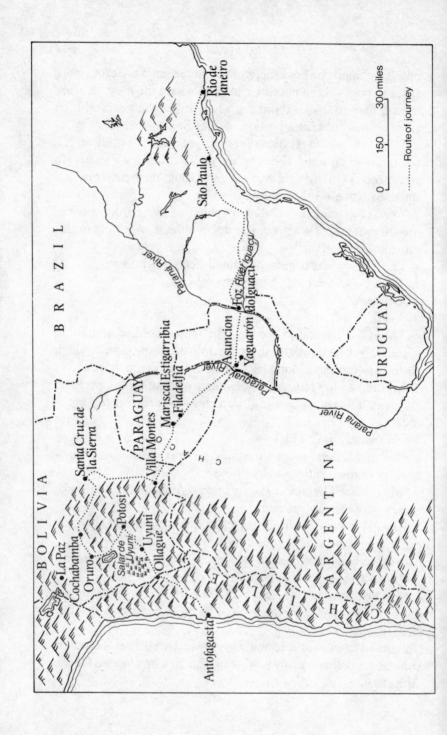

SEVEN

Brazil

I RETURNED to South America the following year by flying from New York to Rio de Janeiro.

It is difficult to enter the life of a modern, frenetically busy city of eight millions whose language you do not speak. Spanish was of surprisingly little use, and raised nationalist hackles. It was understood well enough, but I had difficulties with the replies in Portuguese. I was lonely in Rio.

I stayed, as do most visitors, in Copacabana. The swathe of skyscrapers – each of them individually undistinguished – describes a perfect arc along the beach and is a spectacular sight. This is one of the most densely populated areas in the world: more than 125,000 to the square mile. They crowd into Copacabana to be near the beach which has generated a whole culture, or at least a cult. Every day of the week men and women – but more especially men – paraded themselves up and down in search of admirers. There seemed thousands, and even tens of thousands, of vain men with little else to do. They played football on the beach with consummate skill, turning it more into ballet than sport.

Rio de Janeiro was not, however, entirely carefree. It was the season for the annual riot against the International Monetary Fund; the threat of violence to come hung over the city like the forecast of a cyclone. A commission from the Fund had tried to enter the country *incognito* to have talks about Brazil's mountainous foreign debt with the almost equally unpopular government, but had been discovered at the airport by a group of astute journalists. The attempt at secrecy had made everyone all the more suspicious. The commission would, of course, recommend further belt-tightening, especially by the improvident poor, so that the banks of Europe and New York should not lose their money.

The *favelas*, the infamous slums of the city, clung precariously to the sides of the mountains, as though ready at the first meteorological or geological upheaval to slip downwards and exact revenge on the prosperous suburbs below. But these slums had a life and laughter of their own. If no-one was in full employment, no-one was fully unemployed either. Everyone had some trifling commerce to pursue, selling potatoes or lottery tickets or picking pockets. Unalloyed happiness is rare and fleeting, but so is unrelieved misery.

Below some favelas was Santa Teresa, a hilly and shaded quarter of eighteenth and nineteenth-century houses, still reached by open tram. Pretty terraces, painted pink and green and yellow, lined the narrow cobbled streets. It was the architecture of siestas and quiet evening gatherings; a civilised, humane architecture that called to mind the fastidious novels of Machado de Assis, who dissected human foibles with tolerant irony. But Machado's Brazil, the Brazil of Santa Teresa, was a slave-owning society; the Emperor Dom Pedro II, who spoke eight languages fluently and taught himself Hebrew and Sanskrit, was deposed in 1889 in favour of a republic not because he opposed emancipation, but because he insisted upon it.

In 1945 the giant concrete statue of Christ the Redeemer, 140 feet high and weighing over a thousand tons, was erected on the peak of *Corcovado*, the Hunchback, a mountain that from a certain angle really does look like a vast monolithic Charles Laughton playing Quasimodo. Since then a worship of gigantism has overtaken the city and would have destroyed, but for its incomparable setting of bays and mountains, beaches and palms, ocean and jungle, much of its physical charm. Opposite the seventeenth-century convent of Santo Antônio, for example, is now the headquarters of the state oil monopoly, Petrobras, housed in a building constructed from huge concrete blocks, all of them streaked black with pollution, set at angles to one another, and connected by concrete pillars. The windows are no more than slits in the concrete, as though the bureaucrats inside were afraid of light, especially of it falling on the accounts, or were expecting a siege by the public upon whose heads they would discharge boiling oil. Mindless and brutal, but also unconvincing in its modernity, it illustrates the Brazilian equivocation about the future: Brazil, they say, always has been, and always will be, the country of the future.

I found the new cathedral, dedicated in 1976, similarly unconvincing. A concrete cone 250 feet high and 100 yards across, with four abstract stained class windows running the whole height of the cone, the altar is dwarfed, like a picnic table on an Alp. It is said the cathedral holds a congregation of 5000 seated, 20,000 standing. Thus the Church proves itself as modern as the state oil monopoly.

But Christ the Redeemer is to Rio de Janeiro as the Statue of Liberty is to New York. A constant stream of people makes its way up the mountain to swarm round the Redeemer's concrete feet. Nuns come to pray, everyone else to eat icecreams and spot familiar landmarks below. Some ask whether it is possible to climb inside the Redeemer to reach the out-stretched arms that seem, from a distance, to embrace the whole city; they want to stand on his thumbs and wave, but it is not possible. From a distance the statue is warm and forgiving, but close to it is grey and forbidding, like the character of the semi-fascist semi-dictator, Gertulio Vargas, in whose era it was erected.

I managed to recapture the elegiac mood of the novels of Machado de Assis in the famous Jardim Botânico, founded by Dom Pedro I in 1808. A few people only meandered down the avenues of stately royal palms, a hundred feet high. The humble and familiar trees of Europe were treated here as exotics. I met a Guatemalan engineer whose eyes filled with tears when he recalled the home and family he had left only a few days before coming to learn how to brew beer on an industrial scale. His ambition was to become general manager of the *cervecería nacional*, the national brewery. I said I thought it odd how, in the midst of his country's well-publicised travails, he should be sent abroad to learn to brew beer.

'Ah señor,' he replied, 'you must not believe everything you read about my country. It would be quite safe for you to visit.'

My mood was dispelled for good that evening when I walked down the Avenida Atlântica after dinner – a time when the characters of Machado de Assis stroll, cigar in hand, listening to the waves and reflecting on life in general. The Avenida, which runs along the shore, was now deserted, the life of Copacabana having gravitated inland to the Avenida Nossa Senhora de Copacabana where the neon-lit nightclubs were. A prostitute approached and offered her services. My refusal provoked a barrage of insults. She swung her handbag and hit me over the head with it. She chased me as far as the Copacabana Palace, where I was staying, using her handbag as a gaucho's *bolas*. My precipitate entry into the hotel caused the black-coated and striped-trousered chief receptionist to raise an eyebrow. Going to the revolving door, he told the screaming prostitute to clear off, in language which was less than genteel.

I had decided to cross South America from Rio de Janeiro to Antofagasta in Chile without resort to aeroplanes, and to use only public transport.

I started by taking a bus to Foz do Iguaçu, a town on the Paraná River a thousand miles from Rio de Janeiro. A thousand miles! To European ears it is an immense distance, to travel it a considerable undertaking. But look at a map of Brazil and you will see that the journey from Rio to Foz traverses but the bottom left-hand corner of the country, leaving untouched the vast hinterland provinces each the size of France and with the population of Lyon.

It took twenty-four hours, and even this most populous corner of the country seemed empty. The low, rolling hills of rust-red earth stretched without end, punctuated by one-street towns which were neither rich nor poor, where nothing ever happens. This is Main Street, Brazil, which serves the farmers who make Brazil the second largest exporter of food in the world – though many of its own people never have enough to eat.

I managed somehow to sleep through the whole of Sao Paulo, where a tenth of all Brazilians live. Already the largest city in South America, and one of the largest in the world, it is also amongst the fastest growing. Its frantic pace is said to intimidate even New Yorkers. The size of Luxembourg, it has half of Brazil's industry and makes nine out of ten of its cars. Founded more than four centuries ago, virtually nothing remains from previous ages. In Sao Paulo the future exerts the same fascination that the past exerts in Quito. I do not think it was entirely a coincidence that I slept through it.

At Foz do Iguaçu I stayed at the Hotel das Caratatas, a mile from the famous Iguaça Falls. The deep roar of the water accompanied everything – dinner, sleep, a game of tennis.

Iguaçu means 'great waters' in the Guaraní language, though the Paraná into which it flows twelve miles downstream is a far larger river yet. The falls stretch in a horseshoe a mile and a half across and have twice the volume of Niagara. Rainbows shimmer in the spray as tantalisingly as the visions of utopians. The falls funnel the water by a series of majestic precipices into a boiling chasm below: above them the river is two and a half miles wide, below them a couple of hundred yards. A small wooden walkway juts out to the very base of one of the cataracts, but it has been disused since it partly collapsed, sweeping a large party of Japanese tourists off to their deaths.

I wanted unusual photographs of the falls. It is part of the self-delusive desire of the traveller to have done something different, to have trod where no human foot has trodden before. In a world of 4,000,000,000 people this is increasingly difficult to do especially if, like me, you prefer the day to end with a well-made gin and tonic. Nevertheless, I resolved to clamber up to the very edge of one of the highest cataracts, well away from the laid out paths. ('It is inadvisable,' says the *South American Handbook*, 'to walk away from the main tourist areas; one correspondent has reported the murder of a friend here.') I struggled through the undergrowth of the forest, guided by the roar of the cataract, until I was within a yard of that tremendous leap, two hundred feet above the basalt rocks on which the water smashed itself to foam. A yard before it fell the water ran serenely smooth and clear, unaware of the fate about to overtake it. It was only a foot or two deep. I stepped out on to some slippery rocks in the stream that I might take yet more daring shots. How easy, I thought, just to throw oneself over and have done with it! Not that I was unhappy, but it was a strange and powerful temptation. I began to understand why men wanted to shoot falls in barrels and cross them in a wheelbarrrow pushed along a tightrope. As I stepped out on to rocks further still from the bank I felt myself the plaything of forces incomparably more powerful than myself which gave me, paradoxically, a greater personal significance. But I came to my senses with a jolt, as though wakened from a dream, and trembling with sudden realisation of my danger, I regained the bank.

I walked along the river for several miles above the falls, a wide expanse of lazy, scudding water the colour of tea just after the milk has been added. The other bank was Argentina, now – after the Falklands war – a land forbidden me, and therefore infinitely more attractive than it had ever been before.

I watched the kaleidoscopic clouds of butterflies as they gathered round the small slimy pools near the bank, or landed on any foul ordure they could find. I thought it strange how these beautiful creatures were irresistibly drawn to any vileness on the ground: as though Nature, like Man, were incapable of creating beauty without predicating it on some kind of ugliness.

EIGHT

Paraguay

I CROSSED into Paraguay at Foz do Iguaçu by the Friendship Bridge, so called because Brazil and Paraguay are engaged on the largest hydroelectric scheme in the world at Itaipú. The friendship is slightly unequal, like that between the buffalo and the egret. The dam, costing more than $12,500,000,000, is being built by Brazilian expertise and Paraguayan cheap labour. The Paraguayans have mortgaged their future utterly to the success of the scheme. When it is completed, Brazil will receive cheap electricity for many years while Paraguay – it is hoped – will double its foreign currency earnings.

The town on the Paraguayan side of the Alto Paraná is called Ciudad Presidente Stroessner. If you arrive there by boat it will likely be the M.V. *Presidente Stroessner.* The music played over the boat's loudspeaker system will be the *Don Alfred Polka.* But arrive in Paraguay by air, you will land at the Presidente Stroessner International Airport. I could not help but think of Ernesto Cardenal's line about another Latin American dictator:

Somoza unveils a statue of Somoza in the Somoza stadium.

A large poster of the President's solid and unsmiling countenance over the words, *Paz Trabajo y Bienestar con Stroessner* (Peace Work and Well-being with Stroessner) faced me as a young immigration officer, who seemed surprised that anyone should stray so far from home just to come there, asked me whether I had dollars to change. I did, and with only the merest gesture in the direction of caution, he changed them into *guaranís*, one of South America's stronger currencies.

I took the bus to the capital Asunción, two hundred miles away. Paraguay is still predominantly rural, with no town other than the capital with a population over 50,000. The landscape is gently undulating, the soil a rich red, and the vegetation lush and verdant. Paraguay, or that part of it south-east of the Paraguay River, has long been known as an agricultural arcadia, ruined only by political malfeasance and the distance from any sizeable market. Less than a tenth of the cultivable land is actually worked, a reflection both of its geographical isolation and its system of land tenure. Less than one per cent of the landowners own ninety per cent of the land, and seventy per cent of the landowners own less than two per cent. As a result, landless families squat on the very edges of feudal estates, growing only what they need to live; while the landowners, who live in Asunción, neither know nor care what becomes of their land so long as it provides them with an adequate income. The land being bountiful and the climate benign, the habits of industriousness have never been inculcated successfully; and only those who think that work is valuable in itself believe that Paraguayans have suffered as a result. 'The abundance and richness of his native soil,' wrote John Parish Robertson, the first Briton ever to reside in Paraguay, 'together with the paucity of his wants, permit his idleness at home. Stretched out in his hammock, which is slung in the porchway of his cottage, his delight is to be there in the listlessness of the live-long day, and, in the course of it, to smoke a succession of cigars, and sip some twenty or thirty cups of his favourite maté.'

Thomas Carlyle put it somewhat differently and with more disapproval: 'They are rude people; lead a drowsy life of ease and sluttish abundance.'

We reached Asunción towards evening, as the light began to soften. The city has developed greatly of late, as a result of the fastest economic growth in Latin America, though this has now ground to an ignominious halt. The outskirts were a tangled skein of garages, workshops and warehouses, all bearing the emblems of multinational companies. Yet everything was so clearly built on foundations of mud, with banana trees growing in gaps and chickens being raised in garage forecourts, that even this commercial mess had a certain charm of its own.

And the centre of Asunción, in spite of a handful of recent buildings that pass for skyscrapers (twelve storeys high), still retains a small town atmosphere, where the long siesta is sacrosanct. We pulled up in the Plaza Uruguaya, a tree-filled square where old men sat playing chess or reading newspapers. I was approached at once by a boy who asked me where I was staying. I said I did not know, and he recommended an hotel that was both cheap and comfortable. I had no grounds on which to reject his suggestion and I went along with him.

We set off down the Calle Mejico, in the direction of the river. He carried my bag and would not relinquish it. Travel broadens the mind, but it also induces a state of paranoia: a tendency to imagine that the friendliest act is done with the worst of motives. I divided my attention between possible ambush and the rather charming domestic architecture. The houses were all of one storey, the windows shuttered on the inside, with ornate wrought iron grilles on the outside. Each house was painted a pastel colour and had its own moulded plasterwork decorations. The courtyard was reached down a narrow passageway opening to the street by tall carved wooden double doors. They were not grand or even beautiful, these houses, but – more important – they were on a decent human scale, where a man did not feel overshadowed by Man's creations.

The hotel was at the end of the street and my companion left me, refusing all payment for his help. I felt a momentary stab of guilt at having so mistakenly suspected his motives. I discovered, to my surprise, that the hotel was full of Chinese, singing Catholic hymns in Chinese in an alcove off the entrance hall. I remembered a sentence from a 1923 guidebook to the River Plate and Paraguay: Persons with a criminal record or tuberculosis, or members of the yellow races, are not allowed into the Republic of Paraguay.

My room was an airless box without a window. A ceiling fan revolved spasmodically and unpredictably, disturbing the stifling air (it was only hot inside). The one advantage of this dingy establishment was the view from the verandah: a low bluff overlooking the Río Paraguay. Immediately below, down to the riverbank, was a residential quarter that was not quite slum, not quite respectable. The houses were of whitewashed mud with red tiled roofs, planted on the rich red-brown alluvial soil – comfortably ramshackle houses, whose courtyards were used as playpens and pigsties and vegetable gardens. The river beyond, whose far bank was invisible, seemed to threaten them with inundation: an immense expanse of silver-grey, shining in the evening light like polished pewter. A few small boats stood moored motionless to the near bank, while the river was dotted with *camelotes*, the floating islands of matted water-weeds. Overhead, in the white sky, wheeled vultures. I tried to make out what carrion they had espied: 'Were it not for the occasional headless body floating down the river,' observed one foreign correspondent, 'It might be possible to consider the gaudily uniformed and bemedalled dictator of Paraguay . . . a character out of Gilbert & Sullivan.'

I admitted to a slight sense of disappointment at the apparent lack of headless bodies in the river that evening, which might have given me the gratifications of righteous indignation. But peace has its own compensations. The Chinese mass, with its dismal hymns of joy, had given way to distant, plaintive Argentinian tangos played by a string trio. The records were scratched, or the radio reception from Argentina was poor. It was the music of the dusty provincial towns from the novels of Manuel Puig – strange how potent cheap music is! Below the bluff, on the riverbank, people were going about their Sunday evening business: bringing in the washing, playing cards, carrying a bucket of pig's entrails. I thought that 'brutal dictatorship' did not sum up life, even under a brutal dictatorship.

As the light faded, a neon sign began to wink on the top of the Banco Central del Paraguay:

PAZ TRABAJO Y BIENESTAR CON STROESSNER

I moved next day to a more commodious hotel – the Gran Hotel del Paraguay. It is situated in the quiet and leafy suburb where not long before Anastasio Somoza had been assassinated. The crime – if crime it was – has still not been solved. Almost everyone connected with the tyrant, so beloved of President Reagan that he attended his funeral, has been suspected at some time. Even President Stroessner has been suspected, because Somoza's presence in his fiefdom was attracting light in dark corners, which the President preferred to leave unilluminated.

At any rate, the assassination on the Avenida España was a triumph for German engineering: though Somoza was riddled with bullets – his body contained eighteen – his Mercedes hit by a rocket and the driver mangled beyond recognition, the engine kept running smoothly.

The Gran Hotel is the former palace of Paraguay's greatest national hero, the Marshal-President Francisco Solano López. That he should be the object of veneration rather than universal execration is something that mystifies all foreigners. By a fatal amalgam of incompetence, miscalculation and vanity he led his nation in 1864 into war with Brazil, Argentina and Uruguay from which it emerged six years later with less than half its population still alive. He refused to end the war by the simple expedient, offered on several occasions by his enemies, of exile in Europe on a comfortable pension. The exact number of deaths in the war is not known with certainty, for the demography of the time was rudimentary, but all authorities are agreed that by 1870 nineteen out of every twenty male Paraguayans had died; less than 30,000 remained alive; and that something over half the female population had died too.

And now the man responsible for this immolation – unsurpassed in the history of warfare – has been transformed into *el Héroe Máximo de la Patria*, the Greatest Hero of the Patria. A grandiloquent equestrian statue stands in the centre of Asunción, sword held aloft, his dying words uttered at the Battle of Cerro Corá, the last battle of the war (by which time his 'army' was composed of women and ten year old children given false beards to deceive the Brazilians as to their sex and age), engraved on the plinth:

MUERO CON MI PATRIA

'I die with my country': 'My country dies with me' would have been more apposite.

I reached the centre of the city from the Gran Hotel by one of the rattly old trams (secondhand from Belgium, with signs still in Flemish) that happily continue to operate in Asunción. The heat of the day was not yet upon us, but the city had a sleepy atmosphere. In the Plaza Constitución an old man with a straw hat pulled over his face sat propped up in an arcade against a wall of peeling yellow plaster. He slept soundly. Opposite him was the crumbling and cheerfully undistinguished cathedral. In the middle of the square stood an old Vickers tank, captured in the Chaco War between Paraguay and Bolivia, to commemorate Paraguay's victory over its better armed neighbour. I felt I had not so much arrived in the heart of a capital city, as emerged into the midst of a novel by Graham Greene. Here, if anywhere, was the realm of whisky priests and honorary consuls wrestling incoherently with the ultimate questions of existence.

On the Avenida del Paraguay Independiente which runs from the square stands the Government Palace, said to be the finest public building in all Paraguay. Painted grey, it is supposedly modelled on the Louvre, though any resemblance seemed tenuous to me. In any case the English architect, an engineer called Alonzo Taylor who worked for López and was later tortured by him during one of his fits of paranoia, planted the square tower of a Somerset church in the middle of it. Swarming round the large floral clock in the gardens of the Palace were broad-shouldered men in dark glasses and business suits, looking as comfortable as professional wrestlers at a literary luncheon. They bulged with gun-sized swellings. They stared into the street, while on the flat rooftops of the nearby buildings soldiers and helmeted detachments of the Military Police kept vigil by training machineguns on passers-by. President Stroessner, a man of quiet and frugal habits, rules from the Palace: 'The fatherland,' he once said, 'is founded on the cement of the home. Policy which cares for the moral and material reasons which make homes firm is patriotic policy which fortifies the nation.' I did not stay to outstare the men in dark glasses. The first dictator of Paraguay, Dr José Gaspar Rodriguez de Francia, once ordered that all loiterers in front of his palace should be shot.

Immediately behind the Palace, in full view of the heroic equestrian López, were the worst slums of Asunción, shacks of tin and cardboard on muddy river flats. The river was still shrouded in a mist that the morning sun dispersed slowly. The President is a keen river fisherman, as was the last Spanish governor of Paraguay, General Bernardo de Velasco: 'I order a chair,' he wrote, 'to be carried to the river bank in the afternoon, when I do not ride, from which, with the greatest ease, I throw the line and catch monstrous fishes.'

I walked down the Calle Chile to a remarkable edifice – the Panteón de los Héroes. Designed during López's war by the Italian Alessandro Ravizza (he also designed the railway station), it was completed only in 1937. It is an exact replica of Les Invalides in Paris, on a much reduced scale. Two sailors with muskets stood guard while an officer in a white tunic watched passers-by from among the columns with suspicious and hooded eyes.

The inside was rather cluttered, there being so many heroes to accommodate. Here were deposited the remains of Mariscal Estigarribia, the victorious general of the Chaco War, and those of Carlos Antonio López, the father of the Marshal-President, himself a dictator of Paraguay for eighteen years. A more cautious man than his son, he steered his country clear of foreign entanglements and was known only as The Citizen. He loved his country so much that, according to one historian, he owned half of it. He was so fat, thanks to an insatiable appetite, that, once sat down, he had difficulty in rising from a chair. An Argentine contemporary described him as 'a great tidal wave of flesh . . . a veritable mastodon.'

But the chief glory of the Panteón is the body, or the alleged body, of the Marshal-President. Interred in a coffin draped in a Paraguayan flag and set in a well in the floor just like Napoleon (with whom he liked to be compared), a plaque states: 'Venció Penurias y Fatigas con la Espada en la Mano y la Patria en los Labios al Frente du sus Ultimos Soldados y sobre su Ultima Campa Batalla.' (He Overcame Hardships and Exhaustion with his Sword in his Hand and the Fatherland on his Lips at the Head of his Last Soldiers on his Last Field of Battle.) Whatever is in the coffin, it is most unlikely to be Mariscal Francisco Solano López. He was buried in a shallow grave at Cerro Corá, along with the thousand others who died there, and the remains were disinterred only eighty years later. Asked how it was certain that the bones dug up were those of López, a priest who approved of the cult of the *Héroe Máximo* replied: 'Ah, Señor, a mortal man's remains would have disappeared over the years . . . But Mariscal López was no mortal man!'

I looked at the coffin and wondered how a man who was in most respects a monster of egotism had commanded such loyalty from his people that they fought (literally) to the last man for him, and how he had been transformed into a patriotic cult.

Official historiography has it that the loyalty was entirely spontaneous. It is certain, however, that López employed an elaborate system of espionage, in which every sixth soldier was set on five others to report disaffection. The penalty for failure to do so was death. López was not afraid of executions: anyone whom he considered had not exerted himself sufficiently in the prosecution of the war was shot; he executed two brothers and was about to execute his mother as a traitress when the war ended; on one day at San Fernando in 1868 he executed 368 alleged plotters (the equivalent of 17,000 in a country of Britain's population). His vanity knew no bounds: in the midst of South America's greatest demographic disaster since the Conquest, he extorted a subscription to raise a statue to himself on his birthday and present him with a golden sword. He arrested and imprisoned two British doctors because they attended the wounded after a battle rather than his mother – a chronic hypochondriac – as he had ordered. When his last headquarters were overrun, by which time his army had long been reduced to scavenging wild roots and berries, an ample supply of vintage French wines, cognacs and champagnes was found.

Whatever his positive qualities, this is hardly the stuff of Héroes Máximos. How has the transformation occurred? Everything points to deliberate acts of policy by successive Paraguayan governments. In the aftermath of the Chaco War the totalitarian regime (a title it was proud to claim for itself) of Colonel Rafael Franco felt it needed a military national hero from the past to justify the present domination of politics by the army. López filled the part admirably. Statues were erected and a decree passed annulling all previous laws 'derogatory to the memory of López'. Books which were critical of López, such as R.B. Cunninghame-Graham's *Portrait of a Dictator* and Cecilio Báez's *El Mariscal Francisco Solano López*, were banned from the country (they still are). Cynical hacks set about composing abysmal panegyrics: 'posterity has seen him as a dim twilight, illuminated on the far horizon, treading the earth with his feet, touching the sky with his great brow thoughtful in Promethean sorrow.' Thus Juan Emilio O'Leary, who made a not inconsiderable fortune out of López (and was nominated by the Paraguayans for the Nobel Prize), though his own family had been one of those to suffer most as a result of López's cruelty and megalomania.

But the elevation of López's Irish mistress, Eliza Lynch, from Parisian courtesan on the lookout for a powerful protector to national heroine is, if anything, even more remarkable.

López discovered her while on a diplomatic mission as a young man to Europe. She flattered him – not a difficult thing to do – and was the first to put it into his head that he might be the Napoleon of South America. They returned together to Paraguay where she was accepted neither by Francisco's father, who was still dictator, nor by Asunción society, such as it was, because of her Parisian tastes and manners, and her state of concubinage with López. He could not marry her because she was married already, but they had several illegitimate children. She tried to raise the cultural tone of the capital – always an unpopular thing to do – and she was very spirited in defence of her own dubious position. On a river trip that Madame Lynch (as she was known, and has been known ever since) arranged for all the ladies of Asunción society, with the wife of the French ambassador as guest of honour, she was snubbed by all the guests and not allowed by them to sit at the lunch table on board the river launch. Madame Lynch ordered the servants to throw all the food and wine overboard, and the captain to drop anchor in the middle of the river for several hours. The ladies of Asunción returned that evening hungry and tired, but with deeper insight into Madame Lynch's character.

Once López became dictator himself, however, she became the arbiter of Paraguayan fashion. She maintained her own system of espionage and extorted jewels from the ladies who had spurned her, to finance the war effort. She remained loyal to López to the very end, and legend has it that she buried both her husband and her son after the Battle of Cerro Corá. She returned to Paris where she died in penury and was buried in the Père Lachaise.

In the 1950s two books appeared depicting her as a martyred saint; one of them was declared 'useful for the armed forces of Paraguay' by decree of President Stroessner himself. An orchestrated clamour arose to have her body returned and laid at the side of the Héroe Máximo. The Director of the National Archives, Dr Hipólito Sanchez Quell, duly applied for the exhumation; but the remains suddenly disappeared from Père Lachaise under mysterious circumstances. They were taken by a Paraguayan of Lebanese extraction, Teófilo Chammas, who sent them to Buenos Aires in a sealed casket also containing four kilos of pure Lebanese hashish. The Argentinian customs kept the hashish, but sent on Madame Lynch in an urn.

The day of her arrival in 1961 by gunboat up the river in Asunción was declared *un Día de Homenaje Nacional*, a Day of National Homage. President Stroessner, decked out in one of his best uniforms, spoke at the quayside and called Madame Lynch 'our national heroine, our national martyr'. As chief pallbearer he then accompanied the urn to the Panteón de los Héros where, however, it was not permitted to remain because López and Lynch had never been married, and the Panteón was consecrated ground. If Lynch stayed López had to go, and vice versa. The urn was therefore hurriedly removed to the second floor of the Ministry of Defence, in the Avenida Mariscal Francisco Solano López, where it remained for nine years in the Museo Lynch, together with a book that allegedly contained 87,000 signatures 'in homage'. On the centenary of López's death, the urn was taken to a mausoleum surmounted with a life-sized statue of her, holding aloft two crosses, symbolising both her own and Paraguay's martyrdom.

I had dinner that evening in Madame Lynch's private theatre, now the dining room of the Gran Hotel del Paraguay. It was a large, dimly-lit wood-panelled chamber with a floral frieze and the masks of tragedy and comedy above the words 'In Vino Veritas' – Madame Lynch's private motto. The waiter had been the gardener in the afternoon: he had now donned a white jacket and black bow tie, but his fingers retained traces of his horti-cultural pursuits. He hovered indecisively around the diners, of whom there were only two. The other was clearly English as well. He knew I was English and I knew he was English, but still we did not speak and continued to eat our meals at separate tables: though thousands of miles from home in a land rarely visited by our countrymen, and in need of company, we nevertheless required some other pretext to strike up a conversation. With great skill, we manoeuvred to finish our meals simultaneously, and reached the door of Madame Lynch's theatre at precisely the same moment.

'After you,' I said.

'No,' he replied. 'After you.'

It was the pretext we needed to speak, and we sat down to have a beer together.

He was the representative of a large British pharmaceutical company whose South American headquarters were in Sao Paulo. He was fluent in Spanish, Portuguese and French. He had gone to Brazil without a job and had been taken on by the company on purely Brazilian terms, which meant that he faced the eternal Brazilian problem: inflation. His salary was revised every three months, a great advantage over lower-paid workers whose salaries are reviewed only every six months. Nevertheless, while he felt prosperous at the beginning of each three months, by the end of it he was nearly destitute. People had no faith in money in Brazil: they rushed to convert it to goods as soon as possible.

I found it hard to conceive how economic activity could continue in these circumstances, but he said people had learned to cope. Brazilian accounting was now the most sophisticated in the world. If you borrowed a capital sum it increased at the rate of inflation, thus eliminating the automatic advantage to borrowers of an inflationary situation. As for foreign trade, a system of crawling peg devaluations every two weeks was used, bringing order to what otherwise would have been chaos.

He had come to Paraguay to supervise his company's small operation there. There was not much scope for selling human medicines there because the population was small and most of it was not in the doctor-consulting class. The company sold mainly veterinary products because there were twice as many cattle as people in Paraguay, besides which – he added – they were usually better cared for.

He had lived in several South American countries but liked Brazil the best. The people were friendly, informal, artistic and talented. Argentina, on the other hand, he had found neurotic and self-obsessed. Buenos Aires always had its eye on Paris, Rome or New York to assure itself it was the equal of those cities. The people were simultaneously arrogant and unsure of themselves. They called the Brazilians *macacos*, monkeys, a crude allusion to the miscegenation from which they prided themselves of being free; while they called the other South Americans *tropicales*, tropicals, regarded as uncouth and uncultured.

Unsurprisingly, the subject of the recent conflict over the Falklands came up. He said that while the Brazilian government had supported Argentina, at least verbally, public opinion had been pro-British, not out of love for the British but out of hatred of the Argentinians. Even the government newspapers had dared to doubt the government line, though the radio and television dutifully recounted all the allegations of British atrocities.

Suddenly – the beers began to take effect – he thumped the table with his fist.

'Dammit, they're ours!' he exclaimed. 'The islands are ours. The wops invaded our territory!'

I asked him to keep his voice down. Paraguayans naturally sympathised with their neighbours and someone in the room where we were drinking might speak sufficient English to understand him.

'I don't care,' he said. The beer had made him belligerent, though his pudgy body was decidedly unmartial. 'They're only dagos. We're worth four of them.'

This was not a proposition I was anxious to test. I brought our conversation to a close by saying that I had to get up early next morning. He gave me his card, should I ever happen to be in São Paulo. I heard his angry diatribe trail off as we parted to go to our rooms.

'The islands are as British as . . . as . . . as . . .'

He cast around for a suitable example but could not find one. No doubt in the morning he would think of a thousand such. In the meantime, I wondered about the truth of Madame Lynch's motto.

The next day I had the opportunity to examine the Argentinian side of the question in considerable detail. The news-stands in the Plaza Uruguaya sold mainly Argentinian magazines from two or three months before, coinciding with the invasion (or recovery, as they preferred to call it) of the islands, the war and the defeat.

There was a complete transformation in the mood of the press immediately after the surrender. While the war had still been in progress, the tone was stridently chauvinistic; full of triumphs, with photographs of men celebrating victories they had not won; atrocity stories, not excluding cannibalism; reports of the Pope's unequivocal support for Argentina. Then, overnight, the mood changed to one of luxuriant self-denigration. 'In Argentina,' moaned one headline, 'Nothing is Done Well.' Psychiatrists were asked why the population had been so easily duped by its leaders. The press asked itself why it had disseminated so many lies, and came up with the less than convincing answer that the military communiqués had all been false. No-one admitted to having been eager to embrace the lies they had been fed.

There was a sarcastic interview with General Mario Menéndez, who only a month before would have evoked abject fear and deference from the press that now snapped at his heels. It was possible to feel almost sorry for him, though he had the reputation during the Dirty War in Argentina of being the most brutal and ruthless of officers, a valiant conqueror of grandmothers and children. He gave the impression of being a man of limited intellect who understood little of the events into which he had strayed. He took a pathetic pleasure in the correctness and consideration with which he had been treated by his captors, but showed no awareness of the suffering he had helped unleash on his troops. A stupid rather than an evil man, one thought.

From one of the stands I bought a short book by a former Argentinian foreign minister, Bernadino del Carril, called *La Cuestión de Las Malvinas*. I hoped to clear my mind of all prejudice in favour of my own country, but found Señor del Carril's book did not help me. The scion of a family that had been prominent in Argentine affairs since Independence, he had received an Hispanic and Aristotelic legal education, with the result that his arguments were dry and formal, untouched by the exigencies of life, but at the same time propounded with passion.

He held that the Treaty of Tordesillas in 1494, by which the

Pope divided the unknown world between Spain and Portugal, still had an important bearing on the matter. The United Nations had condemned colonialism; the Falklands were a colony; *ergo*, they stood condemned. That no native people were oppressed as a result was of no account to Señor del Carril, nor that the people actually living there wished to remain a colony; for him, the dry syllogism sufficed.

Having proved that the occupation of the islands in 1833 was an unjustified usurpation (which it was), Señor del Carril let the case rest, as though there were nothing else to be proved. That political arrangements in South America were somewhat fluid at the time, and not immutable, escaped him; his country, for example, did not recognise the independence of Paraguay from Buenos Aires until 1852, and took territory from it in 1870. Nor did he discuss the chaos which his principles of international law would let loose if generally adopted.

Yet, as I refuted in my mind the arguments in the book one by one, I realised I was being sucked into the vortex of South American thinking about history. The British desire to keep the islands was now as irrational as the Argentinian desire to have them. Much better simply to cut the Gordian knot; the minor injustice done to the inhabitants would be more than compensated by the justice of avoiding future war.

I decided to play a small part in improving relations by travelling through northern Argentina. I accordingly applied to the Argentinian consulate, on the floor above the Banco de le Nación Argentina. There was a large map covering one wall of the reception room depicting the Malvinas as undisputed Argentine territory. There were a few Argentinians at the counter, mostly rather desperate-looking men, with several days' growth of beard and slept-in clothes. It would not take much, I thought, to upset them.

I asked a young lady behind the counter for a visa, but when I confessed with a blush that my passport was British, a deathly hush fell over the room and the desperadoes looked ready to rush me. She said she would have to ask the consul in person.

'I am sorry, señor,' she said when she returned. 'But what you ask is completely impossible.'

Thus my diplomatic efforts to bring peace and reconciliation came to an end.

What I really disliked about British policy, I reflected as I walked out into the sunny Asunción street, was that it made it impossible for me to enter a country in which I was interested.

The small town of Yaguarón is thirty miles south-east of the capital. It is famous for its orange groves, from which the *petit grain* used in making perfumes, is distilled. The surrounding hills are not high, but give extensive views of a vast but hospitable emptiness. The red land, inexhaustibly fertile but only semi-cultivated, is studded with dark green trees as far as the eye can see, giving the landscape a cool appearance belied by the fierce sun overhead.

Yaguarón, founded in the same year as Buenos Aires, was for long the centre of the Franciscan missions to the Guaraní tribesmen of the region. Further to the south and east were the missions of the great rivals, the Jesuits, whose *reducciones*, or reductions, were amongst the most remarkable societies that have ever existed. They were perfect, unvarying communist utopias that lasted a century and a half, until destroyed by the envy of their detractors. Two or three Jesuits supervised four thousand or more Indians, whose basic necessities were provided and whose property was held entirely in common. The catechism was the only form of book-learning allowed the Indians, but they were taught animal husbandry, carpentry and other useful arts. Labour was also communal and the *reducciones* were so successful that – at their height they had 100,000 Indians – the other landowners of Paraguay were unable to find sufficient labour. It was this that caused the downfall of the Jesuits in Paraguay.

The Franciscan church of Yaguarón stands in a large grassy field. Its belfry is a tower of wooden scaffolding, standing entirely separate from the rest of the church, and was once used as a lookout for marauding Indians as well. The church itself is a dazzling white rectangle with an overhanging red-tiled roof in whose shade the whole town meets in the evenings. Inside, it is cool, and the elegant simplicity of the exterior contrasts with the phantasmagoria of wood-carving in the interior. The pillars are barley-sugar twists, and everywhere the broad faces of Indian cherubim and seraphim looked out from among foliage and decoration. The pulpit is carved with particular magnificence. It was from here that in 1642 Don Bernadino de Cárdenas, Bishop of Asunción, preached a famous sermon against the Jesuits, whose allegations were to echo down the ages, until they were expelled in 1767. Don Bernadino was a religious hysteric with a genius for self-advertisement: he courted popularity by auto-flagellation and always refusing food in public, saying he was nourished by heavenly sustenance. He alleged that the Jesuits prevented the Indians from paying their taxes; were untrust-worthy and heretical in their theology; and most damning of all, had made themselves fabulously wealthy by exploiting mines in the midst of their lands with slave labour. As late as the nineteenth century expeditions set out to search for Don Bernadino's Jesuit mines, but needless to say, none was ever found for the simple reason that none had ever existed.

Yaguarón was also the home of Dr José Gaspar Rodriguez de Francia, first dictator of Paraguay and one of the most extra-ordinary men of the nineteenth century, though now largely forgotten. His house is a museum, little visited, down an unpaved road that leads straight to the wilderness beyond.

Dr Francia's home is a modest, single-storeyed whitewashed house, not unlike thousands of others. I went there in the hope that it would help me understand something of his enigma – a residue, no doubt, of the primitive idea that after his death a little of a man's spirit remains in the places he has frequented during life.

The house was as simple in furnishing as it was in construction, hardly what one might have expected of a man with such a monstrous ego that he decreed all Paraguayans must wear a hat, be they otherwise naked, so that they might doff it whenever he or one of his functionaries went by. The truth seems to be that Dr Francia was one of those strange austere despots that this normally corrupt continent throws up, whose integrity is terrifying in its consistency, more terrifying by far than any regime of mere peculation could ever be. When Francia died, the public treasury was found to contain 122,000 silver pesos and 87,336 gold, of which latter 36,500 were his unclaimed salary for the previous twenty-five years. He was a Lenin rather than a Somoza.

Francia was born in 1766. His father was for a time the government administrator in Yaguarón, until a petition of the people asked for his removal. 'He threatens the complete desolation of our village by his cruel domination', they wrote.

The future dictator received his doctorate in theology from the University of Córdoba in Argentina at the age of nineteen. He returned to Asunción and applied for the chair in theology at the college there, but it was granted to a man of lesser ability called Bogarín, apparently because of Francia's suspect racial origins (his father had been born in Brazil). But the whirligig of time brings in its revenges: when Francia became dictator he decreed that no-one of pure Spanish descent might marry another, in an attempt to destroy the pride of race that plagues the continent still. His decree was regarded as despotic at the time (a kind of apartheid in reverse), but in the different ideological climate of today it finds its defenders.

He turned to law and was soon an advocate famous for his utter incorruptibility. Francia became dictator because he was the only man in Paraguay with the education and ability to steer the country through the dangerous shoals of Platine politics in the first quarter of the nineteenth century, a fact which almost everyone appreciated. His policy was to secure independence from Buenos Aires and avoid the civil strife that had engulfed the rest of South America. To that end, he drastically curbed individual rights: for example, no-one might enter or leave the country without his personal permission, granted to very few. He attempted to develop Paraguay's economy autonomously, replacing production for export by diversified production for home consumption. On one famous occasion in 1819 locusts destroyed the entire country's crops. Whenever such disasters had struck before, the Paraguayans resorted to their knees and miracle-working Virgins. Francia ordered them off their knees and told them to replant. Thus it was realised for the first time in three centuries that Paraguay's soil and climate could support two crops a year.

As Latin America's problems have appeared more and more intractable, historians – especially those of the left – have rehabilitated the dictator and his policies. At the time, however – and with one very notable exception – writers noticed only his despotic eccentricity, which was indeed considerable.

In 1815 he introduced compulsory prayers for himself (he was known as el Supremo) in church. No decision was taken without him, and he even inspected personally the imported cloth at the government warehouse, finding that the British manufacturers and merchants frequently tried to sell Paraguay short. He lived with his sister (he was a bachelor who furtively sired a few illegitimate children) who rolled his cigars for him, but he always unrolled them again in case they were poisoned. Eventually he dismissed his sister for having sent a government employee on a personal errand.

He was parsimonious with government funds to the ultimate degree. When having a batch of conspirators executed on the lawn in front of the government house he allocated only one musket ball per condemned man. If that failed to kill, the man was hacked to death with a machete. Thanks to ancient muskets and poor marksmanship there was fearful carnage, while Francia looked on from the verandah, calmly smoking a cigar and writing beside the name of each executed man the words *Pax Francia*. There were not many conspiracies against him.

That his justice was arbitrary is putting it mildly indeed. When his horse shied in front of a barrel outside a house, he had the houseowner arrested immediately. He called his torture chamber The Chamber of Truth and prisoners Recluses.

But there was one contemporary writer who found this all

perfectly acceptable, even necessary – Thomas Carlyle. His
famous essay on Francia, published three years after the
dictator's death, is a *locus classicus* of the defence of dictatorship:

> A people that uses almost no soap, and speaks almost no truth,
> but goes about in that fashion, in a state of personal nastiness, and
> also a spiritual nastiness, approaching the sublime; such a people
> is not easy to govern well! –

But at least the trains ran on time:

> And, of course, there was law and order under Francia:
> Whenever a robber could be seized, he was led to the nearest
> Guardhouse; a summary trial took place; and straightway, as soon
> as he had made confession, he was shot. These means proved
> effectual.

The cost of these means was considerable, if an eyewitness is to
be believed (and his account is surely credible, in the light of the
experience of our enlightened century):

> From being the most open, frank and kindhearted people in the
> world, the Paraguayans became the most sordid, low and hypo-
> critical of the human race. The demons of discord, jealousy, and
> distrust took possession of every habitation in the land. The
> over-ruling passion of self-preservation cooled or deadened all
> the softer feelings and affections. The brother informed against
> the sister, the wife against the husband; the son betrayed the
> father, or the father the son; and the bosom friend of yesterday
> became the vile spy and informer of today. All the hinges of society
> were out of joint. No inhabitant of Paraguay could say that the man
> who had broken bread with him today, might not be the instru-
> ment of his destruction on the morrow . . .

I looked at the best-known, perhaps the only, portrait of
Francia, on the wall of his living room. It was crudely done, but
managed to convey something of the severity of his character.

As I gazed at it the three curators of the museum – in excess of
the number of visitors for the last few months – gathered round
me as a kind of curiosity, having broken off their game of draughts

in the garden.

'A great man,' I said.

'Who?' they asked.

'Dr Francia – el Supremo,' I replied.

But they knew nothing of Dr Francia or why they were paid to guard his house while he was away. I signed the visitor's book – a slim volume – and left them to their *yerba maté*, their black Paraguayan cigars and their game of draughts.

I left Asunción early in the morning by taking the Nueva Asunción Bus Company's dilapidated bus to Filadelfia, a small settlement in the Chaco. The Chaco is a vast, inhospitable and still partly unexplored region of Paraguay, Bolivia and northern Argentina that makes up more than half Paraguay's national territory. Fewer than one in twenty Paraguayans live there, and half of those are pure-bred Indians, in the process of gradual extermination. There were only a handful of people on the bus, two of them clutching discontented chickens.

The Chaco begins immediately across the Río Paraguay, which early in the morning is a placid lake rather than a river, the few ripples gleaming and flashing as the sun comes over the horizon. Four and a half centuries after its foundation, Asunción is still a frontier town.

The first part of the Chaco is bisected by the Trans-Chaco Highway, a well-made road a couple of feet above the surrounding land, elevation indeed for these parts. Palm trees dot the landscape which, low and impermeable, is nearly always flooded. It is divided into huge cattle estancias, said to be overgrazed in spite of the apparent lack of cattle. Once, when the bus stopped for no evident reason, a young gaucho on horseback approached us. He trotted up to the bus on his chestnut mount and stared into the bus without any sign of curiosity. He wore a broad-brimmed hat and wide-bottomed trousers decorated with yellow tassels. His boots were spurred, and like all gauchos he had such a perfect understanding with his horse that they seemed more like one organism than two. He reined his horse off to the right and trotted away as mysteriously as he had arrived, and the bus shook itself back to life. The road stretched ahead like a straight grey ribbon, quivering in the distance as though blown by a breeze. The land dried out the further we advanced into the Chaco, and was covered in thorny shrubs punctuated by hardwood trees, the famous *quebracho*, or axebreaker, used for making tannin.

Every fifty or a hundred miles we would pass an outpost. There would be a rancher's house, a tin-roofed structure, with a few domestic animals nearby, a broken down wooden cart, and the rancher himself sitting listlessly in the shade of a tree; or a barracks forming three sides of a square with a tall flagpost at an angle in the middle, flying the red, white and blue Paraguayan flag. The population density – if that is the word – of the Chaco is less than one person per square mile.

After ten hours we reached Loma Plata (Silver Hill, though I saw no hill), the first of the Mennonite settlements. From there it was only another hour to Filadelfia, the largest of the Mennonite towns in the Chaco.

These settlements are the last thing one expects to find in that arid, dry, thorny part of the world. They are suburbs in a desert. The unpaved but well-graded roads are set out in a perfectly regular grid pattern, each with a German name – like Unruh-strasse – signposted at every junction. The shops are clean and the co-operative store, second only in importance to the church as a social centre, has a scrubbed and polished look. The tiled pavements are meticulously swept, and there are bins marked 'Rubbish' in both German and Spanish everywhere within easy reach. There is no litter in Filadelfia.

I went to the Hotel Florida, a Mennonite-run establishment with a spotless new wing of brick with obsessionally neat pointing. The courtyard was being energetically swept by a fresh-faced German girl who, as I later discovered, fought an unceasing battle against the dust of the Chaco (and won). She asked me whether I spoke German and was surprised that I did not: Filadelfia is not a destination for casual visitors.

It was early evening and I walked round the town. At the

southern exit stood a large concrete monument thrusting up-wards, to commemorate its fiftieth anniversary and to thank God for seeing it through hard times to its present prosperity.

For prosperous it now undoubtedly was. There was not much traffic along its broad and dusty streets, but such as there was consisted of gleaming new Volvos. There were also a few horse-drawn buggies, driven at a trot by stolid red-faced farmers with straw hats, often accompanied by small children in old-fashioned frilly bonnets, white or polka-dotted.

The houses were neat and unpretentious, each with its own vegetable garden and citrus orchard. How had the desert been made so to bloom? Was there a skeleton in the cupboard of protestant righteousness?

I returned to the hotel for dinner, 'Food very plain, and rather expensive' said the *South American Handbook*; but nutritious, it might have added, and teutonically filling. It was served on tables upon which it might have been safe, bacteriologically speaking, to perform operations. The waiter, a fair-haired young man who was efficient rather than friendly, put the plates down in front of me with a slap. I was afraid to ask for a beer lest it offend some religious sensibility, but the restaurant was soon filled with ruddy-faced Mennonite farmers come to drink just that, to which their bellies proclaimed them well used. They laughed with deep baritone guffaws: it could have been Munich.

I had come to Filadelfia in the hope of finding a ride into Bolivia across the Chaco – there were no roads, only tracks, and no public transport – and I asked the waiter whether he knew of anyone leaving for Bolivia. He thought the whole scheme slightly mad; he told me traffic to Bolivia was extremely infrequent, not more than one truck a month, the driver might refuse to take me in any case, and I had much better return to Asunción from where there were regular flights to La Paz, getting there in an hour and a half. I explained that I nevertheless wanted to cross the Chaco, having vowed to myself to make the journey between Rio de Janeiro and Antofagasta overland. This did not increase his estimate of my sanity, and he went to join the sensible farmers.

Next morning I walked round the town again, keeping my eyes open for vehicles with Bolivian registration. There was none, but I was prepared to wait. I loitered under a shady tree next to the schoolhouse, where I listened to flaxen-haired children reciting their lessons by rote in German. Their sweet and innocent voices drifted on the wind, but I could not hear them without a chill. By a prejudice too deep for thought, German is for me ineradicably the language of Hitler and Nazism. The oom-pah-pah laughter of the farmers the night before had seemed to me menacing.

I stood on tiptoe to look in at the classroom. The children concentrated with all their might on the blackboard and on what the teacher was saying. There was no disobedience, no distraction, no premature disillusion with the value of education. The habits of thrift and industry had already been inculcated.

As I walked down a street admiring the heavily-laden grapefruit trees in the gardens, a car drew up beside me.

'Good morning,' said the driver in Spanish.

'Good morning.'

'Where are you from?'

'England.'

'What are you doing here?'

'Just visiting,' I said. 'I'm a tourist.'

The man smiled, but without amusement. His questions were laced with suspicion, and I was being interrogated.

'Just visiting?'

'That's right.'

'Well,' he said, changing to perfect English, 'I've lived in Filadelfia all my life, and I've never met anyone before who's just visiting.'

His eyes narrowed as he looked at me. Perhaps I was researcher, an anthropologist or – worse – a reporter come to spoil their Eden. No-one visited Filadelfia just because it was a name on a map. Perhaps I had come to ferret out Dr Mengele, who was thought to be living in the northern Chaco under an assumed name.* (During the war some of the Mennonites, though sup-

* This was written before the discovery of his body in São Paulo.

posedly pacifists, sympathised with the Nazis and a few even returned to Germany.) Or perhaps I had come to smell out the seamy underside of the Mennonite success story – for the world hates nothing so much as success untouched by the breath of scandal.

'Where are you going from here?'

'I hope to get a lift to Bolivia.'

'You may be waiting a long time. I advise you to go back to Asunción.'

I said nothing. In my turn, I was suspicious.

'What do you do for a living?' he asked next.

'I'm a doctor.'

'Really?' He looked hard at me, implying that I might be lying. I didn't look much like a doctor at the time.

'I work on some Pacific islands of which you've probably never heard – the Gilbert Islands.'

He came to the conclusion that I was probably telling the truth and asked me whether I should like to see Filadelfia's hospital. The doctor in charge spoke fluent English and would be glad to see me. He gave me directions and drove off in a cloud of dust.

The hospital was a little way out of town. Though it was winter the weather was sultry, the rays of sun filtering through ranks of high, furrowed grey cloud, creating a greenhouse kind of heat. I walked down a narrow dusty road between dry fields with cacti dotting their margins. These extraordinary tridentate plants, fifteen feet high, had a pretty yellow flower at the summit of one of the prongs. It seemed an inordinate effort to bring forth such a delicate bloom.

Frogs croaked loudly from ditches that ran alongside the fields. I have always found these amphibians attractive and never understood the disgust they frequently evoke. As a child I had once saved up my pocket money to buy an emerald-green South American tree frog with little foot pads that had captured my heart. I bore him triumphantly home (my mother was less enthusiastic) and put him in an apple tree, from which he promptly fell, to my great chagrin, straight into the jaws of my

ever-hungry dog. I have nurtured tender feelings for frogs ever
since that lamentable day, though I have done my share of dis-
secting them with their hearts still palpitating like an Aztec
sacrifice.

I wanted to see the frogs that were croaking so vociferously in
the Paraguayan ditches, but every time I drew near the croaking
ceased, lest they give away their whereabouts. I pretended to walk
away, but the frogs were not fooled. Whether I crept stealthily or
jumped in a single leap up to the ditch, I never saw more of them
than the bubbles which seemed to mock me breaking the surface
of the brackish water. In the end, I decided the frogs were almost
certainly toads, and gave up.

I reached the hospital grounds. A sign requested silence
though there was no traffic to disturb it. The grounds were
carefully tended, with a fine, neat display of tropical shrubs and
flowers. Through these grounds walked – or rather, marched – a
fearful nurse, best bosom forward, whose face seemed to have
been starched along with her uniform. She carried an almost
visible aseptic zone with her, into which no bacterium dared
enter. Her presence would disinfect Hell itself. No patient would
have the temerity to die under her care.

The doctor was a jovial, middle-aged man who spoke too
colloquial English with a strong American accent. He was a
cardiothoracic surgeon who had spent three years in the United
States learning to perform operations that could not be performed anywhere in Paraguay, let alone Filadelfia. Nevertheless,
he said, it had not been time wasted. It had taught him all he
wanted to know about the colossus of the North. It had taught him
also that the paraphernalia of modern medicine saved fewer lives
than commonly supposed. As he grew older he was less carried
away by the drama of cutting people open, and more interested in
the social and psychological dimensions of disease.

We talked a little of the Mennonites, of whom he was one.
They were a pacifist Baptist sect founded in Germany in the
sixteenth century. By the late nineteenth century they were
concentrated in the Ukraine, whither they had fled to escape

persecution. There they had preserved their language (a kind of low German) and their culture; but the Russian Empire and the Soviet Union quickly became intolerant of nonconformist minorities and the Mennonites fled again, first to Canada and then to Paraguay, which was the only country in the world to accept the community's sick and old as well as its young and healthy. A law passed in Paraguay in 1921 gave them generous concessions:

Members of the Mennonite community who arrive in this country as colonists and their descendants enjoy the following rights and privileges:

i To practise their religion and worship with complete freedom

ii Establish, administer and maintain schools and centres of instruction and teach and learn their religion and language, which is German, with no restriction.

The Mennonites settled in the Chaco from 1927 and for many years the colony teetered on the edge of extinction; riven by internal disagreement, blighted by drought, it was attacked by angry and untamed Moro Indians as late as 1955. But in the 1950s the Mennonite colonies underwent transformation. The farms prospered as no others in Paraguay, though initial conditions were far less auspicious. The Mennonites worked hard; they farmed individually, but sold through a powerful cooperative. Now they produced citrus, cotton, groundnuts, sorghum, maize, manioc and dairy produce.

The Mennonites were no longer simple rustics (he mentioned this with a tinge of regret). It would be difficult to find a more highly-educated community in the world. Everyone spoke both Spanish and German fluently, and most of the children English as well. Some of them were sent north to perfect their English. The Mennonites now had their own doctors, engineers, agronomists; they used the latest developments in solar power and wind energy. The colonies were a model for, and a reproach to, the rest of Paraguay, if not South America.

The heart of it all was a religious vision, however, that was unlikely to be adopted wholesale by the rest of the continent. I asked how many Mennonite children who went for education to the outside world failed to return to what, after all, was a restricted life.

'Very few,' said the doctor. 'What we have here is better than the outside world. We are glad to go there, but we are glad to come back.'

By nature an unbeliever in arcadias, utopian visions, and so forth, I wondered whether there was not a worm in the bud, but the smiling affable countenance of the doctor, exuding competence almost like a secretion, assured me that all was as it seemed in Filadelfia: utterly harmonious, except for very occasional causes of psychiatric disturbance, caused by chemical imbalance in the brain.

But behind every great fortune lies a crime, said Balzac; and the achievements of the Mennonites were not without cost to someone. When they first arrived in the Chaco the Mennonites bought 25,000 kilometres of land from the Argentinian firm of Carlos Casado. To prevent the Indians who happened to inhabit that land from being forced off it without due payment, the Mennonites also bought land from them. 'The price,' said a Mennonite report, 'for a 100 to 150 hectare plot consisted of an old pair of trousers, a few metres of cloth or some provisions. The bill of sale, a piece of paper covered in scribbles and rubber stamped with coloured decorations, was handed to the chief, together with a small gift. He would stuff it into the net bag which all Indians carry – next morning the camp was struck and the plot belonged to the whites.'

Forced off the land everywhere, the Indians had no choice but to work for the Mennonites, on their land and in their factories. Squalid encampments called *Arbeiterlager* (Workers' Camps) have sprung up on the periphery of every Mennonite settlement. For many years the Indian workers were paid in tokens redeemable only in the Mennonite cooperative stores. At least one Indian understood the significance of this:

'They pay us in tokens so we never have real money. We have to buy things in their shops. If we never have money we cannot travel – we cannot go to Asunción to complain about the treatment. We are forced to live like this. We are the property of the Mennonites.'

Soon the numbers of Indians settling round Filadelfia and Loma Plata were much greater than the numbers of workers required by the Mennonites, who realised that the surplus represented a potential physical threat. They decided to settle them on small plots in the central Chaco, converting nomads into 'useful members of the Paraguayan nation. To carry this plan through effectively we are absolutely convinced that the Indians need to be brought up as good Christians and that they must be introduced to the message of God and Jesus Christ.'

Building up backward people in a country is the best defence against communism, said the Minister of Defence.

The Mennonites were not the only people in Filadelfia contending for the souls of the Indians. It was also the local headquarters for the New Tribes Mission, an evangelical society founded in Florida in 1942 with the aim of suburbanising aborigines throughout the world. The battle cry is 'Reaching the lost until we have reached the last' – with the Bible and Coca-Cola.

I met a member of the New Tribes Mission, a middle-aged man who might have been an insurance salesman or a minor official of a bank. Theirs is the kind of religion that requires short haircuts. I asked him why missionaries came to such remote places to convert fragments of the world's population when there were so many unbelievers elsewhere. He said he wanted to give the tribes freedom of choice in religion. Without the missionaries, they would never hear about Jesus Christ. If it was freedom of choice he was interested in, I asked, why not teach them about Islam, Judaism, Hinduism, Buddhism or Shinto as well?

Well, he was a believing Christian, so he would only put the Christian point of view, but if the other religions sent their missionaries it was fine by him – only they didn't.

He had spent eleven years in the Brazilian jungle with a

previously uncontacted tribe. It had taken him all that time to learn the fundaments of the language, unrelated as it was to any other, and by the time he left the work of translating the Bible had just begun. I asked how, for example, one translated the episode of Christ driving the money lenders from the Temple into the language of a people without money or temples.

'They have money and temples now,' he replied.

I asked him how many of his tribe had converted, or 'accepted Christ', in the New Tribes idiom.

'We prefer not to head count,' he said, from which I gathered that the number had not been large.

The missionary told me that the uncontacted Indians of the Chaco were bound sooner or later to meet the advance of civilisation: better they should be contacted first by people concerned for their welfare and eternal souls than by rapacious land-hungry farmers. That, at any rate, is the rationale the New Tribes Mission presents to the world. Sometimes they are more forthright.

'I want to give them the chance to hear the Bible,' said one missionary, ' 'cause if they don't, they go to hell and suffer eternal damnation.' They regard the Chaco as Satan's playground, where what Mr Chadband called 'the light of Ter-ewth' has never shone. Norm and Linda, Jerry and Charlene, Gordie and Nancy, have come all the way to Paraguay from Minnesota, Wisconsin and Idaho to shine that light.

Unfortunately, the poor heathen have shown unmistakable signs of preferring their own darkness to the light of others. The New Tribes Missionaries use aeroplanes to spot bands of uncontacted Indians, who throw their spears at the huge noisy bird to frighten it off. Nothing daunted, the missionaries guide pretamed Indians in by radio – Exocet missionaries as it were – to convert the bands. If the Indians flee they are pursued. The New Tribes' books, published by Brown Gold Publications, tell of hardships overcome to bring hymns and hamburgers to the heathen of field and forest, mountain and plain. Of course, as the books admit freely, once contacted the tribes often nearly die out from measles and other diseases: but what is a few years' sojourn in this vale of woe compared to an eternity of ineffable bliss?

As for destroying a culture, one missionary said: 'Destroying a culture? I should hope so – drunkenness and wild dancing; you know, dancing leads to immorality. The idiots had all this witch-craft, the men would drink and dance all night, then go off into the woods with girls and do their immorality.'

For the New Tribes Mission, the world is but a stage for the struggle between God and Satan. Setbacks are the work of the latter, successes of the former. When a New Tribes Mission plane nearly crashes but doesn't, it is because God is co-pilot. When a missionary is released after having been arrested by a Paraguayan policeman, thanks to the representations of the United States consul to President Stroessner, this too is the work of God rather than power politics.

As missionaries have always done, they conflate power with truth. They tell the Indians that it was God who made them rich, and bribe them with the off-scourings of our factories. One is at the same time awed by the sincerity of these complacent people, who spend years in the uttermost parts of the earth for no material gain, and repelled by their intellectual dishonesty and capacity for self-deception.

I waited several days in Filadelfia for my lift. I explored every corner of the small town amd my figure soon became recognised, a little sinister perhaps because no-one was quite sure what I was doing there. I visited the large and modern Mennonite church, built on the assumption that the entire town would worship there on Sundays. I changed a hundred dollar bill in a small workshop run by a man who resembled exactly Dr Ludwig Erhardt, down to the cigar protruding from the jowls. He did not trust me, thought I might be passing a forgery, but in the end his greed overcame his suspicion.

I spent the afternoons in the garden of the hotel, watching the German girl struggle against the settling dust and reading *Facundo*, a classic work of nineteenth-century Argentine literature by

Sarmiento, later president of his country, which explains the barbarism of Argentina in the years after independence by claiming that the gaucho element of the population predominated over the European. Sarmiento's answer to the problem was more European immigration: with what result, the twentieth century has proved.

I was reading one afternoon when I heard a convoy of trucks grind its way into the town. The noise of the engines mingled with music – the anarchic brass band music of South America. The trucks stopped and the music grew louder. I left the hotel to see what was happening. Units of the Paraguayan Army on their way to the border with Bolivia had stopped off for their band to give a concert for the townsfolk.

There were twenty trucks in all, battered and ancient. The soldiers, except for the few officers, were conscripts, speaking Guaraní for preference. They had the broad features of Indians and looked cheerful enough, though no doubt garrison duty in the Chaco was tedious in the extreme. Their uniforms were scarcely uniform: some had helmets, others capes, yet others no boots. As usual with an army of conscripts – it is part of the army's way of informing them they no longer have personal identities – no attempt had been made to fit the size of the uniform to the size of the soldier.

The band stood in no particular order on a street corner. The other soldiers poured down from the trucks in which they had been uncomfortably confined for several hours, leaving their weapons behind, and walked round the town arm in arm. Some of them were drunk; all the band was drunk.

The recital began. The Mennonites gathered round, from Aryan toddlers to the oldest surviving pioneers of the colony. The bandmaster, a short man whose helmet almost covered his ears, was Mussolini's double, and like Mussolini was given to frantic but unsustained bursts of energy. For some reason, perhaps so as not to offend his sensitivity about his short stature, the largest instruments had been given to the smallest members of the band. Tiny men with huge brass tubas strapped to their belts threatened all the time to topple over (their balance was impaired by drink), while flutes and triangles, on the other hand, had been given to men of over six feet.

Since all South American band music sounds as though it is played by men in a joyful state of inebriation, the drunkenness of the soldiery had no perceptible effect on their musical production. But unmistakable sneers appeared on the faces of the Mennonites. What, they were thinking, could ever be made of a nation like this? A rabble, a drunken mob, given over to the pleasures of the moment.

But I liked them. In the ever longer intervals between pieces, when some of the band lit up cigarettes and others disappeared into the Cooperative store to buy chocolate and other military necessities, yet others singled me out as a true foreigner and swore eternal brotherhood with me. They draped their capes over my shoulders and asked for their photographs to be taken while they embraced me. They laughed and tried to teach me Guaraní. In the meantime Mussolini called them back to a semblance of order for the next piece, but they ignored him even when he jumped in the air with frustration.

Eventually the music started again. As it did so, I was approached by an old colonist with a long moustache, pushing a bicycle with a large basket attached to the handlebars.

'We Germans,' he said in heavily accented Spanish, 'like work. Paraguayans like music.'

He shook his head, but I pointed out that Germans had been known for their musical abilities.

'In its place, in its place,' he said, adding that Paraguayans would never make good colonists.

The music came to an abrupt end, and the conscripts came running out of every corner of the town to clamber back up on to the uncomfortable trucks. In a flurry of dust and thick black exhaust fumes the convoy moved off. The Mennonites waved the protectors of their national patrimony off, and they waved back, but the contempt of the farmers was not well-concealed. Among the privileges the Mennonites enjoy in Paraguay is exemption in perpetuity from military service, a privilege indeed in a country so often ruled by Generals. But I had the impression that the contempt of the Mennonites was not so much for military life in general, as for Paraguayan military life in particular.

Shortly afterwards a blue Ford truck without markings appeared in the town. I suspected it was Bolivian, on a smuggling expedition across the Chaco. There is little trade between Paraguay and Bolivia except for smuggling, and only smugglers trouble to make the slightly hazardous journey along unmarked tracks. No two maps of the Chaco seem to agree on the settlements worth marking: one map has an outpost called Dr. P.P. Peña, another, Mariscal Estigarribia; a third, Fortín Avalos Sánchez. Perhaps they are all ephemeral, and it depends on the year of the map.

I asked a man standing by the truck, whose squint, scarred cheek and growth of black beard gave him a formidable and none too savoury appearance, whether he was, by any chance, going to Bolivia. It was a question too fraught with implications for him to answer.

'I don't know,' he said. 'You'll have to ask the boss.'

I waited for the boss. He was an older man, in his forties, with gold teeth and scars on his cheek also. Knife fights, I thought. He was almost as broad as he was tall.

'Excuse me, señor,' I said. 'Are you going to Bolivia?'

He looked at me with hard, shrewd eyes.

'Why do you want to know?'

'I'm travelling across South America.'

He shrugged. He did not understand pointless journeys. Another man, older and toothless, joined us. He was obviously in awe of his master. He and the first man I had asked started to load boxes on the truck.

'Can I come with you to Bolivia?' I asked. 'I'll pay.'

The owner thought of a series of objections.

'We are crossing where there is no border post,' he said. 'You will enter Bolivia without a stamp in your passport.'

'That is my problem.'

'It is very uncomfortable.'

'I don't mind.'

'There is a general strike against the Government in Bolivia. There are no trains, buses, nothing.'

'I still don't mind.'

He had run out of arguments.

'All right. Be here at five o'clock in the morning.'

I took great pleasure in informing the gloomy Aryan waiter that evening that I had found a lift to Bolivia. He still thought I was quite mad.

As the *South American Handbook* recommends that anyone undertaking the journey across the Chaco should take at least a week's supply of food with him, I went to the Cooperative store and bought a sackful of Germano-Paraguayan sausage, cheese, grapefruit, rolls and chocolate.

Next morning I woke up without prompting before dawn. It was cold in the back of the truck, among the contraband whisky and other goods. There were also empty petrol drums: the goods had been exchanged for Bolivian petrol. The road was rough and I was buffeted from drums to whisky and back again, so that by the end of the journey I was covered in a multitude of small bruises.

I shivered with cold and cursed the sun for not rising sooner, though I knew that later in the day I should pray as earnestly for the cool of the night. I debated with myself whether it was better to die of heat or cold, inevitably coming to the conclusion while I was still cold that a heat death was preferable. The lines of Frost kept revolving in my head:

> Some say the world will end in fire,
> Some say in ice.
> From what I've tasted of desire
> I hold with those who favour fire.

The truck was driven without regard for the ruts in the road. A fine red dust soon penetrated my belongings, so that even my toothpaste became gritty. But the road out of Filadelfia was a super highway compared with what came later.

After two hours, with the sun up but warming nothing, we reached Mariscal Estigarribia, a military station which, many hours and kilometres as it was from the border with Bolivia, served as a border post for Paraguay. It was forlorn, the kind of place where men shoot themselves for something to do. It was little more than a clearing in the scrub, leaving a large expanse of dry brown ground. On one side was the commanding officer's house, simple but luxurious by the place's standards, with a verandah facing the parade ground. Fifty yards away was a barn-like edifice – the barracks. Facing both was a large hoarding with a faded picture of President Stroessner and an exhortation to vote for him in the election of four years ago. In Paraguay, exhortations to vote in past and future elections are equally sensible, since the results of both are known with great certainty.

In the middle of the parade ground was a bust of Mariscal Estigarribia, the Parguayan hero of the Chaco War. By the time this war broke out in 1932 the two countries had been squabbling for years over the sovereignty (the legal experts on both sides of the dispute were known as *Doctores en Chaco*). The Bolivians, on account of the superior resources and German advisers, amongst whom was Ernst Röhm, future leader of the S.A., were generally expected to win; but the Bolivian officer class proved so venal and incompetent that the Paraguayans were able to gain victory after victory. So Paraguay won most of the Chaco, at a cost of two Paraguayan and three Bolivian dead per square mile, far more than it has ever supported as mere inhabitants. Most of them died of thirst or typhoid rather than in combat, and the war bankrupted Paraguay for many years. Many South American intellectuals, always with a weakness for conspiracy theories, believe that the war was a conflict by proxy between Shell and Standard Oil, whose concessions were in Paraguay and Bolivia respectively. The truth hardly matters any more: it is always a comfort to know that one's worst and most senseless behaviour is really attributable to others. So far, no oil has been found in the Chaco.

The soldiers of the garrison were engaged on important tasks such as cleaning the ground around the flagpole (it was clean already), painting some steps white (they were white already), and drowning some plants in a sparse flower bed. The commanding officer, *el teniente*, was not yet up, and we could not proceed until he had inspected us personally. In the meantime his deputy, a sergeant, showed an unhealthy interest in my camera.

'Es muy linda, muy linda,' he said. It's very nice, very nice, he said, caressing it as though it were a woman. He asked me how much it had cost: he was hatching a plot against it. I had already resigned myself to its loss – all the other soldiers agreed it was very nice – when the boss of the smugglers whispered something in the ear of the sergeant, and he gave back the camera immediately.

El teniente, in the meantime, had stirred. It was nearly nine o'clock. He appeared in his pyjamas, testing the morning air like a man tests the winter sea before plunging in. He came to the railing of the verandah, surveyed Mariscal Estigarribia, yawned, stretched, and went back to bed.

We waited. I wandered into the barracks: the whole place smelled of urine. It was spartan, with rows of iron bedsteads without mattresses. The conscripts were greeted each morning by a painted slogan near the entrance:

GENERAL OF THE ARMY AND PRESIDENT OF THE REPUBLIC
HIS MOST EXCELLENCY DON ALFREDO STROESSNER
RENOWNED LEADER OF THE STRUGGLE AGAINST WORLD
COMMUNISM

On a table was a cassette, entitled 'Canción A Mi General', song to my general.

Eventually, at ten o'clock, el teniente emerged for the day, definitively clad. He was well-groomed and refreshed, and started to issue orders to anyone in his line of sight.

The boss was obviously a friend of his and a business associate. They passed the time of day, asked about each other's families, cracked a few jokes. I was the only one with a passport, which was duly stamped. Our delay had been more social than bureaucratic.

After Mariscal Estigarribia the road rapidly grew rougher. The warmth of the day made me remember the cold of the night with affection. Soon we were bumping along little more than a track that ran like a scar through the scrub. I was buffeted more than ever, and clung to the sides breathing clouds of dust. Only occasional stops for *yerba maté* provided relief.

'You can come down now, meestah,' said the toothless man. 'You want some *maté*, meestah?'

Every sentence he addressed to me ended with meestah.

'Any complaints, meestah?' he asked eagerly, delighted that they were giving me a rough ride.

'No,' I replied, disappointing them.

I shared my food with them and rose in their estimation. I explained I had brought enough for a week.

'Why?' they asked.

I told them what the *South American Handbook* said. They slapped their sides with laughter.

'We know every kilometre, every metre, of the Chaco,' said the boss. 'We were born here, we have lived here all our lives, we know every tree, every animal. We can never be lost. We will be in Bolivia tomorrow morning – 1000 pesos for you if we are not.' (I later discovered how small a sum 1000 pesos was).

On both sides of the track the scrub was thorny and impenetrable. Without a machete it would have been impossible to go more than a few yards. The leaves of the shrubs were grey-green and thick for the conservation of water, and the firewood for brewing the maté could be hacked directly from the bushes There are peccaries, tapirs, pumas and jaguars in the Chaco (and the New Tribes Mission ran a successful business in jaguar pelts), but we saw none.

I expressed surprise, during the stop for maté, that smugglers should be so friendly with the commanding officer of a border garrison. They laughed at me again.

'Señor,' said the boss, 'everyone in Paraguay is a smuggler.'

So it seems. If contraband were included in Paraguay's trade figures, they would at least double in size. The government is said to have an attitude of 'lucrative connivance'. It is believed that

President Stroessner, 'that great Christian' as General Lemnitzer once called him when he received a present from him, rewards loyal servants with concessions to smuggle certain items, such as radios or whisky, etc. I was seeing merely the self-employed smuggler at work.

We drove endlessly on. At every branch in the track – all unmarked, of course – the driver knew without hesitation which direction to take. We stopped for lunch at a totally isolated adobe house, kept by a woman and a small child who limped. She was expecting us, and served a meal of scrawny chicken (all feet and neck), rice with gravel, and tomato salad. Intense was my disappointment when she brought forth bottles of Coca-Cola – at last, I had thought, I must have reached somewhere beyond the empire of the Real Thing.

The smugglers changed the last of my Paraguayan money for me into Bolivian pesos. Remembering the exchange rates of twelve months before, I was surprised at the generous pile of notes I received in return. Were they mistaken or overgenerous? They did not look the types to make mistakes over money, and I subsequently learnt that they had fleeced me unmercifully.

The longest leg of our journey was after lunch. We drove for fifteen hours without a break. The landscape was monotonously the same for what must have been hundreds of miles. Shrubs, cacti, quebrachos. When darkness fell, and I longed once more for the heat, I lay down among the oil drums and tried to sleep. It was fitful and punctuated by collisions with contraband and dreams like surrealist South American novels: an already dead and bloated President Stroessner, a rainbow of medals pinned across his white tunic, drove me into Bolivia amongst crates containing cocaine. His corpse was arrested over the border and I was appointed his defence lawyer, against charges of crimes against humanity. I made an impassioned speech to the comatose judge: my client had brought stability and even a measure of prosperity to the country. Paraguay had no tradition of democracy or freedom under the law, I said; acquittal was the only just verdict.

The judge woke up, sentenced Stroessner's corpse to be hanged, and ordered the citizens of Asunción to howl abuse at it. There was no excuse, he said, for immersing one's enemies in baths of excrement.

Past midnight, unseen, we entered Bolivia.

NINE

Bolivia

A<small>T ABOUT</small> four in the morning, lying in the bottom of the truck, I saw through a haze of dust and sleep that we had arrived in a dimly lit town. The boss went into a single-storey adobe house to sleep, while the two others climbed up beside me in the back of the truck.

'Sleep, meestah, sleep.'

But not for long. Two hours later, with the sun just rising and filling the world with a watery light, one of the men pummelled me awake.

'Adiós, meestah, adiós.'

I climbed out of the truck into the still-sleeping town of Villa Montes. One or two thin dogs had awoken, their ribs like an abacus, and were already engaged on their day's work: sifting the dust for something edible. Beyond the town rose some green hills, the first I had seen – I realised with a shock – since leaving Asunción two weeks and five hundred miles ago.

I wandered aimlessly in the town until I came across a man in a greasy homburg hat, of whom I asked the way to the police station. There was no police station in Villa Montes, he said, only the army barracks. I went there instead to have my passport stamped.

At the barracks, a miscellaneous collection of structures, I asked a sentry behind some railings whether there was anyone about who could do the necessary. I was too early, he said; I should have to wait for the sergeant to come on duty at seven o'clock. He settled down to the remains of a self-rolled cigarette, while I sat down on a ledge reading *Facundo*, my head filled with unsatisfied sleep.

I heard a rustle of activity behind me. A brass band was forming, of the most diverse and unmartial elements. Some men had protruberant bellies; others looked on the verge of starvation. All had different uniforms. One had an asthmatic wheeze, while several had the red eyes of nocturnal alcoholic over-indulgence. They looked at the world blearily, without enthusiasm.

The barrack gates were opened and the band, with as much disorder as if they had been fleeing from some enemy, stumbled out. Within a few seconds of each other they started to play – a kind of military jam session. As they marched into the town they fell over one another and over pebbles in the road, but somehow they kept playing and their music had that strange uplifting quality that brings joy to the heart. They were Villa Montes' collective alarm clock, marching round the town to tell the inhabitants it was time they were up and doing nothing. Gradually people emerged from their houses, standing at the side of the roads staring vacantly. The band, having awakened the town, marched back to the barracks still playing. As they reached the gates they stood to attention and started to play what sounded like a medley from an unknown Donizetti opera. A man approached me to tell me that I should stand up too – it was the Bolivian national anthem. Everyone stood stiffly erect and the driver of the only vehicle in sight, a large truck, got out of the cab and stood to attention beside it. An intense, deep and uniting patriotism stirred briefly in Villa Montes, which one could not but respect. The idea of a Bolivia unsullied by the venality of governments remained alive.

The anthem over – it was by far the longest anthem I ever heard – the intensity of the moment was dispelled. Mediocrity, futility descended. The band unstrapped its instruments and disintegrated. I went to find the sergeant.

He was in an office, behind some frosted glass. He was reluctant to admit that he was on duty because to do so could only mean trouble. I explained why I had come and he took my proffered passport. He looked at it very carefully but with some caution, as though it might jump. He turned it round in his hands and flipped it over, and back again; then he opened it and examined each page minutely, sometimes upside down. After what seemed a long time, he asked:

'Are you Paraguayan?'

My patience ebbed suddenly. I decided he was a man more used to taking orders than using initiative, so I pointed to the rubber stamp on his desk and told him where to use it. He obeyed my orders with the expression of a whipped dog. The stamp said, *Third Division of the Army Villa Montes.*

Having now legally entered Bolivia I went in search of an hotel. The only one in town was the Hotel el Rancho, about a mile down a pebbly road, near the railway station. It was not very inviting: a long row of wooden rooms with cracks between them and communal washing facilities where the hotel laundry was also done. I asked for a room with a shower of its own.

'No hay,' said the proprietress (There aren't any), with lugubrious satisfaction.

The charge for the room was 200 pesos a night. Remembering that last year the peso stood at 24 to the dollar, the charge of $8.66 for such a room seemed excessive. It was only when I discovered that the peso had slipped to 250 to the dollar (it was soon to slip much further) that I realised the charge was reasonable. While the peso had declined 1000 per cent, the rate of inflation in the same period had been 'only' 200 per cent, making everything a fifth the price (for foreigners).

The proprietress spent all day sitting behind the bar reading sub-Spillane thrillers with lurid covers. Next to her stood a half-witted servant, at whom she barked her orders. Aware of her monopoly position, she took pleasure in denying all requests: 'No hay.' All that was available was a thin coffee essence with colour but no taste perceptible.

Among the Bolivians Villa Montes is known for two things: the highest temperature ever recorded in Bolivia, and an unsuccessful siege by the Paraguayans at the end of the Chaco War. Among the besiegers was a brave young man called Alfredo Stroessner.

Villa Montes was stagnant, as though in some kind of purgatory. The only sign of life in the main plaza was the click of balls
which drifted on the air from a billiard hall. A few days in Villa
Montes make one contemplate the fundamental questions of
existence.

I went to the station to buy a ticket for the weekly train from
Yacuiba just over the border in Argentina to Santa Cruz de la
Sierra. (The general strike was over.) Buying a ticket turned out
to be nearly a full-time occupation. The stationmaster who sold
the tickets was not present at the times advertised and no-one
knew where he was. When finally I ran him to ground, in a bar, he
said he had no tickets, which was odd because the weekly train
was the only train to come through his station. I had to go to the
station five times before he conceded defeat.

The train, when it came, was full not only of passengers but of
their goods: sacks of flour, rice, sugar, and buckets of freshly
hacked quivering meat. I picked my way down the carriage until
my way was blocked, and sat down on a sack. Four mestiza women
on either side of me were very concerned for my welfare and
insisted on yielding their seats to me by turns, though two of them
were old enough to be my grandmother. They were worried that,
as an effete gringo, I was unused to discomfort; and fearing for my
imminent demise by hunger, gave me a larger portion of their
cooked food than they took for themselves.

All the passengers on the train were returning to Santa Cruz
from Yacuiba, having undertaken the thousand-mile round
journey to buy staple foods in Argentina that, thanks to Bolivia's
perpetual economic crisis, were not available in Bolivia. Their
journey had been a great success, having relieved them of anxiety
about food supplies for some time to come, and there was a festive
atmosphere on board the carriage. The passengers by Bolivian
standards were neither poor nor rich but of the middling sort.

The four mestiza women asked me with great interest what I
did for a living. I told them I was a doctor. They asked me whether
I was married. I told them I was not.

'¡Madre mia!' exclaimed one of them crossing herself and beginning a fervent prayer addressed to St Anthony.

She was fat and what the Americans would call homely. In her middle thirties, she had not yet found a husband. To be an unmarried woman in Bolivia at her age was not a comfortable position.

'You do not know why she is praying to St Anthony, señor?' said one of her companions.

'St Anthony is the patron saint of spinsters,' I said.

A gringo heathen was not expected to possess such indispensable knowledge, and the carriage erupted into raucous laughter.

'A gringo doctor would make a good husband, señor.'

'St Anthony,' said the spinster, 'can work miracles. If you pray hard enough and have faith.'

A lively discussion concerning St Anthony's supernatural powers ensued, embracing the whole carriage. Two parties formed: those who thought he did, and those who thought he didn't, work miracles. But even those who thought he didn't work miracles thought he *ought* to: they spoke with the bitterness of thwarted devotion, like Doña Pascuala in W.H.Hudson's *Far Away And Long Ago*:

St Anthony was the saint she was devoted to, and she had taken his image from its place in her bedroom and tied a string round its legs and let it down the well and left it there with its head in the water. He was her own saint, she said, and after all her devotion to him, and all her candles and flowers, this was how he treated her! It was all very well, she told her saint, to amuse himself by causing the rain to fall for days and weeks just to find out whether men would be drowned or turn themselves into frogs to save themselves: now she, Doña Pascuala, was going to find out how *he* liked it. There, with his head in the water, he would have to hang in the well until the weather changed.

Suddenly the atmosphere in the carriage changed. The temperature seemed to drop and a chilly silence descended. At the far end of the carriage four men had entered, dressed casually but with leather holsters and cartridge belts (half-empty, I noted).

'Who are those men?' I whispered.

'Customs,' came a staccato answer.

'This is the third time they have come,' whispered someone behind me. 'Each time a different group.'

The leader of the men, in a red shirt and jeans, was poking a sack in the luggage rack. He pulled it down roughly on to the floor.

'It's rice, only rice,' said the owner, an elderly woman.

'Four hundred pesos,' said the man, leaving the sack on the floor for others to replace.

'But I've already . . . '

'Four hundred pesos,' he repeated without expression.

The woman paid, and the man put the four red notes – bearing the portrait of Simón Bolívar, the Liberator – into his pocket.

The men moved slowly down the carriage, extorting as they came. Occasionally a squabble broke out, but it was always resolved in the men's favour. By the time they reached the couple behind us their pockets were bulging and completely full of banknotes. One of them had found a polythene bag into which to put further exactions.

The couple behind us had decided to fight iniquity. The wife did all the talking: the obverse of *machismo* is outward respect for women. The husband sat tight-lipped, humiliated by his own silence.

'We are poor people,' she said. 'We have gone to Argentina only to find food for ourselves.'

The customs men were unmoved. There were many poor people in Bolivia, mostly too poor even to go to Argentina.

'Six hundred pesos.'

'We are poor people . . .'

The leader signalled with an exasperated sigh to his men to confiscate the couple's goods. They started to collect them.

'It's robbery,' the woman screamed, losing control of herself. 'Locusts! Thieves! Bastards!'

'Are you going to pay, or are we going to take your things?'

asked the leader with studied impassivity.

'Never!' she screamed. 'Never!'

But in the end she paid, just like the others, though 100 pesos less than originally demanded.

The customs men passed me by without so much as seeing me. When they had gone the passengers gradually recovered their gaiety, and laughed when they recalled St Anthony and his miracles. But when a fourth group of customs men came through the carriage extorting yet more money, their equanimity was destroyed for good. A fifth group did not come : they would have been torn limb from limb, guns or no.

The train drew into Santa Cruz several hours late, by a series of violent jerks. The town was in darkness. A single shot cleaved the silence in two.

Santa Cruz was founded in 1561 by an expedition sent out from Paraguay and has remained both a frontier town and ethnically distinct from the rest of Bolivia ever since. Until the 1950s, when the Americans built a road to Cochabamba, it was cheaper to transport goods from Europe to La Paz than from Santa Cruz to La Paz. General Hugo Banzer, while he was president, had a plan to populate the surrounding country with sturdy Boer and Rhodesian farmers.

Santa Cruz had boomed of late, founded on the triple pillars of agriculture, oil and cocaine. It had a reputation for being wild (there is a discotheque called Mau Mau).

The streets have raised and colonnaded sidewalks which induce a cowboy swagger in male pedestrians. There is a wild west atmosphere, a combustible amalgam of impermanence, self-confidence and apprehension.

For these were not good days in Santa Cruz. The Bolivian military government, nearly at the end of its tether, was having to make a show of suppressing the cocaine traffic to gain American loans and credits. The greatest consumer of cocaine in the world had long sought to deprive 100,000 Bolivian producers of their livelihood, on moral grounds. In 1976 Dr Kissinger, who once called South America a dagger pointing at the heart of Antarctica, because 'the axis of history' did not pass through it (a remark more illuminating of Dr Kissinger than of history), flew to Santa Cruz to offer President Banzer $2 million for training the Bolivian police in drug work and $45 million to induce cocaine farmers to grow tomatoes instead. Unfortunately, President Banzer was one of the biggest *narcotraficantes* of all, as everyone knew except Dr Kissinger. When 300 kilos of cocaine were found on Banzer's estancia, all he could find to say was that *someone* must have been using his estancia for illegal purposes.

The Bolivian government, however, was now taking desultory measures to earn the goodwill of the United States. Worst of all for Santa Cruz, the narcotraficantes had fallen out amongst themselves, bringing death and fear to the streets. Abraham Baptista, an army officer who threatened to reveal the connection between the trade and the army because he had been excluded from it, was shot dead outside a pizzeria in the centre of the city. Colonel Emilio Arabe's aircraft had exploded on takeoff. And just before my arrival 'Mosca' (The Fly) Monroy was shot dead on the street.

The days of the murky right-wing terrorist squads that crawled out of the woodwork in Santa Cruz in the wake of the 1980 military coup were not yet over. Klaus Barbie, the SS Butcher of Lyon, still maintained an apartment there. Joachim Fiebelkorn, a young West German psychopath with Nazi ideas, who once worked as a bodyguard to Roberto Suárez Gómez, the doyen of the cocaine trade with a fortune of over $300 million, had formed a gang called *Los Novios de la Muerte*, the Grooms of Death, with a former SS man, Hans Stellfeld, and García Meza's Comptroller-General of the Republic, Adolfo Ustárez. In its officially sponsored reincarnation as the Special Commando Group it terrorised the city for many months.

Also living in Santa Cruz at the time were Stefano delle Chiae and Pierluigi Pagliai, the men who were responsible for eighty-four deaths in the Bologna Station bomb explosion. Pagliai was later shot in the street while delle Chiae escaped to Argentina. It was remarked that where Chile had the Chicago boys of the Milton Friedman school, Bolivia had the Chicago boys of the Al Capone school.

I went therefore with some trepidation to a bank to change fifty dollars. I half-expected a raid. I stood amazed as the teller counted out fifty peso notes (the hundred peso notes were finished for the day, he said). A huge pile built up. The government, believing in an even cruder form of monetarism than that prevailing in some other countries, had refused to acknowledge the fact of inflation and devaluation by printing larger denomination notes. It was good business for the printers, Thomas de le Rue of London, but somewhat inconvenient for me. I had to return to my hotel to find a suitable bag in which to carry my money away.

I sat in the Plaza 24 de Septiembre for several days watching Santa Cruz go by, before moving on. Young men in supercharged American cars used the square as a race track, brakes squealing and tyres burning, to impress young women. Men with macho gaits, women with stiff lacquered coiffures, cripples with shrivelled legs walking on their outstretched arms, and Mennonites, the men in blue denim dungarees and straw hats, the women in floral printed frocks and headscarves, went by. A lone leper sat by the entrance of the pleasant but undistinguished red brick cathedral, begging alms of the pious. I noticed that more gave on the way out than on the way in.

I went to buy a ticket for Cochabamba at the bus station. It was near the airport: the aircraft seemed to rise directly from among the houses, shaking the ground like an earth tremor. The Boeings were used, among other purposes, for transporting political opponents to La Paz where, at el Alto, they were bundled into waiting ambulances and rushed to prison for emergency torture. As the aircraft seemed to hover overhead I wondered whether there were involuntary passengers on board.

The booking office clerk, a mestizo with silver teeth, told me there were no tickets available for Cochabamba for at least a week. I walked away with naive disappointment.

The clerk rushed out of his cubicle after me.

'Señor,' he said. 'My brother is travelling tonight. He is going to Cochabamba.'

'A fortunate coincidence,' I said.

'Perhaps I could persuade him to go another day.' He pulled a ticket from his pocket. 'This is his ticket.'

'How much?' I asked.

'Well, of course he would want a tip,' said the clerk. 'For the inconvenience.'

'Of course. How much would compensate him?'

'As you like, señor.'

He was grateful I accepted his story with good grace and read him no lectures about the evils of corruption. The ticket to Cochabamba cost less than a dollar, the tip still less.

I took the ticket and walked away.

'Buen viaje, señor,' said the clerk with some feeling. 'Buen viaje.'

The bus left at twilight and was uncomfortably full. No-one merely travels on a South American bus: they move house and start a poultry farm at the other end as well. The double seat to which I was allocated was three-quarters occupied by the wide buttocks of a *campesina*, so that I was left to cling precariously on the edge for the overnight journey.

From Santa Cruz to Cochabamba there is a climb of seven thousand feet, but complete darkness soon obscured the view. It was too early to sleep and my companion wanted to talk. She spoke Castilian hesitantly, for Quechua was her mother tongue. She grumbled about the price of everything now, saying that life was becoming harder all the time. Her husband was a tin miner at the Siglo Veinte mine, formerly owned by the Patiños, but now nationalised. He would die, she said, like all the other miners, before he reached pensionable age; whereafter she and her seven children would be turned out of the company house to fend for themselves as best they could. For the privilege of dying of silicosis and tuberculosis before he was forty (his wife looked well past that age already) he was paid twenty-four dollars a month.

I wanted to ask why, then, he still worked down the mine. Were things in Bolivia really so bad that a fatal job in the mines was better than any alternative? I did not ask my question, for fear of sounding ignorant and callow.

'Where you live, señor, do you earn more than my husband?'

My heart contracted with guilt. I was travelling out of curiosity, to relieve boredom, to assuage my restlessness; but my journey was costing more than her husband would earn in *ten years* in the bowels of the earth, if he survived that long.

'A little,' I replied.

'More than . . .' She named a sum equivalent to thirty dollars a month.

'More than that.'

She tutted. If I was rich, why was I taking the bus rather than flying? Why spend a whole night in the discomfort of a bus when I could finish the journey in comfort in half an hour? It was something I could not explain, nor she ever understand. To have replied that I had vowed to cross South America from sea to shining sea overland would only have mystified her.

'The bus is cheaper,' I said.

She understood that.

We stopped at a small town with a half-lit main street for a meal. Most of the passengers entered the rather unwholesome café with enthusiasm, lapping up the greasy grey soup with a thousand slurps. Cheap as the meal was, not all could afford it; those who could not stayed outside, in light that flickered because of the moths that danced round the shadeless bulbs, and bought stale fried snacks that children brought to the nightly bus to Cochabamba.

After dinner my companion made occasional conversation (she had eaten only snacks) while snores began to issue from the back of the bus. Suddenly she let out a piercing scream which woke the sleepers with a start.

'I've lost my purse!' she shrieked. 'I've lost my purse!'

The passengers made to look for it, under the seats, among the chickens, through the cases and bedrolls. They weren't interested in her purse, but they wanted to stop her shrieking.

Then, when it was not found, she started to moan softly. It had contained forty pesos – about fifteen cents – and her husband would beat her for having lost it. (Fifteen cents was an hour underground.) Her sobs were punctuated by convulsive vibrato indrawings of breath. I felt sorry for her, but embarrassed by my own feelings. I hesitated to offer to replace the lost money, lest she be deeply offended. In the end, I plucked up the courage to tender a fifty peso note.

'Please take it,' I said. 'I don't need it.'

She looked at it for a mere fraction of a second, and in one movement removed it from my grasp and stuffed it down the front of her dress.

'Thank you, señor,' she said.

But her gratitude proved short-lived. She was thinking.

'I think there were a hundred pesos in the purse.'

I handed her more money in admiration for her peasant cunning. She said I was very kind, and then we both caught what sleep we could.

Light streaked the grey sky with brilliant silver when I woke; the hills to the east of Cochabamba glowed a rich red-brown; and the valleys between them unfolded deep fertile green as the day gathered strength.

My companion suddenly began to wail again. The keys to her house, she said, had been in her purse, and without them she would be locked out of her own home, perhaps for ever. Not only that, but they had been made recently at a cost of two thousand pesos. She said her husband might leave her for so grievous an offence.

'What shall I do?' she wailed. 'What shall I do?'

I decided against making good the supposed loss of the keys, lest she discover something else was missing. She sobbed quietly all the rest of the way to Cochabamba. When the bus stopped, as everyone gathered up their belongings, she asked me whether her keys were in my bag. Then she accused me in front of the other passengers of having stolen them. Why else should a complete stranger give her a hundred pesos than to keep her quiet? She demanded that I go with her to the nearest police station. I walked away, leaving her screaming her maledictions. I resolved next time to stifle any incipient inclinations to generosity.

I took a room in an hotel in the city centre – one of Cochabamba's best, but still less than three dollars a night. The dining room in which I had breakfast was a cold and gloomy chamber, the waiters almost petrified by cold, far more intense inside than out. I fled the ubiquitous Bolivian coffee essence into the sunny Calle España outside, down which floated the joyous music of a brass band.

I followed the direction of the music and emerged into the city's beautiful central plaza, where a ceremony was taking place at the foot of a column surmounted by a fierce stone eagle, the noble emblem of the enfeebled Bolivian state. The square had a mediterranean savour, with graceful palms and trees ablaze with purple and crimson blooms. The cathedral overlooked the square, another side of which was a splendid colonial arcaded building. The air was pleasantly warm in the sun.

I approached the column. There were two crowds there, an inner and an outer circle. The inner was composed of men and women of European cast. The women – in the majority – seemed overdressed, in expensive suits with elaborate lacework frills at the cuffs and collar. They wore glossy high-heeled shoes, particularly inconvenient for those of portly figure, as most of them were, and their fingers were ringed by gold and jewels. They wore competitive strings of pearls around the neck, and their heavily-applied makeup began to glisten and run in the strong rays of the sun. Mere onlookers, the outer circle was composed entirely of mestizo men, impassive and incurious. The brass band also was mestizo, conducted by a man with the self-important air of a trusted servant.

The speeches began when the music stopped. It was a ceremony to commemorate the founding of the city 440 years before. A rather stentorian lady with a stiffly lacquered coiffure that it would have taken a hurricane to disarrange stepped forth to declaim a message of congratulation from the ladies of Santa Cruz 'on Cochabamba's day of glory', a message flown that very morning from the sister city. The message was grandiloquent, rhetorical flourish completely overwhelming content. Cochabamba, said the ladies of Santa Cruz, had played an heroic part in the wars of Independence, when during a siege the ladies of the city had stood alone against the armed might of Spain, to bring forth a new republic of freedom and justice. A wreath was laid and the national anthem struck up, sung with tremulous but unharmonious emotion by the ladies of Cochabamba.

The anthem over, the band was told by one of the ladies to march round in a small circle playing music to which they might dance. But the dancing was not a success. The men of the inner circle were disinclined to exercise while the ladies were inhibited by their clothes (I suspected the presence of corsets) and a desire to avoid scuffing their shoes. The dancing came to a disorganised end. The band was told to clear off and retreated playing a march, like the defiant remnant of a defeated army; the speechmakers melted away in search of their buffet lunch; while the outer circle of mestizos stayed on, as though expecting something else to happen.

I bought *Los Tiempos* – a Cochabambino newspaper – and sat to read it on one of the benches in the square. It contained an anti-British tirade by a Bolivian lawyer. He inveighed against the evils of colonialism, though I should have said its effects were more to be seen in Cochabamba than on the Falklands' blasted rocks. I wondered whether the British consul would attempt a rebuttal – he lived in the Calle Obispo, in a rather seedy flat – or whether, with the ineffable superiority of British diplomats, he would retain a dignified silence in reply to the ravings of excitable Latins. Subsequent days in Cochabamba proved that he chose the latter course.

A young mestizo sat down on the bench beside me and asked where I was from.

'England,' I said.

'Why did the English kill so many Argentinians?'

Somewhat reluctantly, and wearily, I put the British case and for the first time Roberto, my interlocutor, realised there was such a thing. He asked me whether I should like to see his home, where that afternoon there was to be a gathering of his friends.

We caught a bus, a small vehicle with what seemed like a friendly face. We rattled through the narrow central streets, with overhanging eaves, soon reaching the semi-countryside. Cochabamba is in a valley amidst hills as high as the Alps, but the climate is mild and the soil fertile, making it the most agreeable place in Bolivia to live.

We stopped at a place where the road, for long a mere rubble track, petered out. We sat on some rocks in a pleasant landscape of smallholdings, each with its house of grey-brown mud, separated by cypress trees. The rims of the hills formed an amphitheatre around us. Roberto's arrangements to meet his friends were vague as to both time and location, bespeaking a man less than fully employed. He was a student, he said, but for lack of funds was unattached to any particular educational institution. He wanted to study literature but there was no future in it. He might try a bank or an insurance agency, if a vacancy occurred. We sat on the rocks for two hours, talking of Bolivian literature, of which I knew nothing.

His friends arrived and I was introduced as Roberto's good friend from England. We walked down a lane to Roberto's house. On either side of the lane were cypress trees; ducks paddled in the water-filled potholes; there were goats and a few sheep, fields of wheat and fruit trees. The sun was warm without being oppressive, the scenery beautiful without confronting you with your own insignificance, and the breeze balmy. Like all casual visitors to a rural idyll, I praised it extravagantly, but Roberto and his friends wanted desperately to remove to town, to live in shanties with the offchance of electricity, to join the cadres of vendors of matches and chiclets and lottery tickets and shoelaces and cheap jumping toys which nobody wants in what economists euphemistically call the informal economy.

Roberto's house was the same as the others, dark inside with cheap prints of the Virgin attached to the walls. We sat outside and Roberto suddenly grew ashamed of his own poverty. (He had insisted, though, on paying my busfare.) As guest of honour, he presented me with a warm beer which I did not want but had to drink.

We talked of Bolivia's future. The military regime was completely isolated, without any social support whatsoever. General Vildoso, who had replaced General Torrelio, who had replaced General García Meza, was by no means a democrat but he had announced elections in October as a way of putting an end to the perpetual political crisis and continual general strikes. Some of Roberto's friends expected much of the forthcoming democratic government, others, more circumspect, nothing at all. Was not Bolivia's very instability (there was one memorable day in 1978 when it had six presidents in the course of twenty-four hours), a form of stability in disguise? After all, nothing changed except the government. Democracy or dictatorship, the same poverty and oppression prevailed.

I left them soon afterwards. I had an appointment in Cochabamba, I said; besides which, my presence constrained them. Polite as they were, they did not wish to talk without including me in their conversation, but to do so they had to use formally correct and clearly enunciated language – a limited instrument, at best. We exchanged addresses, swore eternal friendship, and I returned to the bus stop at the end of the lane.

My appointment was an evening piano recital given in the Palacio de Cultura by a young Cochabambino pianist home from his studies at the Warsaw Conservatoire. The recital commenced almost simultaneously with a pornographic film – *Nights of Love* – shown at the cinema next door. The film drew the bigger crowd, of different social composition. Those who came to listen to Mozart, Bach and Chopin were those who had laid wreaths and made speeches on Cochabamba's Day of Glory, while the cinema-goers were those who had stood watching, condemned apparently to repeated acts of voyeurism.

The élite of the city, dressed in furs and other finery, had come, one felt, as much out of social obligation to be seen as out of love of music. The pianist was introduced to the audience with a long rhetorical speech by a man with the goatee beard of an intellectual, the local poet perhaps. The whole city was proud, he said with pardonable overstatement, of its favoured son who had won a scholarship against the stiffest competition from all over the world to the famed Warsaw Conservatoire (there was no mention of political differences). The young pianist, he continued, was certain one day to make an immense contribution to the country's cultural life. Just as everyone thought his speech was over he began to eulogise tonight's composers: they had echoed round the world and down the ages, they had devoted themselves selflessly to the sacred cause of art, they were inextinguishable ardent flames burning in the eternal pantheon of liberators of the human spirit. Before he had finished, everyone began to cough and yawn.

The pianist was a nervous young man who had far outgrown his native city. He played his music with scant regard for the applause of his audience, for he knew much better than they how much or how little he deserved it. Few as such recitals were in Cochabamba, the auditorium was two-thirds empty.

On succeeding days I wandered the city. The three poles of my wanderings were the market called La Concha (the Shell), the best bookshop in Bolivia, and a restaurant where a four-course lunch cost forty cents. Near the market was a flour mill where every morning a long queue of Indian women formed, with babies strapped to their backs by colourful striped blankets, to receive the government ration of flour at a controlled price.

In the market I was seized by the strange delirium that eventually lays hold of all foreigners in South America – the need to haggle. It is fear of looking foolish by paying more than necessary that provokes it, though the sums of money involved are trifling. After much agonizing soulsearching, I bought some strongly but crudely fashioned silverware – for three dollars. I was not entirely comfortable in La Concha. Once again I saw men and women used as beasts of burden, the women carrying bouquets of live chickens tied by their feet and slung over their shoulders, the men with huge baskets of vegetable produce whose weight bent them double. I received many hostile looks: people do not like to be part of a living ethnographical museum for the idly curious.

In the evenings I went to *peñas*, clubs at which Bolivian music was played with wild audience participation, inflamed by *vino nacional*, the rough wine of the country. It is only in its music that South America has succeeded in fusing the cultures of Spain and the pre-columbian civilisations. The guitar, purely Spanish and the *quena*, purely Indian, blend perfectly. The *charango*, a stringed instrument whose sounding box is made from the shell of an armadillo, is a post-conquest invention. The words of the songs switched unselfconsciously from Spanish to Quechua and back again, vibrating with words like *agonía* and *miseria*, lingering over them almost with pleasure. The unattainability of perfect love was echoed in the wider world by the unattainability of justice. The music seemed to resonate with the deepest feelings of the audiences, who enjoyed their catharsis of stamping and clapping to the complex rhythms, leaving the *peñas* fortified against the world's evil.

I took the train to Oruro, a tin mining city three thousand feet higher than Cochabamba. The hundred-mile journey was scheduled to take ten hours, but our departure was delayed by at least half of that. An engineer on the train told me that the essential difference between South Americans and gringos was that the former never expected adherence to a timetable, and were never upset therefore by delays.

My restlessness amused the other passengers. I went outside the station to photograph the scene: foodstalls selling titbits to passengers and their relatives come for tearful farewells, while mangy dogs waited like jackals at a kill. As I took my photographs a Bolivian in the shabby clothes of a junior clerk rushed up to me and began an impassioned harangue. Were these people animals, he asked, that I should take pictures of them? Where was I from? Why was I there? Why had I no respect for the dignity of others? Was Bolivia a museum for my amusement?

I was about to reply (less than truthfully) when he resumed his harangue. Poverty, he said, was a serious matter for those who suffered it, not a diversion for the rich. He shook with anger and said he would call the police unless I cleared off.

Humiliated and chastened, I retreated into the station, not to venture out again until the train jerked its way into the gathering dark, to the sarcastic applause of the passengers.

We arrived in Oruro at dawn. My heart was racing, not from excitement but from altitude. The cold was intense and as penetrating as the dust of the Chaco. The streets were nearly deserted but the sky was already a brilliant, translucent blue. Next to the station was a market just stirring into life. A young man of about twenty called Jaime approached me and offered to show me round the city. Meeting foreigners, he said, was an exciting experience for him, because it reminded him there was a world beyond the cold confines of Oruro.

We breakfasted at a stall in the market: a roasted cob of maize and a plastic mug of savourless but steaming coffee. We went in search of lodgings, all the hotels firmly barred and bolted at that time of the morning. We found a room in a guesthouse whose walls radiated cold (I slept in multiple layers of clothes). The street ended abruptly a few yards beyond the guesthouse in a steep, stony brown hill, to whose scree-laden slopes clung simple adobe houses. A couple of old ladies clad in black struggled up the treacherous scree with water jugs, for the inhabitants of the houses had no other supply.

Jaime took me to a vantage point from which I could survey the city. A statue of the Virgin overlooked the city too, one of the bleakest sights in my recall. Every movement of the air seemed to bring a sharp attack by invisible razor blades. The city below, completely devoid of vegetation, was on the edge of an arid plain of stone-coloured dust which extended to the very gates of the city, which huddled together as though for protection. Fifty miles away, in the crystal air, shimmered some bare mountains, their peaks dusted lightly with snow.

Jaime was a student of engineering and wanted to discover whether his examination results had yet been posted at the university. We walked to the centre of the city (I noticed how carefully everyone shunned the freezing shadows, stepping neatly round their outlines). The university was a comfortless place, bare and functional, without decoration. Hundreds of shabbily dressed students milled in the entrance hall. Theirs was the shabbiness of necessity, not fashion. There was an expectant buzz in the air and I had the impression that it would not have taken much to provoke a riot there – an impression borne out by the history of the place.

The raison d'être of the city is, and always has been, mining. But life at this altitude, and in such a landscape, would be quite harsh enough without the necessity to tunnel miles under the ground for tin, silver and tungsten. The miners have responded by elaborating a complex mythology, fusing Catholic and pre-conquest elements. Above ground *la Virgen del Socavón*, the Virgin of the Cavern, rules as protectress of the miners; but underground is a pantheon of Indian gods whose anger must be propitiated periodically with the sacrifice (in the tunnels) of llamas, gifts of food, cigarettes, alcohol and coca leaves. Whenever a mining disaster occurs, the miners search their memories for rituals incorrectly carried out. Once a year, in February, the streets of Oruro erupt into carnival, in which the struggle between good and evil, represented respectively by the Archangel Michael and Satan (the latter assisted by his temptress wife China Supay), is re-enacted in lavish costumes and masks that have taken the entire year to make. Also re-enacted is another battle between good and evil: between Atahuallpa and Pizarro, ending in a decisive victory for evil. Of late Marxism has been incorporated into the syncretic mythology of the mines, with its own version of the struggle between good and evil, its own Virgins and Satans.

We lunched at the Centro Español, the best restaurant in the city. It was an ordinary unheated house a couple of blocks up the

Calle Adolfo Mitre. The window sills were cemeteries to the flies, and the waiter gave the plastic tablecloth a whisk with his towel as quick as the flick of a serpent's tongue. Nevertheless, this was luxury for Jaime, the greatest Oruro could afford, and he was more than satisfied with his vegetable soup, sardines and banana.

Jaime took me to his home after lunch. He lived with his parents and sister in a new settlement for the middle class on bare land at the foot of a mountain. The bungalows there cost $1000, beyond the reach of most. Jaime was anxious I should see it, but he was also ashamed. The electricity had been cut off, the house was half-finished only, and less than a quarter furnished. His father was a mining engineer with Comibol, the state mining corporation, who drank away his entire salary. His wife, a primary school teacher, earned just enough (at this moment) to feed the family, but there was nothing left to spend on the house. His father rarely went to work but Comibol, as much an inefficient social service as a commercial company, continued to pay him.

Jaime showed me his certificate of army service, without which it was impossible to find employment in Bolivia (and hard enough with it). It contained a book of rules and a credo, which Bolivian soldiers had to learn by heart. Amongst the articles of belief was Bolivia's inherent right to an outlet to the sea. I asked him whether he actually believed it: he said all Bolivians did. Thus is the groundwork laid for a future war.

The longer we stayed in the house – colder inside than out – the more nervous Jaime became that his father might return in his usual drunken rage. An unexpected event such as my arrival was quite sufficient to make him more violent still.

So as not to meet him we went to the cinema in Oruro's *Sala de Conciertos*. The *Sala* was one of the mining magnate Patiño's legacies to the city from the days when he practically owned it. But when the mines were nationalised in a popular revolution in 1952, the concert hall became a cinema: the unwilling or uncomprehending population had associated high culture with the plutocracy. We watched an Argentinian gangster comedy with a soundtrack enunciated through cotton wool. Jaime had difficulty keeping to his faded and flea-ridden plush chair, he laughed so heartily. It was good to see him laugh, for he seemed unduly careworn for his age. He was ashamed, he had told me, still to depend on his mother, but what else could he do? The inflation that had brought me cheap journeys and meals had brought him nothing but the prospect of a ruined life. The second movie was about Australian gangsters. I explained in vain that Australia was not the United States, and he left the cinema convinced he had seen part of the northern giant. I, on the other hand, left the cinema convinced that I was the only Englishman ever to have seen an Australian film in Oruro.

I left the bleak and comfortless city a few days later and went to Potosí. Jaime saw me off and promised to write. A few months later, letters with page after page of irresistible hispanic flattery began to arrive.

The journey to Potosí involved another climb, this time by bus. It is the highest city of any size in the world. The country between the two cities is spectacularly unsuited to human habitation, where even lichens seem to have only a precarious hold. Somehow, occasional herds of alpacas or llamas eke an existence on the windswept heights, foraging for *paja brava*, wild straw, that is too tough for other digestions. And once in a while, more surprising still, there is a farmhouse, a construction of large mud bricks surrounded by a few fields enclosed by low stone walls. Nothing grows in the fields, which are large animal folds: not a tree to be seen, not for fifty or a hundred miles at a view. At one of these farmhouses sat a man propped against a whitewashed wall as motionless as a corpse, as though he had been put out to mummify in the acerbic air. Only a black pig which snuffled its way, snout to the ground, right into the house – where animals are the only form of heating – lent life to the landscape.

Potosí is a well-preserved colonial city where, by rights, no city ought to be. Only human greed could have called it into being. The *Cerro Rico*, the Rich Hill, lowers over the city like a vast and malign pyramid. From the entrails of this one hill alone, over a period of two centuries, was mined a quarter of the world's stock of silver. At a time when instruments of credit were scarce, the *Cerro Rico de Potosi* made possible, in part, the rise of capitalism.

But at what cost! Every year for two hundred years 15,000 men were forced by the *mita de minas* to work in the mines of Potosí whence, according to some authorities, they never returned. Rodrigo de Loiasa, writing in 1586, said: 'If twenty Indians enter on Monday, half may emerge crippled on Saturday.' It is not difficult to see why. A central shaft ran 800 feet deep into the mountain. It was descended by a ladder whose leather straps were twenty-one inches apart. Each man was expected to bring to the surface twenty-five sacks of ore per day, each weighing a hundred pounds – or more than two tons in total. Men were kept underground for five days at a time to avoid wastage of time, and every village from Cuzco in Peru to Tarija on the southern border of Bolivia – a journey that would still take several days – was scoured for labour. The Indians tried either to flee or to pay exemptions to the mineowners. By 1660, such was the reputation of Potosí, the mineowners made almost as much money from the exemption payments as from the silver.

Silver was discovered at Potosí only twelve years after the conquest (the Spanish had discovered all the deposits of silver and gold in their empire within twenty years of their arrival). Within seventy years Potosí had the fourth largest population of any city in Christendom, about 160,000. Its present population being less than half of what it was three centuries ago, accounts for its preservation and its complete lack of modern despoilation. Vast fortunes were won and lost, but it was soon realised by some that the silver was not entirely to Spain's advantage. Complaints were heard in the Cortes of Castile that the silver of Potosí was leaving Spain 'as if we were Indians'. That 'Spain is the Indies of other countries,' became proverbial wisdom. I looked at the *Cerro Rico* and thought of Mrs Thatcher and the North Sea.

I toured the colonial monuments of the city, with its forty sumptuous churches built by mineowners with slightly guilty consciences. The *Casa Real de Moneda*, the Mint, is said to be the largest colonial building surviving in the Americas. Potosí has a famous painter of its own, Melchor Pérez de Holguín, who covered vast areas of canvas with religious allegory, though his work seemed barely competent to me. But in any case it was difficult to fix one's mind on the artistic glories of the place, wrought as they were from such a holocaust: visiting Auschwitz, one would not remark on the fine spring morning. Even Potosí's present return to relative prosperity (its population had declined to less than 10,000 by 1810) is based on the proximity of several tin mines, all exacting their terrible tolls.

I found it impossible to get warm in Potosí.

I took the train to Uyuni. Potosí station was an ironwork structure overlooking a piece of bleak waste ground. I was early for the train – having learnt nothing from the experience – and the only other people in the station were an old Indian couple, the woman wearing multilayered petticoats and a bowler hat from under which emerged a long plaited pigtail. We sat on cold stone benches ten yards apart.

I read Oruno's newspaper, *La Patria*. A man in his late twenties came up to me.

'I want to look in your luggage,' he said.

'Why?' I asked. 'Who are you?'

He took out an identity card. He was a member of the Bolivian Drug Police.

I was apprehensive as he pawed pruriently through my things. There was the possibility he would plant evidence and then extort money – all I had. But he glanced at the Indian couple ten yards away who were watching him; he thanked me and moved on, like a predator cheated of his prey.

When he was out of sight the Indian man came to tell me I had had a lucky escape. Had he not been there, I should have been much the poorer man. I thanked him effusively.

He returned to his seat and continued his silent, seemingly inert vigil with his wife. The station began to fill with travellers, all poor, and their hangers-on: weeping relatives, vendors of sweets, pick-pockets. By the time the train was due the platform was seething, pullulating. The only other gringo and I teamed up together. He was a now middle-aged Dutchman called Frans who dressed in the once-rebellious garb of the Vietnam protest era.

Frans was an unemployed university teacher of linguistics with a particular interest in American poetry. He had been in South America nine months, having arranged for a friend to collect his unemployment benefit and cable it to South America. This was illegal, since people collecting Dutch unemployment benefit were supposed to be seeking work at home. But many of his country-men had discovered that a life of idleness was more supportable in foreign climes, especially in those where the money stretched further.

In any case, Frans had not entirely wasted his time, profes-sionally speaking. He had trekked to a remote valley of the Peruvian Andes, living for six months as the Indians lived, to gather linguistic data. He had compiled a grammar and vocabul-ary of their unknown dialect and hoped that its publication would give him the edge over other candidates for the rare university posts in linguistics that came up. Not only had he reduced a pre-viously unknown dialect to writing, but he had formulated on its basis a whole new theory of human language which would render all previous theories obsolete. I inquired gently whether a six-month residence among people whose ways of life and thinking were completely alien was sufficient for this tremendous enter-prise. How could he be sure that his grammar and vocabulary were accurate?

'It doesn't matter, ' said Frans. 'No-one knows any better.'

Waiting for the train we talked of literature. Frans liked modern American literature, he said, because it was trivial, having got off the treadmill, or out of the strait-jacket, of portentous social realism. He liked literature that played games with the reader, was self-referring, and was linguistically inventive. He did not care for narrative: he wasn't a beginning, middle and end man. He disliked the order that ordinary consciousness imposed on events, preferring instead the kaleidoscopic allusiveness that psychotropic drugs conferred. Our tastes in literature were precisely opposite.

The train was late as usual. Its arrival provoked a near-riot. We joined in the general mêlée to secure seats, lunging at the back of our competitors' legs with our bags; once having secured places, we were able to continue our literary discussion in relative comfort.

We were soon the object of other passengers' curiosity. When it became known I was English, the subject of the Falklands inevitably recurred. By now I had prepared a short speech. To my surprise, Frans thought that Mrs Thatcher had been insufficiently vigorous in her prosecution of the war: she should have exploded a nuclear bomb over the Pampas and in Buenos Aires. Inside every rebel there is a stern authoritarian trying to get out.

Uyuni is a small town of five thousand people at a railway junction. Although at an elevation a thousand feet below Potosi, the latter is a tropical Eden by comparison; for Uyuni is mercilessly exposed in the middle of a plain which borders one of the largest salt lakes in the world, the Salar de Uyuni. Refrigerated gusts of wind blow down its wide dusty streets, and the single storey buildings have long since taken on the colour of the plain.

We arrived at the only hotel, the Avenida, after dark. It was not far from the station. The owner, Señor Don Jesús Rosas, slept immediately opposite the front door, which was locked when night fell. Nearer still to the door slept his half-witted servant, who obeyed his master's instructions issued from under a blanket – but never, apparently, to his master's full satisfaction – whenever there was a knock at the door. These somewhat unusual reception arrangments had been made because low as the nightly tariff was (about 40 cents), a considerable proportion of Señor Rosas' guests attempted to leave the hotel without paying.

The rooms were spartan. There was a barrel of icy water outside in which to wash: one could well understand a certain lack of enthusiasm for cleanliness in the circumstances. Cracks in the windows let through laser-like draughts. I went to bed in as many clothes as I possessed.

Breakfast next morning was fried egg in the English style: cooked until it has vulcanised, and served in so much grease that it eludes the pursuing knife and fork, like a blob of mercury. All the same, we ate it ravenously, and washed it down with warm coffee essence.

Exploring Uyuni did not take long. Outside the hotel was an astonishingly incongruous statue: a huge, square-jawed male mechanic in sky-blue dungarees striding forward in true socialist heroic style, holding a spanner up to the heavens. Why it was there, what it represented, or who put it there, was impossible now to determine. People we asked accepted it as being as immutably existent as the Salar itself, and did not bother with such meta-physical questions. No doubt one day Erich von Daniken will go to Uyuni.

We had another breakfast in a café of cold pork stew, went to the market to buy cassettes of Bolivian music, and decided on a trip into the Salar.

Near the market we found a truck that was about to cross the lake, a hundred miles across. The owner agreed to take us provided we accepted he had no responsibility for our fate once he had left us in the middle of the lake. We climbed up high into the truck, whose every inch was crammed with people and their every possession. Finding a place to stand was not easy; in the end we settled for a narrow gap between an iron trunk and the tailboard which kept us suspended above the bottom of the truck. We hoped for a smooth journey, otherwise our legs would be crushed to fragments. The scores of Indian passengers, for whom this kind of discomfort was part of daily life, were amused by our predicament. Laughing both with us and at us, they were not so much undertaking a journey as migrating in the mass.

We left after an hour of stationary discomfort. The suspension maximised the irregularities in the road's surface, and the truck proceeded by a series of jerks. We endured the first part of the journey with alternate winces and breath-holding. The Indians watched us and smiled happily. But, as soldiers do not feel their wounds in the heat of battle, so we soon became absorbed by the magnificence of the country, and our pain fell away. At the first we skirted the lake, but after a village still more desolate than Uyuni, we turned to drive into it. The lake was dry and the salt stretched out to the horizon, as white as any snowfield. The cloudless sky was an iridescent cobalt blue more intense than any I had ever seen. The shimmering outlines of distant mountain peaks danced and floated ethereally in the sky, untethered to the horizon. It was a world where only two colours existed: blue and white.

A few miles into the lake the owner of the truck asked us whether we wished to go further. Had we done so, we might not have been able to return to Uyuni by nightfall so, to the considerable amazement of the other passengers, who had never heard of such a thing, we climbed down in the midst of this clinical wilderness and waved them all goodbye.

We tested that the whiteness really was salt and not snow by tasting it. Close to its surface crystals glittered like snowflakes. But it was salt all right, and we soon had a dry white crust forming on our lips. We followed the tracks of the truck (our only possible navigational guide on the otherwise featureless field of white). But like children in the first snow of winter we sometimes felt the urge to break the pristine surface of the salt. It was strong enough to bear our weight, so we had to leap and jump to hear the satisfying crunch underfoot and leave our footprints. Gradually it dawned on us we had a long journey and if we did not find a lift it would be nightfall before we reached Uyuni. We walked steadily, with only occasional backward glances at the dancing mountain peaks.

After a mile or two we saw men a long way off, black crumbs on a spotless tablecloth. We diverted to see what they were doing. Working in an area staked out by football pitch flagposts, they were digging salt. They wore darkened goggles against snow-blindness and were well-protected against the biting winds. The backbreaking collection of salt looked a desultory occupation rather than an organised industry. A few small piles awaited collection.

We reached the desolate village. We were tired, thirsty and

hungry, and still had another fifteen miles to walk. The village did not look the kind of place where refreshment would be easily available. It was deserted, apart from one forlorn chicken, pecking at the ground. As we reached the end of the village we saw a man loading some sacks on to a truck. He moved but slowly, yet in the utter stillness of the village his actions seemed almost panic-stricken. We helped him load his truck in return for a lift to Uyuni. Acclimatised as we were, our hearts still knocked against our chests.

We whiled away time in one of Uyuni's cafés, under the stern countenance of the cheaply lithographed Liberator, who presided over the cold and greasy food, the coffee thinner than the atmosphere, and the icy table tops. We talked about the future of the world, if any, and other subjects that expand to fill the time available to discuss them.

That evening I went to a film show in Uyuni's *Teatro Municipal*. Frans said he wanted to sleep: we shook hands, for in the morning he went to Argentina, I to Chile. Ours was one of those strange travellers' meetings in which one learns more about one's companion in a day than in other circumstances would be possible in a year.

The *Teatro Municipal* was one of the few two-storey buildings in the town and the draughtiest I had ever known, like a giant colander. The audience dressed more for a polar expedition than a cinema. At some time in the town's history a megalomaniac mayor had ordered the interior of the *Teatro* to be painted to resemble brown marble. Even before the paint started to peel off the resemblance had not been great. The film was *Invasion of the Giant Spiders*, with subtitles in Spanish, not that they were necessary. Pumpkin-sized arachnid eggs fell to earth from outer space and hatched into giant spiders (magnifications of the garden variety superimposed on scenery) which terrorised a mid-western American town by looming improbably large on the horizon. The Bolivian audience found the hysterical running screams of the American housewives supremely funny, and cheered the spiders on to victory. Alas, in the final reel, after the projectionist had fumbled with it for ten minutes to the accompaniment of jeers, the sheriff of the town restored order by resort to a high technology which was quite beyond the spiders, and the Earth was saved.

I returned to the hotel, past the eagle eye of Señor Rosas, with whom I had found favour by paying for everything in advance. I slept fitfully on my last night in Bolivia, for the train was scheduled at four o'clock in the morning, and in a half-dreaming, half-waking state hallucinated the sound of trains drawing into Uyuni Station just below my window.

TEN

Chile

THE TRAIN arrived at half-past four. The platform was crowded with poor Indians and mestizos even at that early hour (the poor see more dawns than the rich). Everyone huddled together for warmth. Most of the travellers were hopefuls in search of work, though the unemployment rate in Chile admitted by the government was twenty-five per cent, and was probably higher still. But Chile was a powerful magnet for Bolivians all the same: work there, when found, was much better paid.

The carriages of the train were small and covered in green clapboard. I noticed from the footplates that they had been manufactured in Sheffield seventy years earlier. They were unheated despite the cold. I had reserved a seat, but so had many other people and I found myself sitting on a sack of some lumpy commodity. I kept warm as best I could: the temperature on the train often goes to fifteen below zero.

The line to Uyuni was completed in 1889 and was bought by the Antofagasta (Chile) and Bolivia Railway Company, British owned. Other sections of the La Paz to Antofagasta line are owned by different companies. It must once have been a profitable investment, to judge from the lavishness of the wood-panelled interior; but by the mid-1950s the traffic had declined by half and the company was not allowed to shed staff. It lost half a million pounds a year, and no new capital was expended. The once genteel carriages have been thoroughly proletarianised, with the migrating poor taking up every inch of every corner with their veriegated luggage, from bedrolls to fiercely-guarded suitcases.

Among the passengers one man stood out. He was a young Belgian with a bushy black beard, dressed in wine-coloured trousers and a thick white sweater, a boulevard revolutionary if ever I saw one. He read a pamphlet by Lenin translated into Spanish and laughed contemptuously when I asked whether it was not dangerous, in view of the political complexion of the present Chilean government.

He was, it appeared, a voluntary worker, come from Europe to impart the Truth to benighted South Americans. He worked in something called 'community development' and he had just been to a conference of community developers in La Paz. He was returning to the slums of Santiago.

'So you're a kind of missionary,' I said, but it was not an analogy that pleased him.

In any case, he spoke to me only reluctantly, lest it ruin his reputation with the other passengers. He barged into a group of peasant women, whom he dominated with his animated talk and his broad jokes, acting without the inhibitions he took to be the mark of the bourgeois. His condescension, his awareness of being a Lenin fallen among illiterates, was all but palpable, and I thought the peasants sensed it too. At any rate, the more he said, the less they spoke.

The dawn broke slowly across the sky, pink, mauve and yellow by turns. It did not bring warmth. We climbed slowly and painfully, up to 15,000 feet, through land of spectacular barrenness. We stopped at a village near the border, as high as any people live. It was a perfect flat of fine volcanic dust. Built in a rectangle two hundred yards by one hundred, the railway track formed one of its sides. The other three sides were terraced adobe houses with black holes for doors. No trees, no grass, no moss even, grew there. Women stood motionless in the rectangle, surrounded by broods of children. What did these people do? How did they live?

The train dragged itself on. At the back of the carriage was an Indian woman selling *picante de pollo*, a hot chicken stew, which I ate with relish from an aluminium dish. This was hastily dipped in a pail of water, looking like the soup from a Siberian labour camp, after each breakfaster had finished.

We reached the border at Ollagüe, a village of five hundred named for the volcano of 19,000 feet. There were eleven other volcanoes visible, several with wisps of smoke issuing from their craters. Chilean *carabineros* in thigh-length tunics entered the carriages and ordered everyone off. We were made to stand in a single line facing the train from fifty yards away, our backs to the volcanoes. Two more carabineros, their polished leather holsters prominent, short black moustaches glistening with hair oil, marched up and down the line, reading our thoughts. We all felt accused of some nameless crime, the crime perhaps of even daring to exist. Meanwhile, our luggage was forcibly ejected from the train, out of doors and out of windows. We were told to collect our own and return to the line. Not until every piece had been claimed by an owner could the inspection continue. The carabineros looked from owner to luggage and back again, as though that were sufficient to extract a confession of guilt.

We stood for a long time, and someone said the carabineros were waiting for the volcanoes to erupt and bury us. Then all the gringos were called out of the line. There were five of us: a New Zealanders who looked ill (as do all New Zealanders who travel), two Americans and the Belgian, downcast and degraded by being classified a gringo.

'Did you see the movie *Missing?*' whispered one of the Americans. (It concerned the disappearance and death of a young American living in Santiago at the time of the 1973 coup.)

'Don't worry,' replied the other. 'They called us out of line to deal with us first.'

'Or shoot us.'

In full view of the other passengers we were led into the customs shed, where our baggage was cursorily inspected. The *aduaneros* were polite and smiling, and wished us *buen viaje* rather unctuously. This special treatment was gall and wormwood to the Belgian, who wanted desperately to be one of the oppressed. Now he would have to spend the rest of the journey dissociating himself from the other gringos. The South American passengers were not so fortunate. It took four hours and many disputes to clear them.

At last, however, we continued on our journey, into the Atacama Desert where it has not rained for aeons. As we chugged slowly through that land of fantastical shapes, of weird beauty, we had to queue in an old first-class compartment carriage to see the immigration officer. The New Zealander went in before me and emerged some time later, paler still than he had entered, and shaking.

'Christ, that bastard asked me everything,' he said indignantly. 'How much money I had, where was my ticket out, even who I voted for.'

There was something about him, however, that seemed to invite ill-usage. In Bogotá he had been robbed on the street of everything he possessed. He had pleaded with the robbers at least to return his passport. One could imagine the contempt with which they flung it at him.

I entered the walnut-lined compartment in which the officer sat behind a table.

'Name?' he asked brusquely, without looking up.

But on discovering that I was a doctor he became almost obsequious, calling me Señor, and only asking me why I did not intend to stay longer in Chile.

I had noticed an ash-tray full of cigarette ends on his table, and as I left I said: 'Smoking is very bad for the health.'

'I know, Señor, but what can I do?' He shrugged.

I continued through the Atacama on the rear platform of the train's last carriage. The dunes and outcrops seemed to have been arranged by someone of fastidious but ascetic sensibility. The train stopped. Across a plain of light grey ash, a plume of smoke emerged from the geometrically perfect cone of a volcano twenty miles away. In the foreground, the only sign of human endeavour other than the line itself, was a solitary grave, a slight mound planted with a crude wooden cross. Who was buried here? One wanted to linger to contemplate the mystery, but to do so without due preparation would have been to join the deceased. The train moved on, having crossed itself as it were.

The train ride now stops at Calama, an oasis town in the Atacama. The journey is completed by bus along a well-made road, the descent to sea level quite rapid. It is soon obvious that, whatever its present difficulties, Chile is at a quite different stage of development from Bolivia.

We arrived in Antofagasta, the largest of Chile's nothern cities, at dusk. It is built on a narrow strip fringed by bare brown hills around a graceful bay. From my balcony I saw the lights begin to twinkle in an arc. A couple of rusty merchantmen at anchor in the bay lit up too and transformed themselves into elegant yachts. The salt breeze of the Pacific was strong, bringing sudden unromantic gusts of rotting fish. High above the city, in the hills, stood a huge anchor, used as a landmark by all incoming vessels. Standing there, I felt a sense of satisfaction, a promise kept.

I walked through the city, perfectly still and deserted on a Sunday evening. Yugoslav flags flew everywhere – Yugoslavs have flooded into northern Chile and are now prominent citizens, with all the ambivalence of recent immigrants. I passed bookshops, better stocked than any in Bolivia, with the geopolitical works of General Augusto Pinochet Ugarte much to the fore. I strolled up the Calle Prat, named for the Chilean hero of the War of the Pacific, at the ocean end of which stood my hotel. I passed the town gaol, a whitewashed fortress whose ramparts were patrolled by a guard with a machine-gun against the evening sky. I thought it best not to stare too long.

Further up the street, on the first slopes of the hills, the slums began, irregular houses of mud and tin, by no means the worst I had seen. Perhaps the fact that the temperature of Antofagasta never varies from seventy degrees makes them more bearable. On a piece of cleared ground, still stony, youths played football in the declining light, with admiring girls on the sidelines giggling at tackles, goals, corners, at everything that happened. I found myself envying these children of the slums: their youth, their energy, even the environment in which they lived. Even under this dictatorship life was not all misery: and happy the man who can keep alive in his heart the myth of past or future happiness.

I returned to the hotel. Two bourgeois families, children subdued by clean sailor suits and new ribbons, were taking an early evening meal. The women discussed clothes, the men money. I stood on the verandah and stared sightlessly out to sea. Only the phosphorescent white crests of the waves were visible, and the darkness heightened the sound of the rhythmic ebb and flow of the water on the pebbled shore. Five thousand miles away, with scarcely any land between us, were the Gilbert Islands, whither I was heading: slivers of coral a few hundred yards across in an immensity of ocean. There, no land was more than ten feet above the level of the sea; the people lived on fish and coconuts; and nature was bountiful without ever exacting revenge for her bounty by storm or earthquake or tidal wave. But beautiful and peaceful though they were, I dreamt of South America.